OKLAHOMA
foot-loose and fancy-free

OKLAHOMA
foot-loose and fancy-free

By ANGIE DEBO

UNIVERSITY OF OKLAHOMA PRESS : NORMAN AND LONDON

By ANGIE DEBO

The Historical Background of the American Policy of Isolation
(with J. Fred Rippy) (Northampton, Mass., 1924)
The Rise and Fall of the Choctaw Republic (Norman, 1934; New
edition, Norman, 1961)
And Still the Waters Run (Princeton, 1940; Norman, 1984)
The Road to Disappearance: A History of the Creek Indians
(Norman, 1941)
Oklahoma: A Guide to the Sooner State (Ed., with John M. Oski-
son) (Norman, 1941)
Tulsa: From Creek Town to Oil Capital (Norman, 1943)
Prairie City: The Story of an American Community (New York,
1944)
Oklahoma: Foot-loose and Fancy-free (Norman, 1949)
The Five Civilized Tribes of Oklahoma (Philadelphia, 1951)
The Cowman's Southwest, Oliver Nelson (Ed.) (Glendale, Calif.,
1953)
History of the Choctaw, Chickasaw, and Natchez Indians, by
H. B. Cushman (Ed.) (Stillwater, Okla., 1962)
A History of the Indians of the United States (Norman, 1970)
Geronimo: The Man, His Time, His Place (Norman, 1976)

Library of Congress Cataloging-in-Publication Data

Debo, Angie, 1890–
  Oklahoma, foot-loose and fancy-free.

  Reprint. Originally published: Norman : University of Oklahoma
Press, 1949. With a new addendum.
  Includes index.
  1. Oklahoma—Description and travel. 2. Oklahoma—History.
I. Title.
F700.D4 1987   976.6   87–5656
ISBN 0–8061–2066–5 (pbk.)

Contents

Illustrations

Preface

Aɴʏ ꜱᴛᴀᴛᴇ of the American Union deserves to be known and understood. But Oklahoma is more than just another state. It is a lens in which the long rays of time are focused into the brightest of light. In its magnifying clarity, dim facets of the American character stand more clearly revealed. For in Oklahoma all the experiences that went into the making of the nation have been speeded up. Here all the American traits have been intensified. The one who can interpret Oklahoma can grasp the meaning of America in the modern world.

Something of this thought must have been in the minds of the Rockefeller Committee of the University of Oklahoma when they asked me to write this book. It has been a pleasant assignment. I have told something of the physical setting, for people are influenced by their physical environment. I have not written a history, but I am not apologizing for the emphasis on historical background. No psychologist would try to analyze a human personality without careful study of its past. But this is only by way of understanding. In Oklahoma the present is the important thing. That and the future.

For Oklahomans do not believe that their course is run. Nobody knows better than they that mankind is traveling a perilous road, with annihilation perhaps as the not far distant end. But they know it without feeling it. And if they should be building on the edge of a precipice, why building is much pleasanter and even more constructive than looking down into the void. Then there is always the chance that if the building is stanch enough, the precipice may be bridged. And see how bright the prospect is on the other side! Who said anything about quitting? This confidence of course flows out of the experiences of the past, and one generation has felt them all.

I am grateful to the University of Oklahoma for the grant of Rockefeller funds that enabled me to write this interpretation, and to the University Press, for visualizing the possibilities of such a book. And I appreciate the help of Henderson and Dorothy Leake of the Oklahoma Agricultural and Mechanical College, who read and criticized the manuscript, and of Edmon Low, librarian of the College, for his unfailing support and encouragement. I am indebted also to other friends over the state who have given me good suggestions about what they would put into a book of this scope. All this may not have made me a better writer, but certainly it has made me a better Oklahoman.

ANGIE DEBO

Stillwater, Oklahoma
January 1, 1949

OKLAHOMA

foot-loose and fancy-free

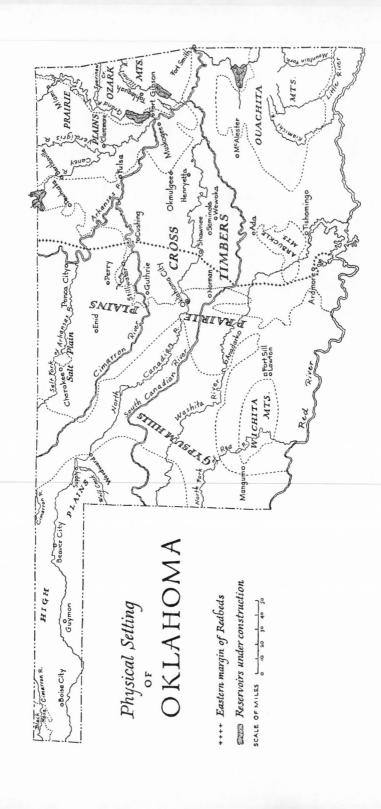

Physical Setting
OF
OKLAHOMA

+++ Eastern margin of Redbeds

▬▬ Reservoirs under construction

SCALE OF MILES
0 10 20 30 40 50

I

The Land We Know

WHEN IT WAS PROPOSED that several pieces of un-
connected territory be put together to form the state of Oklahoma,
someone noticed that the projected commonwealth was shaped
like a butcher's cleaver. If old Bill Murray's memory is correct,
there were members of the Constitutional Convention determined
to adopt that handy utensil as the state seal, and it required shrewd
maneuvering to circumvent them.[1] The figure is graphic if not
poetical; the long narrow strip on the northwest now known as the
Panhandle is the helve of the implement, and the Red River boundary forms its hacked and dented edge.

In measurement Oklahoma is about 470 miles long on the
northern edge, including the handle ("from tip to tip" as it were),
about 320 miles through the greatest length of the blade; its greatest breadth is about 225 miles. It contains about 69,283 square
miles, which ranks it seventeenth in area among the forty-eight
states. It is about the size of North Dakota, slightly larger than
Missouri, almost half again the size of New York, and more than
10 per cent larger than all New England.

Outsiders seem to think every one of the 69,283 miles is exactly
like all the others. For example, Kyle Crichton in an excellent article on Oklahoma's athletic prowess characterized the whole state
from the part he happened to see as "a large flat piece of ground
covered with oil wells, wheat fields, and a crop of long rangy individuals."[2] But it probably has more kinds of country, more kinds

[1] William H. Murray, Memoirs of Governor Murray and ·True History
of Oklahoma (Boston, 1945, 3 vols.), II, 64–66.
[2] "The Eager Aggies," Collier's, October 12, 1946.

3

of weather, and more kinds of flora and fauna than any other area of similar size in the United States.

Geologists have traced these differences to a time remote in the earth's history. The area was apparently a land surface uncounted millions of years in the dim pre-Cambrian ages. Then about the middle of the Cambrian period the sea advanced over much of the region and mile-deep layers of Cambrian, Ordovician, Silurian, Devonian, and Mississippian rocks were deposited. During the ensuing Pennsylvanian period most of Oklahoma stood near sea level, thus forming great swamps in which plants grew rank; but the sea flooded it from time to time, laying down layers of mud and sand, thus covering the vegetation, which was eventually converted into coal. At or near the close of this period there were great seismic movements that folded all these rocks into corrugations—if one can imagine an elongated layer cake crumpled into washboard folds, upbent anticlines, downbent synclines—or even broke and shoved them over each other forming what the geologists call "faults." The tops of these folds have long been worn off, but remnants of the more resistent rocks form Oklahoma's four mountain uplifts: the Ozarks of the northeast and the Ouachitas of the southeast, extensions of similar formations in Missouri and Arkansas; and the Arbuckles and Wichitas of the south central and southwest, both projections of one great upthrust.

During the succeeding period—the Permian, as geologists reckon time—the sea covered only the western part of Oklahoma, depositing red sands and shales. It is these Permian Red Beds that give the characteristic color to the western half of the state. This about finished the job except for a much later invasion of the sea from the south, and the deposit of Comanchean (Lower Cretaceous) rocks along the southern margin, a continuation of the formation extending through Central Texas and far into Old Mexico. Any subsequent change in the land was the work of wind and streams, except for a lava flow that came over the western border of the Panhandle to form the Black Mesa. The rest of the Panhandle is deeply covered with rock debris washed down from the Rocky Mountains.

So much for the geological history of Oklahoma. But in addition to the local movements with their folding and faulting, the

4

whole state is part of a greater fold that bends the entire area east
of the Rocky Mountains into an immense syncline. Strictly speaking one should call it a synclinorium because the whole structure
is wrinkled, just as a washboard may have smaller corrugations
running parallel to the main folds. The trough crosses western
Oklahoma through Alva and Arapaho. (The southeastern end of
this "Anadarko Basin" was the scene of the most active geological exploration in the state during the late nineteen forties.) In
the wide bottom the rocks lie almost level, but on either side the
entire structure rises very gently toward the Rocky Mountains on
the west and the Ouachita-Ozark uplift on the east. Remember we
are not speaking of the surface, but of the fundamental rock structure.

Thus nearly every rock ledge one sees in Oklahoma is tilted
in some direction. In the Arbuckle Mountains this structure is
visible on the surface and can be examined by the layman. Here
rock layers many thousands of feet in thickness that once lay hori-
zontal have been thrust up into an immense wrinkle, with the pre-
Cambrian porphyry and granite at the core and the younger formations arching over it; and the top of the wrinkle has been worn
away, leaving the raw edges exposed. If I place a pencil under
several pages of this book, it forms a ridge; then if I shear off the
top of the ridge, I expose the pencil core and the cut edges of the
leaves. Thus one may walk into the heart of the earth by starting
at the outer portion of the fold and walking from the younger rocks
across the upturned edges of succeeding formations (from Mississippian through Devonian, Silurian, Ordovician, and Cambrian—
limestones, sandstones, and shales) until he reaches the ancient
mass of porphyry in the center of the uplift. Or he may cross these
millions of years in a few minutes by driving north from Ardmore
on U.S. Highway 77, where a geology-conscious Lions Club has
placed road signs marking the steps in this backward sweep of
time. He will see uptilted layers of resistant rock forming conspicuous stripes across the hillsides, and he will notice that each
formation has its characteristic types of soil, topography, and
vegetation.

The variation one sees here in miniature extends throughout
the state. In the Ozark region are timbered hills of limestone cov-

ered with a loose mantle of chert. These are the "flint hills" of north-eastern Oklahoma. In the Ouachitas are shales and sandstones, the most resistant of which form pine-clad mountains rising nearly two thousand feet above their base. West of these uplifts is a prairie region of shale and limestone grading west into a belt of sandstone hills covered with scrub timber. The Arbuckles thrust up their many-folded strata through the south end of these sandstone hills.

Next come the Red Beds along a line roughly dividing the state into eastern and western halves; and strangely enough, the settlement of Oklahoma followed almost exactly that line of cleavage between white pioneers to the west, Indians to the east. Along this Permian boundary the Red Beds have eroded into rugged shapes merging into the older sandstone hills to the east, but through most of the area the soft shales and sandstones have weathered into level prairie. In the southern part of this region the Wichita Mountains obtrude their bare granite masses five hundred to eleven hundred feet above the plain. Their structure is almost certainly identical with that of the Arbuckles, but the Permian deposits have covered all but traces of the older formations on their flanks. Farther west, even the core of the uplift is completely buried; but it continues beneath the surface across the Oklahoma border to form the hidden Amarillo Mountains of the Texas Panhandle oil field. Also under these level central prairies lie the buried Nemaha Mountains, starting near Mill Creek in the Arbuckle region and running north across the state, and bearing the greatest oil fields of Oklahoma on either side of their huge granite axis.

In the western part of the state, ledges of white gypsum alternate with the red soil to form picturesque flat-topped mesas or escarpments along the streams. The most conspicuous are the so-called Glass Mountains near Fairview, where a transparent form of gypsum known as selenite catches the rays of the sun and throws them back with dazzling effect. The surrounding area is wild and barren with the banded red and white soil carved in "bad-land" topography, and the surface strewn with sparkling crystals washed down from the hills. The whole "gyp hills" region rises rapidly toward the west, merging in the northwest into the High Plains.

The High Plains are deeply eroded at the eastern margin and

6

The Land We Know

along the streams to form rugged bluffs. Especially picturesque are the barren Antelope Hills, once a landmark for early travelers, near the western boundary of the state on the South Canadian River. But this is only the edge of the High Plains. On top, at some places in the Panhandle they are so level that they have no drainage; not even the smallest rivulet cuts their surface, and surplus rainfall gathers into saucerlike lakes.

Distinct from all this, is the narrow Comanchean strip bordering the Red River. It may once have extended along the full length of the state, but now it appears only along the eastern half. Here the structure dips gently toward the south and southeast, forming parallel east-west outcroppings of sand, limestone, and shale. A very sandy belt, once an ancient coastal plain, lies along the northern margin, then a band of black waxy soil like that in North Texas, and to the south another strip of coastal plain.

The whole surface of Oklahoma slopes from northwest to southeast: the altitude on the top of the Black Mesa in the northwestern corner of the Panhandle is 4,978 feet; on the Red River next to the Arkansas line, it is 324. Many long rivers flow in parallel lines southeast across the state. Perhaps one should not say "flow" of these twisting, shallow sheets of water moving lazily over wide beds of sand. In the western half each of these streams is bordered along the northeast by a strip of sand two to eighteen miles wide blown up out of the river by the south wind. It can still be seen rising from the dry bed on any windy day. White and thick it covers the Red Beds, held down by vegetation except where it has been unwisely put in cultivation. In only a few places it forms naked dunes; near Waynoka on the Cimarron River several great wind-rippled drifts are rolling north over the upland, covering elm and cottonwood trees as they advance.

Thus Crichton made a true characterization of all these rivers when he described the Cimarron as a "historic stream" lacking only water. But sometimes they are filled with water, which sweeps down in a swirling torrent bearing soil and uprooted trees, breaking over the low banks, destroying farms and tearing out bridges. In earlier days pioneers trying to cross the treacherous fords were drowned in these sudden rises or engulfed in quicksand.

But it would not be like Oklahoma to have only one kind of

7

river. From the Ozarks and the Ouachitas come clear streams rippling over rocky beds. There are no more agreeable combinations of shade and waterfall and mossy bank than one finds along the Illinois, the Sallisaw, the Poteau, the Kiamichi, or the Mountain Fork. The rainfall also varies from an average annual precipitation of less than seventeen inches in the western Panhandle to fifty-one inches in the southeast. One can draw parallel lines almost straight north and south across the map to connect the points of equal precipitation.

The Oklahoma climate is of spangled sunshine—with variations. Spring comes early with a flash of mockingbirds' wings, moving across the land in power like an army with banners. Summer is dry and scorching with cool breezes at night. Autumn is golden and perfect; it begins about the first of September and lasts till after Christmas. Properly speaking, there is no winter; the period is filled with weather left over from the other seasons—spring days alternating with autumn days, an occasional summer day, and once in a great while a howling blizzard. But all the seasons are likely to be jumbled—snow in May, hot winds in March, spring showers in November, with hailstorms or even tornadoes thrown in for good measure. (Only sultry days are practically unknown.[3]) On United States weather maps showing the generalized path of storms, Oklahoma is a little white island surrounded by sweeping black lines—a fortunate isle set in a tempestuous sea. But when a storm strikes, it strikes hard.

At such times the thermometer may drop in twelve hours from eighty degrees to below freezing; and most of the drop comes in the first hour or two after the wind swings to the north. I remember very well a change of that kind that occurred, I believe, about the middle of April in 1938. It was the noon hour of a perfect spring day, and I was sitting under a tree enjoying it all. I happened to be facing the north when I felt—I could almost swear I saw—the wind veer sharply, and an icy blast swept across the bright landscape. By the middle of the afternoon the snow was whirling, and

[3] The Oklahoma climate has changed in the 1980s. It now has sultry weather in summer. (Angie Debo, June 16, 1986.)

by night the railroads and the highways were blocked with drifts. Hundreds of school children from three states were at Enid to march in the spring band festival. Even the wires were down so that frantic parents could not communicate with their thinly clad offspring. Enid took them into its homes until the roads were opened. Of course the drifts soon melted, but the trees had to put out a second crop of leaves and spring had to start all over again.

Oklahomans like to tell weather stories. There was the man out in the field with his team, when the sun shone so hot that one of the horses fell and quickly died. While the discouraged farmer was removing the harness, the wind changed to the north; and before he had finished his task, the other horse froze to death. Then there was the drought so severe that when the fish swam up the creek, they raised a dust cloud; but when the rain finally came, the water rose with such fury that it tore the bricks out of the pavement and bore them away on the surface of the flood. And weather proverbs have passed into the common speech: "Anybody who tries to predict the weather in Oklahoma is a newcomer or a fool"; or "If you don't like this weather, just wait a minute."

During the fifty-odd years of white settlement there have been three serious dry cycles: there was the one beginning in the fall of 1893, which almost broke the pioneers; there was the terrible summer of 1910, and two or three years following; and there was the drought of "dust bowl" ill repute in the middle nineteen thirties. Even in normal years the western half of the state has an occasional day when the wind blows hard and the sun is a white ball in a red haze and the air is a lurid darkness. These days are trying, but they come seldom. The sifting dust is not so hard on the temper of housewives as the smoke pall that lies over Eastern cities, and the obscurity is not so depressing as the fogs of less sunny climes.

For Oklahomans like to take their weather straight. They like their clear atmosphere and brilliant sky. The most scorching sunshine suits them better than a cloud; even in times of drought when their very living depends on getting moisture, a half-day's rain is about all they can take without grumbling. And they have much sunshine. Oklahoma City has an annual average of 166 clear days, and most of the others are only partly cloudy. St. Louis has 139,

Chicago 117, Detroit 99, New York City 105, Pittsburgh 87, and Washington 128. Even sun-kissed Los Angeles has only 179.

With all kinds of soil and all kinds of weather Oklahoma should—and does—grow many kinds of plants. Botanists say that only about 5 per cent of our species are found in all parts of the state; in other words, nineteen out of twenty reach the limit of their range here. And in unspoiled portions of this still new land the abundance as well as the variety of wild flowers beggars description. Sheets of color blot out the green of the prairie; banks of color glow through the timber. And flowers bloom every month of the year.

The mountainous eastern end of the state is heavily forested. In the northeast is hardwood—oak, elm, hickory, maple—and some pine (southern yellow pine); south of the Arkansas River is hardwood and much pine, and in the extreme southeast along the sparkling streams grow the tulip tree and the cypress. The largest tree in Oklahoma is an ancient cypress near Eagletown; it measures fifty-six feet in circumference and is ninety feet high. Here in the spring is the breath-taking beauty of the flowering dogwood; in the winter, the waxy green leaves and bright red berries of the holly.

West of this, in the great reaches of prairie, the bluestem grass —so say the old-timers—once grew as tall "as a man on horseback." Washington Irving, who traveled over this parklike region in 1832 described it as a land "of flowery plains and sloping uplands, diversified by groves and clumps of trees, and long screens of woodland; the whole wearing the aspect of complete, and even ornamental cultivation instead of native wildness."

Crossing the state from north to south through the rugged sandstone hills and extending into the eroded margin of the Red Beds lies the belt of tangled blackjacks and post oaks known—and dreaded—by early travelers as the "Cross Timbers." Fingers of the same blackjack–post-oak jungle extend northwest on the sand hills that flank the rivers. Again quoting Irving: "The Cross Timber is about forty miles in breadth, and stretches over a rough country of rolling hills . . . very much cut up by deep ravines. . . . The fires made on the prairie by the Indian hunters, had frequently penetrated these forests, scorching and calcining the lower twigs and

10

branches of the trees, and leaving them black and hard, so as to tear the flesh of man and horse that had to scramble through them. . . . It was like struggling through forests of cast iron."

Through all this land west of the mountains, whether prairie or scrub timber, fine trees formerly grew along the streams (the largest ones are gone now): walnut and oak, cedar—partial to the Cimarron and its branches—and pecan, from which the nuts were gathered and shipped in quantity long before the white man came. Through much of the state these trees are decorated in the winter with green knots of mistletoe, which also is shipped commercially. This plant was loved by the pioneers—it is said because it was used in funerals in bleak days when no other growing plant was available—and it is still the "state flower." As one follows the streams west and the other timber falls away, the cottonwood becomes increasingly conspicuous. It is poor for fuel and worse for lumber, but how could dwellers in a prairie land live without the beauty of its craggy white branches and its polished, twinkling leaves? Also extending far west are the wild plum—in the spring a white drift of bloom, in the summer good for marmalade—and the redbud, the "state tree," most popular of all Oklahoma plants. And on the broad flood plains of the rivers, especially the Cimarron and Red, the tamarisk raises its slender gray-green or lavender-pink sprays.

The great continuous plain of the Red Beds once formed a sea of grass starred with flowers. Here, about the center of the state, the rank bluestem of the east began to shade into the short, dense buffalo grass of the west. Most of the grass is gone now, and the prairie is an ocean of wheat. But its green waves still roll to a far horizon, with the curled plumes of timbered streams seeming to float on its restless surface.

As the plains grade west into a drier climate and a ragged land of gyp hills, the grass becomes bunchy and the blackjack thickets on the strips of river-blown sand give place to shinnery oak and sagebrush. Increasingly common is the yucca ("soap weed" or "bear grass") with its sharp spearlike leaves and its tall stems of fragrant, waxy flowers, and the cactus—especially the prickly pear ("hog-ear" cactus)—with its fleshy, thorny body and fragile blooms. In the southwest grow the tough but delicate-look-

11

ing desert willow *(Chilopsis linearis)* with its lavender flowers, and the mesquite *(Prosopis glandulosa)* with its dainty foliage and hanging pods.

Here is a familiar story about the mesquite—this frail-seeming tree that grows mostly underground. It is a Texas story, but since this part of Oklahoma once thought it belonged to Texas, it is not inappropriate. A tenderfoot ranch hand was directed to climb the windmill tower to turn on water for the stock. Then he was put to digging mesquite roots for fuel. But this time he balked, expressing a fluent opinion of "a —— —— country where you have to climb for water and dig for firewood."

In the Panhandle, sagebrush and clumps of grass still grow on the sand hills bordering the streams, but the flat top of the plains is indeed the "short-grass country." In this land of shimmering mirages and overpowering sky the curly buffalo grass once grew as tight and thick as the nap of a carpet. Flowers bloom here, too, mostly yellow flowers; and that strange plant, the locoweed, favorite of "Western" fiction writers, once was a minor hazard to the owner of livestock. The Russian thistle, not a native, but a weed brought in with impure seed, breaks from its roots and tumbles—a great, loose ball—across the fields or drifts high along the fences. On the rugged lava-capped Black Mesa grow piñon trees *(Pinus edulis)* strayed from New Mexico, and a few western yellow pine. Thus Oklahoma flora runs the gamut from the great cypress of warm, low southeastern valley to the brave piñon of wind-swept height.

Zoologists say that the range in species of native Oklahoma animals is probably greater than that of any equal area in the United States. Denizens of the timbered East were at home in the Ozarks and the Ouachitas; Rocky Mountain species strayed to the western sections; Great Plains animals found the prairies their natural habitat.

Most of the wild life is gone now. The bears have been killed, the great herds of buffalo have disappeared except in parks, the panther's scream is seldom heard in the timber, the fierce gray lobo no longer menaces the cowman's profit, and the prairie-dog towns are vanishing from the western flats. But a few protected deer still live in the northeast and southeast and one small band of wild antelope fleets across the Black Mesa; the farmers still join together to kill the predatory coyote; the jack rabbit lopes across the wheat fields as once he loped across the grassland; and small game and fur-bearing animals still seek refuge in the timber.

The birds also find Oklahoma a meeting place of North and South, East and West, plain and timber. There are more than 250 varieties, 200 of which stay the year around. Prairie chickens and wild turkeys, once very numerous, have been almost destroyed; quail on their way to extinction have been restocked. Geese and ducks fly over, flocks of sea gulls from the Gulf of Mexico visit the state, and dense clouds of blackbirds wheel and twist, and settle on feed lot and pasture. Meadow larks and cardinals stay all winter, filling the air with their clear notes on every sunny day. Robins also remain the year around. Every spring some unobservant Oklahoman goes into ecstasies on seeing the "first robin" that hopped around his lawn all winter. Crows also stay all the time, probably in order to plot more meanness. Sometimes they become such a nuisance that they are killed with dynamite in great numbers at their roosting places.

Of the migratory birds, orioles, hummingbirds, mockingbirds, catbirds, kingbirds, and the scissor-tailed flycatcher are among the most common. The mockingbird is the universal favorite. All day and all night he pours out his joy (one wonders when he eats), his slender body atilt on treetop or house roof, or floating up into the air borne by the surge of his song. Once in a while a belated one stays all winter, when he may be heard singing rather sadly on some crisp night.

Oklahoma also has tarantulas with hairy legs spreading to a terrifying distance and hairy body "as big as a hen's egg." (I never saw any that big; one is likely to overestimate their size when he is scared.) It has centipedes ten inches long, repulsive looking and really poisonous. It has scorpions, always in a fury, and able to deliver a painful sting with their lashing tails. It has harmless lizards darting about, and innocent horned toads spreading themselves flat and turning their grotesque little heads up wisely.

Oklahoma also has people. They have been greatly written about these later years, and as they have writhed under distorted portrayals, they have developed an abnormal sensitiveness to pub-

13

OKLAHOMA

lic opinion. For they are not Wild West characters nor Joads, but
people. And yet they do have traits that set them apart from their
fellow Americans. There is a distinctive Oklahoma character—
partly the product of physical environment, but even more the
result of a peculiar history.

14

II

"Red People"

ALTHOUGH OKLAHOMA is young as a state, the region came early within the scope of the white man's imperial ambitions. In the summer of 1541—less than fifty years after Columbus first set the prow of his ships toward the Western world—the weary but still glittering cavalcade of Francisco Vásquez de Coronado, who had come from far-off Mexico in search of golden cities, was winding across the trackless reaches of its western plains. And that same fall Hernando de Soto, who had been pushing his intrepid way through the tangled forests and mighty rivers of the Gulf region, made his winter camp close to the present eastern boundary.

Other expeditions followed: priests, soldiers, and courtiers —dim but heroic figures driven by the restless genius of Spain. But they found only immense herds of "crooked-backed oxen" and bands of wandering hunters. Today their memory lingers only in the names of western rivers and the oft-recurring legends of buried treasure and lost Spanish mines in the Wichita Mountains.

In 1682, Robert Cavelier, Sieur de La Salle, came down the Mississippi and claimed all the basin of that river (including Oklahoma) under the name of Louisiana for the king of France. During the succeeding century his countrymen penetrated eastern Oklahoma—even maintained a short-lived fur-trading post near the present Chilocco—and the French influence still lives in the names of streams and mountains of this section. Conflicting claims and the changes arising from European wars made Louisiana at one time French, at another Spanish, and finally by purchase in 1803 a part of the United States.

15

OKLAHOMA

Neither President Jefferson nor any of his advisers knew the extent of the land they had acquired, but by a treaty negotiated with Spain in 1819 the southwestern boundary was fixed at the Red River and the one-hundredth meridian. Thus all of the present Oklahoma except the Panhandle lay within the American domain. For administrative purposes it was first joined with the Territory of Indiana. Next it was governed from St. Louis. Then, as territories were carved out of the Louisiana region, it was included first in the Territory of Missouri, and finally—except for a strip along the northern part—in the Territory of Arkansas.

All this is written on the map. Take for example the name of the Ouachita Mountains and the Washita River, pronounced the same with the accent on the "wash." This word in the Choctaw language means "big hunt," and it preserves the record of successful hunting trips from the tribal home in Mississippi. But the French spelled it in Arkansas and eastern Oklahoma, and the English-speaking Americans wrote it their way in the west.

For the Oklahoma region soon came within the sphere of American activity. Military and scientific expeditions, travelers, and adventurers mapped its rivers, studied its flora and fauna, and entered into friendly relations with the wild Indians who hunted over its plains. At the same time the advance guard of American settlement began to penetrate the eastern part of the state: half-savage frontiersmen built cabins along the streams; and trading firms, especially the great Chouteau family of St. Louis, established remote outposts to carry on their traffic with the Indian tribes. Chouteaus still live in the state, proud of their ancestor, one of the founders of St. Louis, but prouder of their century and a half of Oklahoma enterprise; and they carry on a perennial dispute with historians about the date and location of the "first white settlement." But the controversy is mainly academic; for the real colonization of Oklahoma by a civilized people began with the arrival of immigrant Indians from the Southeast.

The ancestors of the Cherokees, Choctaws, Chickasaws, Creeks, and Seminoles were living in the Gulf and southern Appalachian region when De Soto came. They were then a prosperous agricultural people with highly developed political and social institutions. During the next three centuries, and especially after

16

1800, they learned much from the white man. They acquired live-stock and cotton, obtained Negro slaves, and began to lay out plantations; they had come in contact with Christianity, and were building churches and schools; and they were beginning to adopt written constitutions and law codes. It was at this time that the Cherokee, Sequoyah, reduced his native language to writing, and the whole tribe became literate. The Choctaws were doing the same with the help of missionary translators.

But the white man coveted the rich Gulf cotton lands, and so the same period that marked the Indians' most rapid advancement brought about a demand for their expulsion. During 1817–37 all these tribes were persuaded or forced to exchange their lands in the East for wild tracts beyond the frontier, where—so said the treaties—they might govern themselves, and no state or territory would ever be erected over them without their consent. Eventually they owned all of present-day Oklahoma except the Panhandle.

Some of them submitted peaceably to the Removal. Others, especially the valiant Seminoles, were dragged from their homes by military force. Whether they entered upon their exile with heart-broken submission or were driven as sullen, desperate captives in chains, their suffering on the "Trail of Tears" forms one of the most tragic episodes in American history. Incidents of the journey are still fresh in family tradition, and the march as a whole forms an Oklahoma epic.

There was danger that these broken contingents of evacués might fall an easy prey to the wild Indians who already inhabited the region. The government accordingly established forts to protect them: Fort Smith, at the present western boundary of Arkansas, in 1817; Fort Gibson at the "Three Forks" of the Arkansas, Verdigris, and Grand rivers, in 1824; Fort Towson, near the mouth of the Kiamichi, in 1824; Fort Washita, a few miles above the confluence of the Washita and Red rivers, in 1842; Fort Arbuckle, on the north slope of the Arbuckle Mountains, in 1851; Fort Cobb, where Cobb Creek empties into the Washita, in 1859; and several others of less permanent importance. These lonely outposts of American authority maintained an active social life, served as centers of Indian councils, and formed the base of military expeditions to more distant frontiers. Fort Gibson, especially, became

a sort of focal point in American history. Two of its military person-
nel and one civilian living in the vicinity later became presidents:
Zachary Taylor of the United States, Jefferson Davis of the Southern Confederacy, and Sam Houston of the Texas Republic. Also
stationed briefly here were future military leaders on both sides
in the Civil War: Robert E. Lee, J. E. B. Stuart, Braxton Bragg,
Albert Sidney Johnston, George H. Thomas, Edmund Kirby Smith,
John B. Hood.

As soon as they had time to recover from the Removal, the
Indians began to prosper in their new home. They laid out farms,
planted orchards, and accumulated cattle and horses and hogs.
Even today one may find the site of an old grist mill or an abandoned salt works where native business once flourished; and substantial houses built by mixed-blood aristocrats now stand vacant
in eroded fields. Here and there were traders' stores owned by
mixed bloods or white men licensed by the federal government. A
few intermarried white men lived among them, but intruders
bothered them very little. They were protected theoretically by
their treaties and the Indian Intercourse Acts, but actually by their
remote location beyond the frontier.

Steamboats of shallow draft came up the Arkansas and Red
rivers bringing furniture and farm implements and striped calico,
and taking back cargoes of pecans and furs and agricultural products. Several great trails led across the country: the Texas Road,
through present Vinita, Muskogee, and McAlester, crowded by
white emigrants with their covered wagons pointed south, and occasionally a herd of cattle moving north to market; the California
Trail, used by gold seekers moving west from Fort Smith up the
Arkansas and Canadian rivers; and the Santa Fé Trail, with its
great freight trains from Independence, Missouri, cutting southwest across the Panhandle.

The immigrant Indians were settled in the eastern half of the
present state, but they made periodic hunting trips west to the
buffalo plains. To distinguish them from the wild natives of the
region, they were usually called the "Five Civilized Tribes"; and as
the states of Missouri, Arkansas, Texas, and Kansas were formed
on their borders, their land became known as "the Indian Territory." But relying on the guarantees of the Removal treaties, they

steadfastly refused to form a territorial government, which they knew would be dominated by white people. They held many councils and established friendly relations with each other and with the wild tribes, but each little republic governed its citizens under its own laws.

A list of Oklahoma "firsts" shows the importance of this Indian background in the development of the state. True, the first county government with the first court was established by the white man while the area was still a part of Arkansas; Miller County in the southeastern corner was organized in 1820, and the first post office was opened at Miller Courthouse in 1824. But Arkansas authority disappeared, and most of the squatters were moved out when the land was settled by the Choctaws.[1] Also in 1821 the first Protestant mission station—Union Mission in the northeast—was established by white men for the wild Osages; and when the Creeks and Cherokees moved in, it became a center of influence for them. But the first church organization in the state so far as is known was a Presbyterian church formed in 1830 among the recently arrived Creeks near present Muskogee. Another Presbyterian congregation organized by the Choctaws near Millerton two years later erected a sturdy stone building in 1846, which still stands as the oldest church building in the state.

Oklahoma elections go back at least as early as 1831, when the Cherokees chose their tribal officers. And although the missionaries, with the active co-operation of the Indians engaged in educational work, the first public-school law in Oklahoma was passed by the Cherokees in 1832; it provided for five English-language schools, and appointed Sequoyah under an annual salary to teach his characters informally throughout the settlement. Probably the first constitution framed in Oklahoma was the one adopted by the Choctaws in 1834—a continuation of the constitutional development that started in the East. The first book was printed at Union Mission in 1835; it was probably a Creek primer, *I stutsi in Naktsokv*, prepared by a missionary with the help of native converts, although it may have been a Cherokee or a Choctaw al-

---

[1] A similar situation arose in the northeastern part of what is now the state of Oklahoma with the organization and subsequent extinction of Lovely County before the arrival of the Cherokees.

manac, for the three publications bear the same date. In 1838 the Choctaws built the first capitol in the state—a hewn-log building near the present Tuskahoma.

The first newspapers in Oklahoma were bilingual Cherokee-and-English publications beginning in 1844. Baptist missionaries published *The Cherokee Messenger* for a short time near present Westville; a month later came *The Cherokee Advocate,* a tribal publication which, under the name of *The Cherokee Phoenix,* had been launched in the East in 1828 and discontinued during the stress of Removal. The first Masonic lodge in Oklahoma was chartered in 1848 at Tahlequah with a Cherokee membership. This same Tahlequah, the Cherokee capital, was incorporated under tribal law in 1852—the first incorporated town in Oklahoma. And so it goes. A few years ago when I wrote a history of Tulsa—young, beautiful oil-built Tulsa—I found it really began in 1836 when a band of Creek immigrants from Alabama selected the site and founded the town with a formal ceremony of dedication. Oklahoma is not new; it is only the white man who is a newcomer.

All this promising Indian development was interrupted by the Civil War. It was inevitable that the Five Civilized Tribes should join the South. Their leading men held slaves. The former federal agents to the tribes were all Southern men. They were hemmed in by seceded states on three sides. The federal garrisons hastily abandoned the military posts in the territory and retreated to Kansas; new federal agents appointed to take the place of the secessionists stopped in the same safe refuge. Their country was overrun with Confederate envoys explaining that the Union was severed, and advising them to cast their lot in with their own section. There was nobody to dispute the overwhelming evidence that in that area the United States had been superseded by a new government.

But a conservative fullblood element of the three most northern tribes—Cherokees, Creeks, and Seminoles—was unable to make the shift. These Indians left their homes and collected in a great camp on the Deep Fork of the Canadian, and sent frantic appeals for help to the United States government. But no help arrived. The Confederates attacked them, and they fled to Kansas, where great numbers died in refugee camps. Later their men enlisted in the

Union Army and joined in recapturing the Indian Territory. Then it was the Southern Indians who fled to refugee camps along the Red River. Meanwhile both sides enlisted the support of the wild tribes of the western prairies. Some bands joined the South, but more with Northern encouragement raided enthusiastically on the Texas frontier.

As the war progressed, guerrilla bands from both sides ravaged the Indian Territory, and citizens of Kansas carried on an organized business of driving out the Indians' cattle and selling them to army contractors. When soldiers and refugees, whether Northern or Southern, returned to their homes at the close of the war, their country was completely stripped.

Worse for the Indians than the war itself was the great Western expansion that followed it. Once again white settlers wanted their land. For a time it looked as though the Indian Territory would be thrown open to homesteaders; but it was finally decided to take away the western—and unsettled—half of their country and colonize other Indians there. All but the Chickasaws were also induced to grant citizenship to their former slaves. An elaborate plan was drawn up for an intertribal council that was to be the beginning of an Indian state. These provisions were embodied in treaties which the Five Tribes signed at the close of the war.

During the negotiations in Washington the delegates discussed the governor of the proposed commonwealth. What should be his title? Allen Wright, a Choctaw delegate, spoke up instantly. No doubt he had been reading the old treaties, which repeatedly referred to "the Choctaw Nation of Red People." In the Choctaw version "Red People" reads *Okla Homa.* The name was fresh in his mind. "We will call him 'governor of Oklahoma,'" he said— governor of the Red People. And so it was written. No Indian commonwealth was ever formed, but a state does bear the name "Oklahoma." Incidentally Muriel H. Wright, a granddaughter of that Choctaw delegate, is one of its leading historians.

In the years following the Civil War about twenty-five tribes of Indians were given reservations in the ceded western half or the small northeast corner of the Indian Territory, and one tribe bought citizenship with the Cherokees. Most of the smaller tribes— Delaware, Shawnee, Sac and Fox, Ottawa, Wyandotte, and others

21

—were Eastern Indians, victims of the former Removal policy. They had purchased lands beyond the frontier at the same time as the Five Tribes; but when Kansas and other states were formed, they were again surrounded. Other tribes, like the Osage, Cheyenne and Arapaho, Pawnee, and Kiowa (with an affiliated Apache band) and Comanche, were hunters of the Plains; and the more agricultural Wichitas were assigned to reservations to confine their wanderings to the Indian Territory.

A chain of military posts was established through the Southwest to hold the wild tribes in check. Fort Supply (1868), Fort Sill (1869), and Fort Reno (1874) were in the present state of Oklahoma. The great Civil War generals, Philip H. Sheridan and William Tecumseh Sherman, George A. Custer of later "Custer Massacre" fame, and Nelson A. Miles, the well-known Indian fighter, were all connected with the early history of these posts. The military reservation at Fort Supply now belongs to the state of Oklahoma and a mental hospital has been built there; a federal reformatory occupies part of the Fort Reno site; and Fort Sill is still a great military post, the Field Artillery School of the United States Army.

But in the late eighteen sixties and early seventies these forts were the stations of Indian fighters. They found plenty to do. The wild tribes were not ready to surrender their spacious prairies; but their hunting grounds in Kansas, Texas, and Colorado were rapidly filling with settlers, and the vast buffalo herds, which formed the basis of their living and their culture, were being exterminated by hide hunters. The Indians retaliated by raiding the frontiers, and the whole Southwest flamed with violence. Their resistance was finally broken in 1875; then they settled down on their reservations in the Indian Territory, herded up by government agents, and painfully acquiring some of the outward forms of civilization.

In 1870, at the very height of hostilities, the United States called an intertribal council at Okmulgee, the Creek capital, as the first step in the united Indian government envisioned by the treaties. Here leaders of the Civilized Tribes met the painted, befeathered war chiefs of the Southwest and delegates of the broken tribes recently removed from Kansas; and now in polished parliamentary procedure, now in native symbolism of peace pipe and beads, they tried to work out a policy based upon a common Indian interest. Over and over they emphasized the importance of agriculture and education as their only chance of survival, and the need of guarding the Indian Territory as the future home of their race. But the Great Father at Washington objected to their independence, and after a few years the council was discontinued. It had an important influence; as the wild tribes saw the fields and herds of their civilized neighbors, they began to understand that they, too, might learn a way of life that would compensate them for the loss of the buffalo.

The Five Tribes were again prospering. They had rebuilt their dwellings, set out new orchards, planted their weed-grown fields, and were once more acquiring extensive herds. As their property gained value, their courts dealt with increasingly complex questions of civil and criminal law. The land belonged to the tribe, but each citizen was protected in the use of as much as he cared to cultivate.

The Indians also replaced their ruined school buildings and re-established their educational systems. Each tribe supported neighborhood schools taught by native teachers, and boarding schools for higher training. At least two tribes—the Choctaw and Creek—sent selected young people to outside colleges at public expense. Literacy in the native languages was general, and more than half the population could read and write in English. Each settlement had its Presbyterian, Methodist, or Baptist church, usually served by a native pastor.

But the Indian Territory had lost its protected isolation. The first railroad—the Missouri, Kansas, and Texas ("Katy"), following the old Texas Trail—was built across the Five Tribes area during 1870–72, and the construction of other lines followed. At the stations white men laid out active little towns with boundless ambitions. And white settlers began to establish farms, perhaps under some form of lease from an Indian, perhaps with no legal status whatever. Others began to cut and ship the timber from the tribal domain in spite of the Indians' protests. Then through a compromise with the Choctaw government extensive coal mines were opened near McAlester, operated under a royalty agreement and worked by imported laborers. The tribes tried to regulate all this immigration by a system of "permits" to traders and legitimate laborers, and expulsion of intruders; but it soon broke out of control. The first federal census of the Five Tribes area, made in 1890, showed a population of 109,393 whites and 18,636 Negroes (former slaves of the Indians reinforced by Negro intruders) to 50,055 Indians.

These noncitizens could not own land, form city governments, or establish public schools. The Indians had no jurisdiction over them. During most of the period they had no civil courts, and in criminal matters there was only the federal court for the Western District of Arkansas at Fort Smith. Outlaws accordingly flocked to the region. United States marshals ranged through the territory collecting the most notorious criminals and bringing them before the famous "hanging judge," Isaac C. Parker, at Fort Smith. But although a specially constructed gallows dropped them in simultaneous batches, they multiplied faster than even Judge Parker could exterminate them.

Cattlemen also began to occupy the Indian Territory. First they drove their herds across the domain of the Five Tribes from Texas to northern markets. Then they shipped on the Katy and on the Atlantic and Pacific (now the St. Louis and San Francisco— "Frisco"), which soon built from the northeast corner of the territory to Tulsa. But they had discovered the richness of the rank bluestem, and they brought in many thousands of head and turned them loose on the Indians' ranges. The tribes tried to collect fines on the longhorned intruders, but if a tribal officer attempted to seize them, he was brought before Judge Parker and convicted of larceny.

Meanwhile, on the vacant prairies of central Oklahoma, far to the west of the Five Tribes settlements, the greatest cow traffic of all was beating the path famous in song and story as the Chisholm Trail. Literally millions of head were driven up to the Kansas cow towns, first to Abilene, then—as the railroads advanced south— to Wichita, and last to Caldwell on the border. Great freighters' wagons pulled by mules or many yoke of oxen moved down the trail with supplies for the Indian agencies or the military posts, and lighter stagecoaches carrying passengers on government business. The stations at which they stopped are now thriving towns and cities on the Rock Island Railroad—Pond Creek, Enid, Bison, Hennessey, Dover, Kingfisher, and so on down the line. U. S. Highway 81 also traverses the route, appropriately marked by spreading horns symbolic of the first travelers. A few years ago the Oklahoma Highway Commission took aerial photographs and laid them end to end to form a long map; here, after more than half a century of cultivation, the marks of the great rutted thoroughfare still show as a continuous scar across farmland and stream.

A little later and farther west, the Western Trail became another notable cowpath. It crossed the Red River at a supply point known as "Doan's Store," traversed the Kiowa-Comanche-Apache and Cheyenne-Arapaho reservations, passed by Fort Supply and the stage station of Buffalo, and on to Dodge City, wildest of Kansas cow towns. South of Fort Supply a branch came from the southwest, connecting with Fort Elliott and the ranches and cow towns of the Texas Panhandle. Still farther west the Jones-Plummer Trail from the Texas Panhandle to Dodge City crossed the Oklahoma Panhandle, with a stage station at Beaver "City."

It was very easy for the drovers to turn their cattle off these trails to graze on the Indian reservations. Some were allowed to remain near the agencies to supply beef to the Indians, who had lost their buffalo and had not yet learned to farm. Others with the consent of the agents made irregular leasing arrangements with the tribes.

But the most extensive ranching region of all western Oklahoma was the Cherokee Outlet or "Strip," which lay 60 miles wide and 180 miles long on the Kansas border. It had been taken from the Cherokees as a home for other Indians, but after several tribes had been settled there, more than six million acres still lay unoccupied. The Cherokees collected grazing fees—when they could—from individual cattlemen, until the Cherokee Strip Live Stock Association was chartered under Kansas law in 1883. This ranching corporation then entered into a contract with the tribe by which it paid a yearly rental of $100,000 for the entire tract; it fixed the boundaries of each member's range; and it recorded brands, arranged roundups, and offered rewards for the extermination of gray wolves and cattle thieves.

Thus, in spite of Indian farms in the east and Indian reserva-

25

tions and military posts in the west, all of Oklahoma had become a part of the fabled Western empire of grass and longhorns. Every community in the state still has aging men of clear eyes and bow-legged gait who have not forgotten the techniques of trail and range, the heraldry of brands, the sweat and songs and pranks of the cowboy.

Meanwhile the frontiersmen of the surrounding states had their eyes on the Indian Territory; and they protested equally against its possession by Indians and its occupation by cattlemen. They were backed up by the thousands of intruders living among the Five Tribes. Working under cover to foment the agitation were the officials and stockholders of the Katy and the Atlantic and Pacific railroads, which had received grants of land along the right of way conditioned upon the extinction of the Indian title. They subsidized newspapers in the railroad towns of the territory to urge the opening of the country, and the border press of the surrounding states freely joined in the campaign.

By 1880 these forces had become strong enough to prevent the settlement of any more Indian tribes in the territory. It was mainly through their influence that much of the land ceded for that purpose at the close of the Civil War remained unoccupied. Obviously, if the country was filled with Indians it would not be available for *them.* They also influenced members of Congress to introduce the so-called "Oklahoma Bills" for the formation of a territorial government and the opening of the country to settlement. But the Civilized Tribes sent their ablest citizens to Washington to defeat these proposals. The agitators then adopted other tactics.

In 1879 the railroad interests began to advertise the fact that a tract of nearly two million acres ceded by the Creeks and Seminoles in the center of the Territory had never been assigned to another tribe; and they argued that these "Unassigned Lands" or "Oklahoma Lands" were therefore open to homesteaders. Stories of the fertility of the region were circulated throughout the United States, and colonies of "Boomers" under the lead of a Kansan named David L. Payne began to invade the country. The Civilized Tribes in alarm appealed to Judge Parker. He ruled that the Indians had ceded the land conditionally for other Indians only, and fined Payne for trespass.

"Red People"

But the invaders continued to drive stakes in the prairie and lay out townsites. The law carried no penalty but a fine, and imposing a fine on these penniless adventurers was a pure abstraction. Soldiers from Fort Reno would convey them to the border, but they would return immediately. They found the country occupied by cattlemen, who had come in without permission from anyone and established ranches with camps and corrals and well defined ranges. The poor homeseeker *vs.* rich cattleman motif then entered into the agitation, with public sympathy on the side of the nester. In 1886–87 the Atchinson, Topeka, and Santa Fe Railroad was built—this time with no corrupting land grant—from north to south across the Indian Territory, passing through the "Oklahoma Lands"; and lonely stations—Guthrie, Oklahoma [City], Edmond, and Norman—were laid out along its right of way.

Finally the United States purchased an absolute title to the land from the Creeks and Seminoles, and announced that on April 22, 1889, it would be opened for white settlement. Meanwhile in 1887 Congress had passed the Dawes Severalty Act, providing that all the Indians except the Five Tribes should be forced to take individual "allotments" of land (and United States citizenship), and that the remainder of their reservations should be opened as soon as possible to homesteaders. Thus the long-cherished plans for an Indian commonwealth were definitely abandoned. The land of the "Red People" was to become the frontier of the white man.

III

The White Man Builds
in Oklahoma

T<small>HE</small> "O<small>KLAHOMA</small> L<small>ANDS</small>" had already been surveyed and divided into quarter-section (160-acre) tracts marked with cornerstones. Now two government land offices were hastily constructed—at Guthrie station on the Santa Fe, and Kingfisher stage stop on the Chisholm Trail—to receive filings of homestead entry. Prospective settlers were warned that anyone who should cross the border before high noon on the opening day would be disqualified to hold a claim; and soldiers were stationed there to guard the empty land against intrusion.

The great horse race known as the "Run" grew out of these circumstances; obviously if the homeseekers were forbidden to enter until a certain hour, they would all enter at once, and the one who could outdistance his rivals would have his pick. And they came by the tens of thousands. From Kansas they cut through the ranches of the Cherokee Strip, or they flowed down the Chisholm Trail in one continuous stream of covered wagons and riders; and they fanned out along the northern and western borders. They came from a percarious sojourn among the Creeks and Cherokees and waited along the east. Others came up from Texas and the Chickasaw country and camped on the south; theirs would be a perilous entry by ford across the treacherous Canadian, which formed the southern boundary. Still others planned to enter by rail. The Santa Fe officials promised to run trains in from each direction, starting at the signal and holding the speed to that of a man on horseback; the passengers, packed in or holding on, would drop off along the way to stake their claims. All these were the honest homeseekers; an unprincipled minority known as "Sooners" managed to seep in and settle on choice locations before the time set for the opening.

On April 22 the sun rose clear on a bright land. The encircling line grew tense. Finally came twelve o'clock, and the starting gun, the wild yell, the thunder of hoofs, the whistle of the trains. This, too, is an Oklahoma epic. Men still like to tell how they drove a stake in the prairie, feverishly located cornerstones, and rode to the land office to record their choice. And near the railroad stations promoters were laying out townsites, and men were swarming over them to stake lots and set up tents. When the sun went down that night, the age-old solitude was broken by the campfires of homesteaders and the cheerful confusion of populous towns. Nobody knows how many came in that first day; the federal census of 1890 showed a population of 53,822. The same enumeration listed 5,883 inhabitants for Guthrie, 4,151 for Oklahoma City, and 1,134 for Kingfisher.

On the first day or during the first week, men in the towns started banks, published newspapers, opened stores and restaurants, and set up lawyers' and doctors' offices—all confident that skyscrapers and busy streets would soon replace the huddle of tents and shacks. Religious services were held in the open air the first Sunday. The settlement of the land was a little less rapid, for after they had completed their filing, most of the men returned to their old homes and spent some time in preparation for the venture. But by fall there was a family on every claim. The land was dotted with dugouts and sod houses, wells were dug, the sod was broken for planting, and neighbors from widely separated states entered into community relations based on common needs.

Often a chance conversation will show the dramatic speed of this development. Recently I talked with an elderly man, still hale and active, who was visiting in Oklahoma City. It was the first time he had seen the place since a few days before the Opening; he had been too young to file on a claim, and so he had gone away and had only read of what had happened there. He had a clear memory of a little railroad station by a river, a green valley with bordering blackjack hills, a teepee or two where some wandering Indians camped, and steel rails stretching across the emptiness to the outside world. He saw towers of business rising from the flat, mile on mile of residences spreading across the upland, tentacles of industry reaching to the suburbs. Everything he knew was covered up. But I have seldom seen anyone so moved by the feeling that he had looked in on the stuff of history.

For more than a year this surging frontier in the heart of the Indian Territory had no organized government. But life was surprisingly safe, and as for property, that existed mainly in the imagination of the builders. Whenever it became necessary, the settlers acted together through mass meetings and informal elections.

Guthrie and Oklahoma City organized provisional governments the first week, mainly to bring order into the platting of the townsites. Two days after the Opening, Guthrie set aside ten acres on "Capitol Hill" for a territorial seat of government; and the *Oklahoma Times,* printed in a tent in Oklahoma City, pointed out on May 9 that a near-by tract still occupied by a detachment of soldiers would make a fine location for the capitol. Kingfisher and other ambitious towns, some of which have since disappeared from the map, cherished similar ambitions. During the summer, delegations from the different settlements met in conventions to organize a territorial government, but nothing came out of these meetings but capital fights.

Then on May 2, 1890 Congress created a Territory of Oklahoma for the western half of the present state. It would have a governor appointed by the president, a system of courts also appointive, and a legislature elected by the people. The Territory would have no voice in national elections except that it might choose a delegate to Congress, who could speak but not vote. Guthrie was designated as the temporary capital—an advantage it managed to hold throughout the territorial period. The area settled the previous year was divided into six counties.

This Organic Act also added the Panhandle to the new territory as a seventh county. For a long time it had been known as "No Man's Land." Lying on the Spanish side of the boundary set in 1819, it had become through successive revolutions a part of Mexico and then of Texas; and when Texas entered the Union, it became a part of the United States. But when the present boundaries of Texas and New Mexico were fixed by the Compromise of 1850, and Kansas and Colorado were carved out of the public domain, this strip was left outside any state or territory. Mexican sheep-herders drifted across the western end, cowmen divided its ranges, nesters built dugouts along the valleys, and promoters laid out townsites. It was entirely without law or government. In 1887 the settlers met in a sod schoolhouse at Beaver "City" and organized a "Territory of Cimarron," but Congress never legalized their action. A provisional legislature did convene and pass a few "laws." One eloquent of the plight of the settlers imposed a fine on any non-resident who should gather buffalo bones, cow chips, wood, grapes, or any other "territorial products." When the "Oklahoma Lands" were opened in 1889, many of the discouraged squatters moved to these greener fields. Only 2,674 were left to be counted in the census the next year. More than one hundred miles lay between them and the 1889 settlement.

Meanwhile the President appointed deserving politicians as governor and judges of the new territory; and in August the first legislature convened in Guthrie for a four months' session. The legislators spent so much time wrangling over the location of the capital and other state institutions that the law code hastily drawn up just before adjournment contained a section regulating Oklahoma's seaports. But they did create an educational system for the territory.

Public schools had of course been impossible before a government was organized, but most of the towns had held tuition schools the first winter, and some of the rural communities had gathered their children in log cabins or dugouts and employed a neighbor to teach them on a "subscription" basis. Then the next spring the Organic Act carried a federal appropriation of $50,000 to support the common schools until it would be possible to assess and collect taxes. The legislature accordingly provided for the election of superintendents, the certification of teachers, and the organization of school districts. The law was passed so late in the session—December 5, to be exact—that the schools did not open until spring. Most of them were operated for about three and one-half months. By the next winter the territory took over the financing, but for several years the pitiably small amount of taxable property in rural neighborhoods limited the term to three months. Thus the surprising literacy of the first generation of Oklahomans is based on the use of three or four textbooks for a three months' term in a sod or log building with homemade benches.

The first legislature also located—after much jockeying among the different towns—three territorial colleges. Two were opened in churches the next fall: the Normal School at Edmond on the Santa Fe with twenty-three students; and the Agricultural and Mechanical College, generally known as A. and M., at the village of Stillwater, with forty-five. The University of Oklahoma opened a year later—in the fall of 1892—in a rented store building at Norman with a president and three other teachers. Soon each of these institutions was housed in a pretentious building that loomed above the struggling town and the newly turned sod of the campus like a symbol of the people's faith. The one at the University has since burned down, but "North Tower" at Edmond and "Old Central" at A. and M. still stand as rallying points of student affection.

Old settlers at Stillwater remember a young man from Iowa who hauled freight over a trail through the blackjacks west of town. The event of his day's drive was a distant view of the stark building on the hillside, which to him meant Ambition and Opportunity. His name was James Brooks A. Robertson, and he later served as governor of Oklahoma.

Thus the conquering white American established institutions on the new soil of Oklahoma. Its centers of such development grew rapidly. As soon as Indian tribes accepted allotments under the Dawes Act, the surplus lands were thrown open with another Run and the conquest of another frontier. There was the Run into the Iowa, Sac and Fox, and Shawnee-Potawatomi reservations to the east of "Old Oklahoma" in 1891; the opening of the Cheyenne-Arapaho country to the west the next year; the greatest Run of all on the north the year after that, when the United States purchased an absolute title to the Cherokee Outlet and opened it, with the Tonkawa and Pawnee reservations; and the small Kickapoo Opening in 1895. The settlers in their turn wrestled with the same problems of food and shelter and community building, and their new counties were added to the older government.

Another area of white pioneering came from the settlement of a boundary contest between the United States and Texas. It was undisputed that the Red River was the boundary; that had been settled by the treaty with Spain in 1819. But the stream has two forks. The United States said the South Fork was the real Red River; Texas, a little cramped for space, claimed the land up to the North Fork and began to settle it. The country was first occupied by cattlemen; then nesters and townsite promoters began to come in, and in 1886 the region was organized under Texas law as Greer County with Mangum as the county seat. The census of 1890 showed a population of 5,338. But in 1896 the United States Supreme Court decided that the South Fork was the main stream. The land was then added to the growing Territory of Oklahoma, and several thousand Texans were thereby automatically changed to Oklahomans.

Meanwhile the Kiowas, Comanches, and Apaches and the Wichitas and some affiliated tribes had chosen allotments, and the surplus land of those two reservations was ready for settlement. As the time approached for the homesteading of this large and fertile area in the southwest, it became apparent that the contest for free farms would surpass all previous land rushes. It was decided therefore to open the region by lottery. In July, 1901, people from all parts of the United States camped at El Reno in "Old Oklahoma" and at Fort Sill and registered their applications for claims. The names were then drawn from a box, and each recipient of a lucky number was permitted to select a quarter-section of land. Thus without noise or strife, but with the same deep, creative forces of growth, this wild tract of prairie also became a land of farms and schools and striving towns.

The reservations of the Poncas, the Otoes and Missouris, the Kaws, and the Osages were also broken up into individual allotments and these Indians became citizens of Oklahoma. But there was no Run into their country, for they divided all their land among their members without leaving a surplus for white settlement.

Thus from 1890 on, the Territory of Oklahoma was a region of Indian reservations and a succession of white frontiers. The name "Indian Territory" was now confined to the eastern half of the present state. It was owned and governed by the Five Civilized Tribes and by several fragments of tribes in the northeastern corner. These "Twin Territories" were approximately equal not only in size but in population. The census of 1900—before the opening of the Kiowa-Comanche and Wichita reservations—showed 398,331 inhabitants for Oklahoma, 392,060 for the Indian Territory; a special enumeration made in 1907 listed 733,062 and 681,115 respectively.

These figures show how rapidly the region was filling up with white people, and they indicate that the movement was only slightly retarded by the tribal status of the eastern half. The separation of the two areas was more apparent than real. In Oklahoma Territory were the Runs, homesteading, and the organization of government; in Indian Territory was an extralegal infiltration almost as rapid, but the dominant fact was the same.

Of course the white residents in the Indian Territory were dissatisfied with their status. Naturally they besieged the federal government for redress; and the senators and representatives from adjoining states and the delegate from the Territory of Oklahoma worked actively in their interest. Finally in 1893 Congress created a commission to persuade the Indians to surrender their control and prepare for statehood. It was headed for a time by former Senator Dawes of Massachusetts, the same man who had given his name to the Severalty Act under which the western reservations were being broken up. The Indians quoted the guarantees of the treaties, but after five years of fruitless negotiations Congress passed the Curtis Act forcing the allotment of their land and the abolition of their governments. The "Dawes Commission" then carried out the liquidation of their affairs under this law or under separate agreements made with the tribes.

This was a complex task requiring years for its completion. The communal property of each tribe had to be divided equally among the citizens. These five great estates comprised an area totaling 19,525,966 acres, with rich valleys, rugged hills, and forests of pine and hardwood. All this had to be surveyed and appraised so that each Indian would get his share of land and money; and the Indians and inrushing whites had to be protected in some way during the period of transition.

First the townsites were platted and sold; and it became possible for white city builders to own lots, organize municipal governments, lay taxes, and establish schools. The land was divided

34

as equally as possible—taking account of its fertility—among the tribal citizens, except for a surplus of three and three-fourths million acres, belonging mostly to the Choctaws and Chickasaws, which was sold at auction. The individual allotments were at first not subject to sale, for the Indians had requested this protection until they could gain experience in the new system of landholding; but this restriction was gradually removed, so that white people began to purchase their farms. Thus while there was never a Run into the Five Tribes area, the ultimate result was the same.

The public buildings were sold. Some of them are now owned by the state of Oklahoma or its divisions. The tribal governments were shorn of their powers, and the Indians became citizens of the United States. Congress borrowed laws from Arkansas to form a legal code, and established a system of federal courts to enforce it. The Indians' rural schools were enlarged to admit white children; later they became a part of the public school system of the state.

All of these arrangements were complicated by the discovery of oil, on the allotments first of Cherokees and then of Creeks. This brought a new kind of "Run," as drillers, promoters, representatives of large corporations, and shoestring operators, from the oil fields of Pennsylvania and other states, rushed to some hole in a trampled wilderness where millions of dollars might be lost or won. The strife and violence, the unpredictable chances of this industry brought the blood and thunder strangely lacking in most of the state's history. The village of Tulsa—once a Creek Indian settlement, next a cow town on the Frisco—managed to capture this business; and began its dramatic growth as an oil town.

But the Dawes Commission went on with its work. At the same time the small tribes in the northeast had been induced to break up their reservations and accept individual ownership under the Dawes Severalty Act. By 1905 the end was in sight; the Indian Territory was ready for statehood. The tribal leaders objected to union with Oklahoma. With a few white men who joined the movement, they held a convention at Muskogee and wrote a constitution for a "State of Sequoyah." But Congress ignored them, as it also denied the aspirations of Oklahoma Territory for separate statehood. With a logic more apparent in the long view than it was during the brief years of separation, the Enabling Act passed during the following session provided for the union of the "Twin Territories" to form the state of Oklahoma. Thus, out of the conflict between the Indian's love of his homeland and the creative forces of the last white frontier, a new commonwealth was ready to enter the sisterhood of states.

Under the terms of the Enabling Act, fifty-five delegates from each territory and two from the Osage Reservation—still in process of allotment—were elected to write a constitution. To the surprise of political observers ninety-nine delegates proved to be Democrats and only thirteen Republicans. Most of them were young men. Many were farmers, and all were agrarian in outlook. Several were mixed-blood Indians. Again to the surprise of observers, the "east side" dominated the group through alliances made at the Sequoyah Convention the previous year. The president was William H. ("Alfalfa Bill") Murray, a young Texan, who had come to the Indian Territory to practice law, had married a cultured Chickasaw girl, and had been employed as private secretary by her uncle, the Chickasaw governor. Another leader was Charles N. Haskell, who had recently come from Ohio to Muskogee to build railroads out of imagination and brass. A third was Robert Lee Williams, a college graduate from Alabama, who had been living for ten years in the Choctaw country. Still another was Henry S. Johnston, born in Indiana, and admitted to the bar in Colorado, who had settled in the new town of Perry after the opening of the Cherokee Strip. All four of these were destined to become governors of the state they were forming.

The constitution drawn up by the convention was a product of the progressive movement just then stirring the United States and the world. It was a long document—printed, it would make a book half as large as this. The delegates wanted to provide in black and white for every contingency; they were taking no chances with "implied powers." Murray has since complained of governors who were not familiar with constitutional provisions, but relatively few persons have read the document through since its adoption. It provided for the initiative and referendum to give the people control of legislation, and the mandatory primary, that new device by which the people would nominate their candidates for office. It established numerous boards and commissions to regulate all manner of activities and businesses—especially to reduce corporations from boss to servant. It made nearly all offices elective. Murray now realizes this was a mistake. He attributes it to the people's unhappy territorial experience with federal appointees.[1]

When the document was completed, it was submitted to the voters, who ratified it by an overwhelming majority. At the same election they adopted a "prohibition" clause, which has never been modified except for the legalization in 1933 of 3.2 per cent beer. They also chose state and local officers and members of Congress. The Democrats elected all the state officers, a large majority of the legislature, four of the five representatives, and both senators. Charles N. Haskell was chosen governor. President Theodore Roosevelt then issued a proclamation declaring Oklahoma a state of the Union, and on the same day—November 16, 1907—the new state officers were inaugurated at Guthrie.

Oklahoma at that time had a population of 1,414,177, of which 5.3 per cent was Indian. It had all the proud poverty, the buoyant self-confidence, and the crude strength of every American frontier, complicated by the restrictions still remaining on Indian land and the requirements of an industrial age. At the time of its admission it was the leading oil-producing state, lead and zinc mining had become important with the break-up of the small Indian reservations of the northeast, and coal mining had been carried on in the Choctaw country, and to a lesser extent in the Creek country, for many years. Railroads were flung across the land, villages towered into cities, factories were established with feverish impatience; and in all this restless surge of growth, the destruction of natural resources and the creative forces of building were closely joined.

Oklahoma almost doubled in population between statehood and 1930. As oil field after oil field spouted gold in ever increasing streams, Tulsa, with a population too small to count in 1890, climbed from 7,298 inhabitants in 1907 to 18,182 in 1910, 72,075 in 1920, 141,258 in 1930. Oklahoma City, the capital since 1910, less specialized than Tulsa in its economic base, rose from 32,452 to 185,389 during the same period; at the last date its own sky line

[1] Murray, *Memoirs*, II, 44–45.

37

was a forest of derricks, for the greatest oil pool of the state lay beneath its busy streets. Attendance at the University rose from 384 students of college rank in 1907 to 740 in 1910, 2,763 in 1920, 5,416 in 1930; the enrollment at A. and M. grew by similar leaps to 4,298.

After 1930, Oklahoma paused in its rapid growth. The depression and drought of that decade hit hard, and the next census showed a population decrease of 59,606, or 2.5 per cent. This loss was due to the larger farm units of a mechanized agriculture, the decline of rural villages through motor transportation, and a depression industry too slack to absorb the overflow.

But 2,336,434 sturdy Americans (as counted by the 1940 census) still live in Oklahoma. It will be the task of the rest of this book to show how they live and what manner of people they are. One of their most violent forms of expression is politics.

IV

A Seething Caldron of Politics

$\mathbf{H}$ERE IS THE BASIC CAUSE of Oklahoma's political turmoil: a people agrarian in outlook and Jacksonian in politics had to cope with industrial problems developing with a speed never before attained in American history. As late as 1935 a survey made by the Brookings Institution found that "Oklahoma is advanced materially but retarded politically. It is economically developed, but governmentally immature." Former Oklahoman George Milburn expressed the same idea more cleverly: "Oklahoma is to sociology as Australia is to zoology"—a place of social and political survivals as outdated in modern life "as a duckbill or a kangaroo."[1]

This condition did not originate with statehood. The leaders of the Civilized Tribes, great native statesmen though they were, were unable to control the powerful financial interests that contended for their possessions. Elections became factional fights between sinister forces that lurked behind the forms of democracy, confusing the issues. Administrations were manipulated by the same hidden influences. I wish I had space for William H. Murray's story of how he worked through Chickasaw constitutional forms to keep one thousand claimants off the tribal rolls.[2] There was fully $4,000,000 involved, for Chickasaw citizenship was worth $1,075 in cash and 320 acres of average land. Murray's tactics on behalf of the Indians were matched by similar methods on the part of their opponents. Any politician trained in that school knew all the tricks of the trade.

[1] In "Oklahoma, the Misfit State," *Everybody's Digest*, August, 1946.
[2] Murray, *Memoirs*, I, 241–43.

39

Oklahoma Territory's sixteen years of political life had also been stormy. There was bitter rivalry between cities bursting with civic pride, and between individuals striving for personal advancement; and the party organizations were torn by factions fighting for control of federal patronage.

This situation was complicated by the political protest of the homesteader struggling to hold his bare 160 acres against the extortions of banks and loan companies charging up to 60 per cent interest, excessive freight rates imposed by the railroads, and inflated prices of farm machinery padded by tariff protection. This protest grew louder with the depression and the terrible drought of the middle nineties. (No Oklahoman will admit that he blames the party in power for the weather, but radical political movements certainly thrive during drought cycles.)

Of course the settlers joined the agrarian revolt that was then sweeping over the West and South of the United States; they met in sod or log schoolhouses to form a Farmers' Alliance, gathered in groves for Populist picnics and oratory, and argued in blacksmith shops and crossroads stores for the curbing of privilege and more direct democracy in government. It was characteristic that James B. Weaver of Iowa had taken time off between running for president on third-party tickets to be an Oklahoma eighty-niner; he hit the prairie of Oklahoma "City" a few minutes after noon on April 22 and began to lay off a townsite, and before night, standing in a wagon, he addressed the crowd in the interest of a city government to reconcile the claims of rival promoters.

The Democrats and Populists usually fought each other, thus throwing the election to their Republican enemies; but sometimes they "fused" and thereby gained control of county governments and the legislature, and once they elected their delegate to Congress. Their enthusiasm for William Jennings Bryan and free silver could not have been greater had they been allowed to vote; even the Republicans felt they could pay their debts more easily if they had twice as many dollars.

Thus the motives of Oklahoma political leaders had been less frankly mercenary, their quarrels more open, and their alliances more casual than those of their Indian Territory contemporaries. When the two groups met for the first time in the Constitutional Convention, the "east side" organization controlled by Murray rolled over the "west side" delegates with a silent smoothness that flattened them out before they even saw it coming.

Murray has published his reminiscences along with his pronouncements on a variety of subjects in a three-volume work entitled "*Memoirs of Governor Murray and True History of Oklahoma, together with his Biography, Philosophy, Statesmanship, and Oklahoma History, Interwoven.* Whoever will read it through will find a complete cross section of early Oklahoma political thought.

Thrown on his own resources at the age of twelve, he managed to put himself through some sketchy schooling, with a thirst for knowledge akin to Lincoln's. Small wonder he thinks that by reading a few books he became a classical scholar, an economist, and an authority on international affairs. Many of his contemporaries, never having read any book, have accepted his valuation.

He practiced every kind of political trick, but he was financially incorruptible. His poverty was not the pose of the demagogue, but a fact of his life as real as that of the homesteader in his dugout. His family life was pure, and he trained his children in integrity and self-reliance. He judged men according to whether they opposed or supported him; some of his brightest heroes are men he should not have trusted.

One thing he knows and reveres—the Constitution of the United States. And he knows the Constitution of Oklahoma as no other man has ever known it; he repeats it word by word, loving every cadence. His ideas on agriculture—which he also knows—are statesmanlike and practical. But in all things beyond the limits of his hard-won experience his misconceptions are startling. One who understands his mind and character can interpret Oklahoma politics.

The Jacksonian conviction that one's friends are patriots, while one's opponents are enemies of the state has brought the spoils system in its very worst form to Oklahoma. It had been bad enough in territorial days when appointments to the Dawes Commission or the federal judiciary were made to reward the friends and relatives of some Republican politician from Illinois or Connecticut; but it was worse when presidents and faculties of the state colleges

41

were appointed on the basis of their service to Oklahoma Democrats. Some institutions have finally managed to build up a tenure based on an enlightened conception of public service, but it has been a slow process.

In the middle nineteen thirties I was carrying on some research of my own in the files of an important state office. A craze for stamp collecting had struck that wing of the capitol, and the employees gathered in such excited huddles to discuss their hobby that citizens who came in on business could hardly make themselves heard. Finally, during a lull, the appointed official in charge turned to me and said with complete seriousness: "I've been neglecting my stamp book. You know how it is at home; a person can always find something else to work at. I believe I'll bring it up here to the office where I have plenty of time." This is a typical incident of that era. It would not be typical now. But even yet, too many positions in the public service are held by unqualified people.

A part of this "rotation in office" philosophy was embodied in the constitutional provision that forbade the governor and several other elective state officers to succeed themselves. This was to keep them from forming a "statehouse gang" to plunder the public property. But they soon learned to exchange offices and support each other's campaigns. If they are honest, this practice of "swapping keys" gives them experience in administration; but if they are corrupt, they are seldom disturbed. The voters are helpless. There are too many elective offices. Probably no Oklahoman has ever gone into the polling booth without having to mark his ballot largely by guess—and the guess is often wrong.

The dominant political influence of the first twenty years of statehood was the systematic plundering of Five Tribes allottees. It had been done before. Even the same techniques had been used in Mississippi, Alabama, Kansas, Indiana—wherever Indian reservations had been broken up and placed under individual tenure. But the spoils had never been so vast or the spoliation so rapid as in Oklahoma. The Indians had the same legal protection—in theory —as other citizens; but they were unfamiliar with deeds, mortgages, and oil leases, and distrustful of the white man's law. Thus they were stripped of their property through deception, forged instruments, kidnaping, even murder, and the plundering of estates by guardians through the probate courts.

The same process went on to a limited extent when the smaller reservations of the "west side" were allotted under the Dawes Act. Only with the Osages did it reach scandalous proportions. That tribe had divided only the surface—657 acres of rolling grassland for each of 2,229 citizens—leaving the minerals under communal ownership. Then oil began to gush from the Osage hills in such quantity that the share of every man, woman, and child on the roll was at one time more than one thousand dollars a month. Some through the inheritance of several "headrights" received ten times that amount. White men who stood to profit could even speed the inheriting process by murder. The probate court of Osage County, which comprised the former reservation, was busy handing out guardianships of minors and "incompetent" adults; and helping the Osages spend their money to the tune of about twenty million dollars a year became the community's major industry.

Historians have been inclined to pussyfoot in this field of Indian exploitation, but nobody who ignores it can understand Oklahoma politics. The Indian allotments added together formed an area about the size of Indiana, rich in farmland, coal, and timber, and richer in oil production than any other state of the Union. This was a prize worth seizing. Rival combinations of guardians and attorneys fought each other to control the courts; public sentiment supporting the business was strong enough to dominate the legislature; and, with a few honorable exceptions, the press was purchased and the church was silenced by the profits of the unholy traffic.

The plunder was somewhat slowed down by the restrictions on the sale of Indian land, and so the Oklahoma delegation in Congress worked as a unit to abolish these impediments. They succeeded only in part; hence a small acreage of restricted land is still held by the allottees. Oklahomans also, like the Georgians of a century before in their contest with the Creeks and Cherokees, became violent champions of "states' rights." Federal protection of the Indians was feeble enough in all conscience, for Indian Service employees and federal court officials in the state were largely appointed by the spoils system, which placed them under the control of local politicians; but even so it was fiercely resented by a citizenship determined to have a free hand with the Indians' holdings.

After about twenty years of statehood the Indians' property had been scaled down until it no longer invited wholesale exploitation. At the same time there was a reform in the Indian Service throughout the United States. Thus with less to steal and more protection to the stealees, the business of robbing Indians dropped to a minor place as a political influence. Some of the exploiters were discredited, a few were punished, more graduated into respectability and forgot how they started their climb to power and influence; but gradually a new generation took over the leadership of the state.

Thus Oklahomans, no better and no worse than other frontiersmen, seized the greatest opportunity for wholesale looting that was ever placed before any American population. Moreover, even where Indian ownership was not a factor, the oil industry was so vast and its rewards so unpredictable that it broke all controls. Its political influence began early. Murray, who served as speaker of the House, gives convincing proof that several members of the first legislature were bribed by the oil interests.[3]

It was in fact evident immediately after statehood that Oklahoma had a bad combination of powerful forces bent on plunder and an unwieldy constitution. No matter how much the average citizen might desire reform, he found himself defeated because the rules were too complicated.

Murray ran for governor at the expiration of Haskell's term. He still maintains that he was counted out by a dishonest tabulation of the votes.[4] The office went to Lee Cruce, a Kentuckian who had married a Chickasaw girl and gone into the banking business at Ardmore. Cruce was a man of pleasing personality, but he was not a strong executive and things got out of hand. An investigating committee of the legislature uncovered extensive corruption in several state departments, but nothing was done about it. These futile investigations became a familiar pattern in Oklahoma government. Under the constitution the governor has no control over

[3] Murray, *Memoirs*, II, 134.
[4] Murray, *Memoirs*, II, 152–53.

the other executive officials. The people elect them (by guess) and then forget about them.

It was also at this early time that Oklahoma began to get a bad name for pardoning criminals. The practice began—believe it or not—through the good will of a pioneer society where everyone was friendly to his neighbor, good or bad. In later administrations the business of buying and selling pardons became an open scandal.

Governor Cruce was unwilling to send any man to his death, and so he commuted all capital sentences to life imprisonment. The lieutenant governor was a childish old man who enjoyed sitting at the governor's desk and signing papers; he was easily influenced to sign pardons. If Cruce was called to any duty outside the state, the acting governor was likely to release a group of prisoners. The Governor therefore became almost a prisoner himself, reluctant to step across the state line for any purpose.

At the next campaign, Al Jennings, a former territorial outlaw who had dramatized his career in a book, even sought the Democratic nomination for governor. He received a substantial number of votes, some of which were from Republicans who crossed over into the Democratic primary to give their opponents an unacceptable candidate. But the nomination and subsequent election went to Robert L. Williams, who had been serving as chief justice of the supreme court; and Jennings eventually went to California and got a job writing for the movies.

Williams proved to be a strong executive, but a man of his own time, surprisingly like Murray in his intellectual outlook. He served during the war years when farm prices soared, oil wells spouted, and the state throbbed with energy. The Oklahoma National Guard was first sent into Mexico to join the futile attempt to catch Villa; then when the United States entered World War I, Oklahomans with their fellow Americans went overseas. The anguish of this experience brought out all the crude violence of a still young society, at first fiercely isolationist, then as fiercely determined to see it through. "Slackers" were compelled to buy bonds, civil rights were forgotten, and "traitors" were ferreted out, as the whole strong state was swept with patriotic fervor. Well, not quite the whole state. A group of underprivileged whites and Seminole Indians and Negroes living in the tangled timber along the

South Canadian began to burn bridges, dynamite water mains, and tear down fences as their protest against conscription. But their revolt was soon quelled. Probably, if the truth were known, they were allottees despoiled of their property through the forms of law, and poor whites who had watched the process and concluded everything was rotten.

It was evident that the ideas of the common man as written in the constitution had failed to bring the expected Utopia. Moreover, somebody had to be blamed for the drought cycle that began in 1910. This time the discontent expressed itself in socialism. (It is significant that only the Socialist party took a definite stand against the legalized robbery of Indian children through the probate courts.) The vote grew from 9,740 at statehood to 52,703 in 1914. Then came the war and the Socialist argument that one can have peace by refusing to fight. This did not fit the mood of a people swept by a mighty anger. Socialism died, and has never been resurrected.

Oklahoma has always had a good many Republicans. In the election of 1920 in the middle of J. B. A. Robertson's term, they swept everything: a senator and five of the eight representatives, the electoral vote for Harding, and a majority in the lower house of the legislature. Fundamentally the cause was a strong isolationism that reacted instinctively against the League of Nations; but the good work was helped along by an alliance between Harding's "Ohio gang" and Oklahoma oil. Later when the scandals began to break at Washington, it was a little difficult to decide whether the Republican party had purchased Oklahoma or whether Oklahoma oil had purchased the United States government.

The Democratic state administration still had two years to go. The state senate also had a Democratic majority because half of its members held over from the previous election. The political strife of this period was the worst Oklahoma had ever known—between the Governor and the legislature, between Republican factions battling for federal spoils (and control of the Indian oil money), and between rival guardians contending for the favor of the probate courts. At the same time came a general price collapse, bank and business failures, and unemployed former service men. Then out of the emotional stress of the war and the economic strain

that followed it was born the Oklahoma Ku Klux Klan. Oklahomans learned to parade in white sheets, to trample on minorities,
to fear rumors, and to vote by mass hysteria.

Meanwhile, in North Dakota the farmers through the Non-
Partisan League had got control of the state government. Organ-
izers had come to Oklahoma as early as 1917, but times were too
good to make converts. Now in the postwar deflation, Oklahoma
was again ready for a radical movement. In the fall of 1921 farmers,
laborers, former Socialists, and Non-Partisan adherents met in
convention at Shawnee and formed the Farmer-Labor Reconstruc-
tion League. They drew up a platform advocating public ownership or regulation of utilities, mills, and grain elevators; a state-
owned central bank and reduction of tenantry by credits to farmers
and home builders; tax exemption on farm improvements and
equipment; labor legislation; and free schoolbooks. (It is strange
how public policy eventually catches up with these radical platforms!) In the following election John Calloway ("Jack") Walton
received the League's endorsement for governor. He was a very
ambitious young man, Iowa-born, Nebraska-bred, who had come
to Oklahoma to work as a civil engineer, gone into politics, and
become mayor of Oklahoma City. His campaign made headlines
throughout the United States. He traveled with a jazz orchestra,
speaking to immense crowds, and won by a big majority. Then he
invited his supporters to an inaugural barbecue, where they surged
about long fire trenches and huge pots of coffee, eating and drinking and generally celebrating the triumph of the common man—
and provoking more headlines about strange Oklahoma.

His administration was a series of bitter fights—with the Klan,
which he tried to suppress by placing the whole state under martial
law; with the colleges, which he attempted to dominate through
patronage; and with his former Farmer-Labor supporters, who
tried to dictate his appointments. Before his first year in office
ended, the legislature was ready to impeach him. But it was not
time for the regular session, and the Governor understandably refused to call a special session. When the lawmakers tried to assemble on their own call, he stationed the National Guard in the capitol
and dared them to enter. Finally through the initiative, the people

47

authorized the legislature to convene itself. Then it met and made short work of impeaching the Governor.

Lieutenant Governor Martin Edward Trapp, who succeeded him, was an eighty-niner, with all the word implies in pioneering hardships. He was only twelve years old when he came with his father from Kansas to settle on a claim near Guthrie. He attended a few brief terms in a one-room school, went to business college, taught a little, entered county politics, and at statehood was elected to one of the state offices. He knew how to get along with the legislature, for he was serving his third term as lieutenant governor. His administration was the most peaceful the state had yet known.

Edna Ferber said in *Cimarron* that "governor after governor" of Oklahoma "was impeached with musical comedy swiftness and regularity." Perhaps the state partially deserved that comment, for it did impeach two governors. Henry S. Johnston, who went into office after Trapp in 1927, was not a strong executive and the legislature again got out of control. The quarrel seemed to be mainly personal. The supreme court had set aside the self-convening law, and so again the country was treated to the spectacle of a governor dispersing the legislature by force of arms. This time the lawmakers went back home and waited until the regular session. Then they impeached Johnston on eleven charges, but convicted him of only one—"general incompetency." His term was finished by young Arkansas-born William J. Holloway, the lieutenant governor, and again a strange calm descended upon the capitol.

Oklahomans have always been ashamed of Johnston's removal. They felt that he was probably as "competent" when impeached as he had been when they elected him. Indeed, if removals are to be made on that score, it might be cheaper to require all candidates for office to qualify by an aptitude test.

The next election came in 1930, when the end of frontier exploitation and the beginning of the general depression were slowing down the gay merry-go-round of Oklahoma life. William H. Murray had just returned from a grandiose colonization project in Bolivia. With no backing but the friendship of his old associates and the confidence of plain people everywhere, he swept into the governor's office with the greatest majority ever gained by a candidate in the state. He had a stormy administration, but when his

48

opponents threatened to use the impeachment formula again, he likened them to "a bunch of cotton tail rabbits trying to pull a wild cat out of its den."[5] Then somebody invented the novel "constitutional" principle that if a state impeaches three governors, it automatically loses its statehood and reverts to territorial status. This rumor certainly had a deterrent effect; and it is surprising how many people still believe it to be law. It fits in with the humble mood brought about by Johnston's impeachment: a sneaking suspicion that perhaps Oklahoma has shown itself unworthy of statehood.

The suffering of the depression years was intensified by the unprecedented drought. The crops dried up, and the wind tore the soil from the fields and piled it in rippled drifts or bore it in curdled clouds that thickened the atmosphere. But Murray met human problems with the practical directness of one who knows all about poverty. He cut his living expenses to the bone and spent much of his salary on relief, and he forced state employees to contribute to the fund. When some of the cities began to jail men for the crime of seeking work, he ordered their release—and made the order effective. But his administration of relief was not as efficient as he likes to believe. He established a record even in Oklahoma for his frank use of spoils, and many of his appointees were incompetent.

In 1932 he made a bid for the presidential nomination, but gained little support outside Oklahoma. He became a bitter opponent of Franklin D. Roosevelt and all New Deal measures, thus ironically ranging himself alongside the very conservative forces that had fought him throughout his career.

The New Deal in fact became the most hotly contested issue in state politics during the nineteen thirties. It denied the whole course of Oklahoma history—the quick and ruthless acquisition of natural resources, the freedom from restraint, and the meteoric rise of individuals. No wonder industrial leaders and landowners hated Roosevelt and his kind with a bitterness based on fear. This feeling expressed itself in the election of E. H. Moore, a Tulsa oilman converted to Republicanism, to the United States Senate in 1942. On the other hand, the restraints, the more equitable distribution, and

5 Murray, *Memoirs*, II, 386.

the conservation of human and material values promised by the New Deal appealed to a great mass of the inarticulate who had no frontier to open in their generation. They voted with enthusiasm for Roosevelt and his Oklahoma supporters.

Ernest W. Marland was elected governor on a New Deal platform in 1934. A Pennsylvanian who had come to Ponca City to enter the oil business, he had quickly gained and more suddenly lost a fortune, and then had taken up politics. In his days of wealth he had been a philanthropist, and as governor he worked for social legislation. First he invited the Brookings Institution to make the first scientific survey that had ever been made of governmental problems in the state. Then under his leadership homesteads were exempted from taxation; the state fitted its governmental structure to the federal Social Security Act; a Department of Public Safety was established, with a highway patrol and drivers' licenses and a dramatic reduction of traffic deaths; the public schools received state aid; and a Planning and Resources Board was created. All these have been permanent reforms. The state also co-operated actively with the alphabetical federal relief agencies of those depression years. But unfortunately Marland was not a good administrator: the public debt mounted, and general inefficiency and corruption touched even some of his closest advisers.

Leon C. ("Red") Phillips, born in Missouri but educated at the University of Oklahoma, was speaker of the House of Representatives. A strong and stubborn man, he fought every step of the way against most of the Governor's program. Then, running on an economy platform with the support of anti–New Dealers and a general revulsion against the cynical improbity of the Marland era, he was elected the next governor. He dominated the state administration, and he did effect some economies—though partially at the expense of education and other public services. He entered into a violent controversy with the federal government to stop the construction of two great power projects, the Grand River and Denison (Red River) dams. He failed there, and public sentiment apparently did not support him.

After a little more than a generation of turmoil, the administration of the state government since 1943 has been strangely calm. This may be due to the expanding economy and full employment

50

of the war years, but I am tempted to believe the cause is deeper: that Oklahoma has at last reached political maturity. The state has passed the pioneer era when a strong people came in to seize and build; it has passed the economic and emotional crosscurrents of the stormy nineteen twenties and the disillusionment of the depression years. The first is gone forever. The problems of the last two may return, but they will be met by a new generation, Oklahoma-trained. And that training has been good. The steady work and quiet lives of the great majority add up to a mightier force than the clash of titans; and that influence has finally come into its own. I think it is deeply significant that these six years of peaceful administration have been under the leadership of the state's first native-born governors.

Robert S. Kerr, who served from 1943 to 1947, was born in the Indian Territory on a farm his father leased from a Chickasaw Indian. He even looks like an Oklahoma product; his whole family is so tall that special beds were installed in the governor's mansion. An oilman with constructive ideas about industry, he ran the state like a good business. He was fortunate in an expanding revenue that enabled him to spend money for useful services, pay off debts, and still build up a surplus. Except for a few quarrels inherited from previous years, all departments worked together harmoniously. Even the relations with the federal government were bloodless.

Governor Kerr traveled a great deal outside the state—200,000 miles by his own estimate. He delivered the "keynote" speech at the Democratic National Convention in 1944. The people back home felt that the "good impression" he made on these trips brought the state "valuable publicity." (Always that pathetic longing for approval!) Certainly he does not remotely resemble a wild Indian on the warpath or a starving Okie. Apparently his interest in politics is permanent, for in 1948 he was elected to the United States Senate.

The present governor, Roy J. Turner, is also typical of the native Oklahoma generation. Born on the claim his father staked in the Run into the Iowa Reservation, he learned accounting, worked at several jobs, prospered in the oil business, took up ranching as a profitable side line, and encouraged farm boys to raise live-

51

stock. He became interested in politics only recently through school laws and oil legislation, and as a result of these contacts he decided to run for governor. As usual there were plenty of Democratic candidates for the office, and a few mud balls sailed through the air during the campaign, but his administration is running smoothly. The dove of peace could be brooding over the dome of the capitol—except that there is no dome.

These later years have shown a tendency to approach governmental problems through scientific study. The Brookings survey was one step. The University of Oklahoma also exerts an influence. In 1913 the Department of Government organized a Municipal League, through which city officials meet to discuss planning, revenues, utilities, zoning, and other municipal problems. This has become very active in recent years, and as a result, city government is usually good in Oklahoma. Another influence comes through books published by the University of Oklahoma Press. *State Control of Local Finance in Oklahoma* by Robert K. Carr, a government professor, is outstanding in this field; it is a critical analysis of the state's haphazard system of taxation and expenditures.

Here I pause to do battle with the modesty of my publisher. I cannot interpret Oklahoma life without appraising the influence of the University of Oklahoma Press. And so over the protests of the director I shall refer to it frequently in the following pages. I hope there will not be ragged holes in my manuscript where these references have been deleted by the censor.

Do political leaders pay any attention to these studies? There is increasing evidence that they do. In 1945 the legislature set up an interim committee to study taxation and finance, and several of its findings were enacted into law by the 1947 session. This latter session then created a permanent legislative council of ten senators and fifteen representatives for intensive study of basic state problems. A paid director was employed, and meetings have even been held with governmental leaders of neighboring states to work out a system of regional law. The recommendations of the council will certainly help to guide the policy of subsequent legislatures. This is a great change from the turbulent politics of other days.[6]

[6] One tragic event in this 1947 session did receive wide publicity. A

A Seething Caldron of Politics

The legislature of 1947 also passed a bill submitting to the voters the question of calling a convention to write a new constitution. Certainly good government will always be difficult so long as the state retains its cumbersome organic law. But the powerful *Daily Oklahoman-Times* newspaper combination of Oklahoma City endorsed a plan to have the document drafted by a small, specialized group; and arguments favoring the plan influenced Governor Turner to veto the convention measure. Then during the ensuing two years the legislative council gave serious study to constitutional revision, which also has strong backing from civic groups. This new Oklahoma-born generation may eventually take control not only of the functioning of the government but of its fundamental principles.

But whether in present peace or former turbulence, the pages of Oklahoma's political history have been spattered with oil. The same greasy shower has made everything in the state spring into growth. To know Oklahoma, one must know oil.

young, former service man, member of the House, walked into the Senate chamber and shot a senator. He was committed to a veterans' hospital for mental disorders, and the wounded man expressed only sympathy for him. The incident has no significance so far as the general legislative character is concerned.

V

"Lakes and Rivers of Oil"

"EVERYBODY IS RICH FROM OIL" is a popular misconception about Oklahoma. But a surprisingly large proportion of the population has received small amounts—say $160 a year for leasing the home farm—and these sums mount in the aggregate. A few persons through sheer luck have become millionaires.

Right here I am expected to tell about the wild doings of ignorant yokels dazzled by sudden riches. Such stories make good copy—they pander to a sort of hidden envy in the reader—but they are almost wholly fictitious. When a hard-working farm couple begins to think in five, six, or even seven figures, the first thing they do is to assist their children to buy land and farm equipment. Then they adopt a modest comfort in living. Their imagination seldom goes farther. With the remainder of their fortune they try to make good investments, many of which—like the investments of more experienced people—were swept away in the late depression. A recital of this sort is very tiresome, and not at all what one likes to read about Oklahoma.

It is true, however, that the majority of Oklahomans have been affected in their thinking by the unpredictable chances of oil. The hard-pressed farmer struggling through a bad year hopes that Santa Claus in the form of a lease man will bring that dollar an acre to pay the interest on the mortgage. Any trapped individual turns instinctively to "If I could only sell some royalty—" And almost everyone has moments of letting his imagination range over "If I were rich—" Why not? It has happened to his own friends and relatives. And this has increased the already restless and adventureous spirit of a frontier population.

"Lakes and Rivers of Oil"

Oil has influenced Oklahoma life in more tangible ways. It has furnished job opportunities for the landless generation; many a husky boy has started in as a roustabout at the near-by field, and worked up into the highly specialized—and highly paid—labor of the industry. On its higher levels the fierce competition of the oil game has affected business and political morality. And the scrambled hell and violence of the oil boom towns attracted underworld characters from Oklahoma and other states to ply their criminal trades. The boom towns are all gone now; they grew into cities with clean streets and civic ambitions, or they dried up and died with the depletion of the field. But the stories told of their heyday when life was cheap and the pace was fast are all true—and less than the truth.

"All Oklahoma Indians are rich and perform ridiculous antics" is another generalization that cannot be supported by facts. Only the Osages, with their undivided mineral interest, benefited as a tribe by oil development. The land of the others had been allotted, and most of it had passed out of their possession before oil was found. But in remote fullblood settlements a few still retained their allotments, and some of these were elevated to dazzling wealth and publicity. Usually such oil-rich individuals were more notable for the wrongs they suffered from corrupt courts and guardians than for their own escapades. But a few— like a few Eastern playboys or Hollywood darlings, who also are not typical— lacked the disciplined intelligence to control their new affluence. Their income has progressively declined since the late nineteen twenties, so that even this irresponsible class has ceased to make headlines. But while they lasted, they made the best copy of all— the motif of "Ignorant Indians throwing their money around when I could spend it so wisely if I only had it," or the even more attractive "What a good boy am I: I stuck in my thumb and pulled out a plum and gave it to the Indians."

Oil development did begin on the Indian side of the state. It is not known when the first seepages were discovered; but as early as 1846 "oil springs" in the Choctaw country were reported to be valued for their supposed medicinal properties. It was in 1859, as all the world knows, that the oil industry began its spectacular career in Pennsylvania; and in the same year other puny wells in

55

Kansas and Texas prompted the prospecting that became very active in those states during the eighteen eighties. At this latter period promoters entered the Indian Territory and helped the tribal leaders to organize companies and obtain drilling franchises from their governments. Thus in the middle eighteen eighties wildcats were drilled near Tahlequah in the Cherokee Nation and near Atoka in the Choctaw country. About the same time in the Chickasaw Nation a hand-drilled well 425 feet deep brought oil flowing from the top of the hole. The oil was used locally for lubrication, but nobody recognized this as the "discovery well" of the great Healdton field of later fame.

A white man named Edward Byrd next obtained a lease from the Cherokee Nation, and in 1889 he began drilling shallow wells near Chelsea. None of them produced much, but in the Cherokee archives I once found a record of sixty cents paid to the tribe as royalty for six barrels of oil sold from this lease during the quarter closing September 30, 1892. That seems to establish the first "commercial" production in Oklahoma—until somebody digs up an earlier record.

About the same time, companies of Creek citizens made leases to outside capitalists, and drilling began at Muskogee and Eufaula. A showing of oil was found at Muskogee in 1896, but no important strike was made. It was also in 1896 that the Foster brothers, wealthy Rhode Islanders, obtained a blanket lease of the Osage Reservation. The next year they drilled a shallow well near the Kansas line, capable of producing fifty barrels a day, but they capped the hole because the production was too small for profitable operation. Again, in 1897 oil was discovered in the Cherokee Nation in what is now the Johnstone Park in Bartlesville. But it was not marketed for several years, partly because of lack of transportation facilities—the drilling rig had been hauled seventy miles overland to the location—and partly because the Dawes Commission was even then taking steps to divide the Cherokee land.

Meanwhile Tulsa started on its way through a greatly publicized strike in the Creek country. Just across the river from the lively little town some shoestring promoters were drilling at the tiny hamlet of Red Fork. On June 25, 1901—no good Tulsan has ever forgotten the date—a little gas-driven oil sprayed feebly from the hole. Carefully planted headlines did the rest. Telegrams poured in from Kansas and distant Pennsylvania; promoters flocked to the location; and the first oil boom—a phenomenon to be repeated many times in Oklahoma's history—was in full swing. But leasing had to wait on the transitional status of Indian land.

In 1903 the government issued regulations for the making of lease contracts with Five Tribes allottees. This was a signal for oilmen to rush to the Indian Territory, where the Mellon, the Standard, and other great Eastern interests and daring young operators barely able to finance one well all entered into the most unrestrained rivalry. The Johnstone well was brought into production at Bartlesville, and the town blessed by two new railroads began to develop as a center of the industry. A producing region was rapidly opened from the Kansas line south, and other wells were brought in near Chelsea, Coody's Bluff, and Alluwe. By that time the Foster interests had developed a field west of Bartlesville in the Osage country.

There was also extensive wildcatting throughout Oklahoma Territory, with a showing of oil in many places and one good field at Cleveland, which soon spread across the Arkansas to enter the Osage country from the southwest. In 1904 the "Twin Territories" had almost five hundred producing wells with an output of more than one million barrels of oil.

But the first spectacular production came from the Glenn Pool south of Tulsa. This famous lens was discovered in 1905 by two wildcatting partners operating on a margin so small that they are said to have cut expenses by drilling without a casing. It soon became the most sensational small field in the world. As every operator raced to tap the rich sand in as many places as possible ahead of his rivals, production soon outran transportation. Millions of barrels of oil spouted from the wells and were caught in "earthen tanks" (just ponds) or flowed down the creeks. Eventually pipe lines were constructed—to the Standard refineries at Whiting, Indiana, and to the refineries and exporting terminals of The Texas Company and the Gulf Oil Corporation on the Gulf of Mexico. In the summer of 1907 the pool had 516 wells producing 117,440 barrels of oil a day. When Oklahoma was admitted to statehood that year, it had a production of 43,500,000 barrels, 26.2 per cent of the nation's output, almost half of this coming from the Glenn Pool. Many Oklahomans whose names are still notable in oil history got their start from this rich field.

For the next twenty years Oklahoma alternated with California as the leading oil state. To the initiate, its years of supremacy (1907–1908, 1915–22, and 1927) call the roll of fabulous strikes. The development crept from the Indian country west to the land of the homesteaders: through Marland's discoveries Ponca City was launched as a center of the industry by 1912; and fields were opened during the next few years near Blackwell and Garber. The huge Cushing Pool in the tangled hills of the Creek country was opened in 1912. At its peak it produced more than half of the gasoline of the United States. The year after Cushing came the Healdton field, which made Ardmore an oil city. In 1920 the fabulous Burbank pool was discovered in the Osage country east of Ponca City; and the next year a less spectacular field was opened near Tonkawa. Several scattered developments in the Seminole area culminated in dramatic discoveries in 1926. The next year the seven major pools and many smaller units of the Greater Seminole field produced 136,000,000 barrels, 10 per cent of all the oil produced in the United States. Then in 1928 the Oklahoma City field blew into production. At the same time scores of lesser fields were opened in various parts of the state. Oil derricks became a characteristic feature of the Oklahoma landscape, and it is entirely fitting that the state capitol itself should be surrounded by the slender steel towers of one of the great oil fields of the world.

The waste that accompanied this development was enormous. According to the "rule of capture," oil and gas belong to the man who brings them to the surface by drilling. Thus every operator rushed to sink his wells and get his share of the oil before a rival drained the pool, without regard for the ultimate production of the field.

Natural gas, which always accompanies oil, is an important natural resource. It is more than that: gas pressure drives the oil to the well and, in the case of flowing wells, forces it to the surface. Obviously every unit of gas should be made to carry out the greatest possible amount of oil. But if the wells are allowed to flow wide open or if the reservoir is tapped by too many wells, much of this

58

expulsive force is wasted. As the pressure diminishes, flowing wells have to "go on the pump"—a great expense—and eventually the pumping wells stop producing, leaving the rest of the oil in the ground. This is the ultimate end of all oil fields, but it has been greatly hastened in Oklahoma—and throughout the rest of the United States for that matter—by the speed and fury of competitive drilling. In the flush fields the gas was conveyed aloft in pipes and set on fire, so that the whole scene in the wavering lights and shadows of these flares looked like something out of Dante. At Cushing, where more than two thousand giant torches burned, it was estimated that the yearly waste of gas was equal in heating power to more than five million tons of coal, and an incalculable amount of oil was lost past recovery.

Another result of this cutthroat competition was overproduction. At the beginning of a field, lack of pipe lines was the bottleneck; then after these were provided, the flood of oil would break the market. It was a tragic waste to bring oil that could not be handled out of its safe storage in the earth to run down ravines and back up against feverishly constructed dams, where the best part evaporated. Even worse from the producer's standpoint was the effect on prices. But nobody could afford to stop drilling and let his competitors drain his lease.

Oklahoma oil first brought a market collapse throughout the United States by the enormous production of the Cushing and Healdton fields. By 1916 the posted price of crude had dropped from $1.05 to 35 cents a barrel, with actual sales often far below the latter figure. And still more oil came out of the earth. The producers talked of constructing a co-operative tank farm to hold it off the market, or of "pinching back" their wells to curtail production, and the state Corporation Commission tried to limit the spacing and drilling of new wells. But nothing came of these plans. Then World War I demands pulled the industry out of its depression, and the price soon rose to $3.50 a barrel.

Production mounted with the development of the Burbank and lesser fields during the early nineteen twenties; and in 1927 the production of the Greater Seminole field again broke the world market. Officials of the major companies, faced by a ruinous price collapse, agreed to a total production figure for the field, with each well placed on a quota basis. They chose Ray Collins of Tulsa as umpire to enforce this "proration" and requested the Corporation Commission to give him authority. The arrangement was soon enacted into law; the Corporation Commission assumed control and fixed "allowable" production limits for all the flush pools of the state. Hence, except during World War II, Oklahoma has never operated at capacity since 1927. In that peak year it produced 277,775,000 barrels, or 30.8 per cent of the nation's output, and for the last time headed the list of oil states.

The Oklahoma City field was developed under proration. The result was apparent to the industry in a reasonably stable price structure—at least this great field with an estimated potential capacity of more than 1,500,000 barrels daily did not break the world market. But proration is not all of conservation. It takes no account of the gas-oil ratio required by each individual well to move the oil, and also, by limiting the production of existing wells, it may even encourage excessive drilling. In Oklahoma City the wells were spaced too close. It has been estimated that 750,000,000 cubic feet of gas were wasted every day in this field during the period of flush production—twice the daily consumption of the state in the coldest weather.

Even nature did not always co-operate. The wells came in with such stupendous gas pressure that they sometimes broke out of control and defied puny man-made "allowables." "Wild Mary Sudik" at Oklahoma City achieved international notoriety. She produced, according to one estimate, more than 2,000 barrels of oil and 10,000,000 cubic feet of gas an hour during the eleven days of her rampage. She was an awesome sight throwing a great rust-colored spray high in the air. Although she was some distance out in the country, there were large areas within the city where people were forbidden to strike a match even to cook their meals and in residential sections more than ten miles away droplets of oil fell thick on houses and parked cars. All drilling operations were halted near the wild well. It took six months to tame Mary down to a quiet production of one thousand barrels of oil an hour.

But in spite of the rumpus raised by Wild Mary and several of her contemporaries, the Oklahoma City pool was developed without the thunder and greed and the unleased passions that cast such lurid shadows over the oil-soaked earth of Glenn Pool, Cushing, and Seminole. The quiet extension of the field through block after block of residential sections without disturbing the beauty of the lawns brought drama of another kind. Finally it reached the capitol, and oil drained from beneath the grounds through wells set on a slant poured royalty into the public treasury to erect the tall office building that houses several departments of the state government.

The stability the industry had so hardly won lasted through two years of the Oklahoma City development. Then in the fall of 1930 a lone wildcatter stretched his credit to drill one more well in East Texas and brought in a field so mighty that it made all of Oklahoma's great pools look like "teasers." All this in the midst of the general financial depression.

Oklahoma proration began to fall apart. Small producers needing money in a hurry and landowners eager to cash in had always opposed it. Governor Murray, who had just come into office, said there was other opposition: he said there were powerful oil magnates scheming to depress the market in order to fill their tanks with cheap oil and make a killing. Apparently the law was on their side. The Oklahoma Supreme Court ruled that while the proration statute was legal, no penalty could be imposed for its violation; and the federal district judges issued an injunction forbidding the Corporation Commission to enforce it. The price of Oklahoma crude plummeted to sixteen cents a barrel. In Texas, crude oil was selling for ten cents, with some sales reported as low as two cents. The whole industry was on the caving brink of ruin. This was in the summer of 1931.

For once Murray questioned his own authority. Then through the days and nights of a solitary week end he reasoned out his problem. He thought of King John and Runnymede, and he concluded he had all the executive powers that had not been abrogated by kings or forbidden by constitutions. Once convinced, he worked quickly and secretly. He placed the National Guard in readiness, and then suddenly he issued an order to close all the oil wells in Oklahoma except "strippers" pumping not more than twenty-five barrels a day. The guardsmen immediately took over 3,108 wells in twenty-nine pools—the same wells that had been under the

61

futile proration order of the Corporation Commission. Oklahoma was used to seeing its militia carrying out strange orders; now it saw its young khaki-clad civilian soldiers armed to the teeth pacing the platforms below the silent derricks, while newsboys on the street screamed the headlines.

The "inferior" (Murray's word) federal courts folded up when Murray got into action; eventually the United States Supreme Court sustained him. Governor Ross Sterling of Texas followed his example and proclaimed martial law in the East Texas field; but he finally lost out before the high tribunal. The price of oil began to climb, until before the end of the year Murray opened the wells and put them back on proration. In January the price reached one dollar a barrel.[1]

But the troubles of the industry were not over. Obviously, the problem was not one to be solved piecemeal by states acting separately. Uniform control was first attempted by the federal government through the short-lived NRA. Then, through a series of conferences growing out of a meeting of oil-state governors at Governor-elect Marland's residence in Ponca City, the states of Texas, New Mexico, California, and Oklahoma with the consent of Congress entered into an agreement known as the Interstate Oil Compact. At the present time there are twenty-one member states working through an Interstate Oil Compact Commission. Each passes its own conservation laws, but the Commission carries on research and makes recommendations, and the federal government helps out through the Connally Act forbidding interstate transportation of oil produced in violation of state law.

The Commission has been careful to stress conservation and avoid mention of price stabilization. (After all there are antitrust laws, although Marland was inclined to ignore them—he said nobody could put a state in jail.) But the two go together; the system has protected both the industry and the oil resources. And with states, landowners, and oilmen all scrambling to get their share of the business, there is no possible danger of restricting production at the expense of the public.

Not only through interstate action but in its domestic policy Oklahoma now leads all the states in oil conservation. The Cor-

[1] Murray, *Memoirs*, II, 502–13; III, 489–95.

poration Commission has power to fix a spacing pattern and to set "allowables" based on the gas-oil ratio required in each particular field. It also may order a "unit plan" by which the operators in a given field pool their interests, and one company develops the field at the most efficient rate of production. This seems to be an ideal conservation measure, but its acceptance has been slow. It was not until 1945 that the legislature authorized its use, and two more years passed before it was put into effect.

Oklahoma oil development has been unspectacular since 1930. The Oklahoma City field has passed its flush period and gone on the pump. The Fitts Pool was discovered near Ada in the southern part of the state in 1933. The most significant activity of the war years was the development of the great West Edmond field north of Oklahoma City. Its wells spaced a quarter of a mile apart have hardly disturbed farm operations, and its production has been strictly prorated. But even here 250,000,000 cubic feet of gas were vented into the air every day. Finally, in the fall of 1947 the Corporation Commission, with the approval of most of the leaseholders and operators, for the first time applied the unit plan; and the Sohio Petroleum Company was chosen manager of the whole four-county field. It is estimated that this procedure will prolong the life of the field twenty years and save 60,000,000 barrels of oil that would otherwise have remained in the ground. Of course it cannot repair the damage already done to the reservoir.

Conservation had to stand on its own merits during these later years, for, with war and postwar demands, the industry did not need price stabilization. And there are still people who must have their oil money immediately, even though they kill the goose that lays the golden eggs. They brought considerable pressure on the 1947 legislature to repeal all the conservation laws. Three or four oil companies opposed the adoption of the unit plan at Edmond; and they are now challenging the constitutionality of the law before the courts. Then, when the Corporation Commission ordered unit operation of a second field—the Medrano zone of the West Cement Pool near Chickasha—the farmers and royalty owners formed an organization to fight it. They, too, appealed to the courts and carried on a campaign to elect a legislature friendly to their cause. Thus the matter is not settled at this writing, but the

63

general sentiment of the industry seems to be with the conservation forces.

In production, Oklahoma is now not even in the running with Texas; it is regularly outdistanced by California; and in 1943 it was surpassed for the first time by Louisiana. But it still produces much oil—142,094,000 barrels from 53,540 wells in 1947. And the American Petroleum Institute estimates its oil reserves (based on known and recoverable deposits) at 898,186,000 barrels. Here the state again has dropped to fourth rank—and this time we are looking at the future. But nobody can be too sure. The decline of existing fields in Oklahoma has usually been the prelude to the discovery of new ones. Oil development has moved steadily west, usually through deeper drilling. Oklahoma City was once out of the picture; the earlier tests had all been too shallow. Wildcatting is now very active throughout the western half of the state.

Several good fields have already been discovered in the southwest in a region once considered unpromising; and the Golden Trend—the oilmen's name for a complicated miscellany of producing zones of the Anadarko Basin in Garvin and McClain counties—is the most spectacular of present developments. The deepest well in the world was sunk to explore the Anadarko Basin a few miles north of Fort Cobb. Drilling began in April 1946, and stopped fourteen months later at a depth of 17,823 feet—more than three and one-half miles. It was drilled as a "tight hole"—that is, no information was given out except about drilling progress—but the company kept a careful record of the formations encountered, and it is expected to yield important geological data to guide future operations in that area.

For in those days of rising demand, the industry was frantically searching for new fields. A "wildcat," as all Oklahoma understands, is an exploratory well—a well drilled in "unproven" territory. All the great fields of the state were brought in by persistent wildcatting. But how does one know where to start a wildcat?

VI

The Know-how of the Oil Industry

DURING THE EARLY YEARS of the industry, discovery of oil depended more on luck and persistence than on scientific method. Even superstition was employed. There was for instance the age-old technique of the "water witch"; a forked willow wand in the hands of a man with peculiar powers was supposed to turn sharply down when passing over an oil pool. Then there were intricate contraptions known by oilmen as "doodle bugs" guaranteed to locate oil by "molecular dynamics" or "subterranean osmosis." But most practical men located their wildcats where the surface features resembled those of some producing field. That was not such a bad method with shallow wells, where the top of the ground really might indicate what lay beneath. Then eventually through the science of geology, men discovered the relationship between the presence of oil and the internal structure of the earth.

It is now known that oil has been formed from organic matter, animal or vegetable, deposited in layers of sediment on the bottom of the sea. These layers have been covered with other sediment, hardened into rock, and pressed into gigantic folds. There are no "lakes and rivers of oil," and the word "pool" is only a figure of speech. The oil fills the spaces of such porous rocks as sandstone or crystalline linestone. (When the oilman speaks of the Wilcox "sand" or the Hunton "lime," he is referring to sandstone and limestone.) With its accompanying gas it has a tendency to rise until stopped by impervious rock. An oil pool therefore is often found under a stratum of impenetrable rock bent into an arch or anticline. Other pools are found where the oil has been trapped by a "fault"

65

or fracture—the rocks have slipped and placed a resistant formation against the oil-bearing stratum. In still other cases, an oil-bearing rock formed a sand bar in an ancient river or at the edge of an ancient sea, and the whole has been covered by more resistant formations. Wherever oil is found, the gas—which is lighter —will be on top, then the oil, and under it water—salt water. Thus, paradoxical as it may seem, when the driller strikes salt water, he has a "dry hole," because if the oil had been there, he would have touched it first.

The geologist's task is to map these hidden structures. If any rock layers are exposed, he studies the inclination. Obviously if he finds two outcroppings of the same rock formation tilted towards each other across a considerable distance, he works out the location of an anticline. If the ends are also tilted to form a "closed" anticline—shaped like an inverted saucer—he has found the answer to a geologist's prayer. But these ancient domes and folds are often deeply buried; and the geologist must then resort to the core drill. This device consists of a bit with a sharp cutting edge, which is rotated to remove a cylinder of rock as it bores shallow holes into the earth. By keeping a record of these cores and comparing them with other cores obtained by drilling over a wide area, the geologist can work out the dips and folds of a given rock formation. A study of the fossils also helps; if the geologist knows what kind of life existed on the earth at the time the rock was laid down, he can determine its age and its relationship to other formations known to be oil bearing.

The science of geophysics has become an increasing aid to the geologist. The geophysicist studies the structure by testing the characteristics of the buried strata. Many devices are employed: an electric drill or a series of electrodes can throw a current through the rock and measure its resistance; the magnetometer determines the mineral content of rocks by their magnetic attraction; the torsion balance and gravimeter weigh the rocks by the pull of gravity; and—most important of all at the present time—the seismograph starts a small earthquake and tests the formations by the speed and intensity of its vibrations. (Those colored strings fluttering from the weeds and fence posts along so many Oklahoma farms indicate seismograph surveys.) Radar offers the newest possibil-

ities, but it is still in the experimental stage, and so far as I know
has not been tried in Oklahoma. It picks up radio impulses from
a dome or anticline and bounces them off a reflecting target to a
centrally located instrument.

There has even been some attempt to detect the presence of
oil by chemical analysis of the surface soil, on the theory that minute quantities of gas will escape even through the mile or more of
impervious strata overlying an oil deposit. Drillers also keep a
"log" of their progress and the formations they encounter, and this
record is preserved and used in working out adjoining structures.
Indeed, a well like the Fort Cobb wildcat, where constant corre-
lation was maintained between the rock samples and the seismograph interpretation, is equivalent to one gigantic core.

By a combination of all these methods the underground structure is carefully mapped. Leases are then obtained from the landowners, and drilling begins. The odds are more than four to one
that the wildcat will not turn out to be a "discovery well." Of the
843 wildcats completed in Oklahoma in 1947, 150 (127 oil wells,
23 gassers) were successful. But the percentage of failure is very
much higher when the location is made at random or by unscien-
tific methods. And drilling is an expensive process. In the early
days of oil development in Oklahoma, $5,000 would put down a
hole, but the cost has increased with the depth of drilling. The
3,844 wells completed in the state during the peak production
of 1927 were drilled at a total cost of $124,161,200, an average of
$32,300 a well; the discovery well in the Oklahoma City field cost
$150,000, but the expense declined somewhat as the pool devel-
oped; the wells in the Golden Trend are costing from $60,000 to
$250,000 each; and the cost of the Fort Cobb wildcat probably
reached $1,500,000. With these figures in mind, the operator is
glad to spend money on scientific methods to reduce the proportion of dry holes.

The development of scientific methods in locating oil has been
paralleled by improvements in drilling machinery. The first wells
were drilled by cable tools; a steel bar at the end of a cable was
lifted and dropped to pound its way through the rock. Now the
rotary method is usually employed. A serrated or flanged bit is
fastened to a shaft of pipe, and rotated so as to grind the rock into

67

powder and gouge its way into the earth, and a thick mud is forced into the hole to flush out the pulverized drillings. When the bit needs to be sharpened or changed, the pipe is disjointed as it is pulled up, and then screwed together again as it is let back into the hole. This is a tedious business as the well grows deeper, and the cumulative weight of the three-mile-long shaft in the Fort Cobb wildcat is enough to stagger the imagination. The visitor to an oil field will often observe these dismantled lengths of pipe standing upright against the side of the derrick, and he will pause to watch the practiced rhythm of the drilling crew in screwing or unscrewing the sections. A lively painting of this operation at a well near Oklahoma City was made by Mead Shaeffer for the November 9, 1946, cover of the *Saturday Evening Post*. That was one Oklahoma picture that pleased the natives.

For there is beauty—and in these days little of noise or smell or greasy spray—in an oil field. In the day there is the grace of tapering towers and the burnished symmetry of tanks; and at night when drilling is active and the derricks blaze with electric lights against a velvet sky, there is no more glorious sight on earth.

In cumulative figures, since Edward Byrd first began to pump oil out of his Cherokee wells, about sixty thousand wells in forty-four of the seventy-seven Oklahoma counties have produced about six billion barrels of petroleum worth almost eight billion dollars. A vast hidden network of more than fifteen thousand miles of pipe line transports this product to the refineries. More than half of it is refined outside the state, for even in oil, Oklahoma's processing industries are relatively undeveloped. But in spite of that, petroleum refining is by far the state's most important manufacturing industry—important enough to rank Oklahoma sixth or seventh among the states of the Union. The refineries are located in sixteen counties. Some of them produce gasoline, kerosene, and fuel oils; others turn out lubricating oils; and a few manufacture an amazing and rapidly increasing number of chemical derivatives.

Natural gas is the most important by-product of the petroleum industry. But in the first oil fields of the Indian Territory there were no pipe lines for taking care of it and no facilities for using it. A "gasser" was almost the same as a dry hole, and was usually left open in the hope that it would subside into oil production. As for

68

the gas coming from oil wells, that was allowed to escape through the casing head as the oil was piped off.

By 1905, however, gas was being used as fuel in half a dozen towns. Then a Kansas promoter planned to lay a pipe line to transport it to outside cities. The Tulsa Commercial Club and other new state builders became aroused. They reasoned that they had an important fuel; and if they kept it at home, they could force industry to locate at the source of supply. They won the Constitutional Convention to their view, but the gas company built up to the Kansas line ready to cross over in the three-hour hiatus between Roosevelt's statehood proclamation and the time set for the inauguration of the new government. Then Governor-elect Haskell, listening with the wires open, took a private oath the instant the President signed the paper, and stopped the construction.

But factories did not immediately come to Oklahoma. The only result of the gas embargo was the continued waste of a product that could have been marketed in other states. Domestic consumption was increasing—almost half a million dollars' worth of gas was used the first year of statehood—but about eighteen million dollars' worth was wasted. Then the federal courts ruled against the Oklahoma law, and pipe lines were constructed to Eastern centers.

The waste, as has been seen, continued; the gas was saved or vented according to the convenience of the operators. But enough was run into pipe lines to place Oklahoma near the top of the gas-producing states. It now ranks fourth, with an output of about three hundred billion cubic feet a year from an estimated reserve of six and one-half trillion cubic feet. The gas is widely distributed —in fifty-six of the seventy-seven counties. Nearly half comes from casing-head sources, but an immense field in the Panhandle (extending into Kansas and Texas) and several smaller fields produce only gas. It grades from the "wet" gas, which contains readily separated gasoline, to the "dry" gas, which is never liquefied in commercial practice.

The dry gas is transported by more than eleven thousand miles of pipe lines. About one-fourth is sent to other states. The rest is used at home for heating purposes and industry; the state stands high—often at the top—in volume of consumption. The general use of gas explains the shining cleanness of Oklahoma cities. A relatively new industry is the manufacture of carbon black by burning gas with insufficient oxygen—in other words, make it smoke and collect the soot. (This is *not* a clean process.) This product is an essential in rubber compounding and is used as a pigment in inks and paints.

The wet gas is liquefied under pressure or by absorption to form the extremely light and volatile "natural gasoline" used as a blend in motor fuel. For the past thirty years Oklahoma has ranked among the three leading states—often standing at the head of the list—in its production. Other liquefied petroleum gases are propane and butane, with a present use as fuel (in the stoves and refrigerators of Oklahoma farmers off the gas mains) and a constantly expanding number of chemical derivatives important in the rubber, plastic, and lacquer industries.

The varied demands of the oil industry require skills, and Oklahoma began early to develop them. The University of Oklahoma offered its first course in geology in territorial days in 1900. Now its School of Geology and its School of Petroleum Engineering are internationally known. The major oil companies have begun to help the good work along by establishing university fellowships in these fields. The College of Petroleum Engineering of the University of Tulsa also has a high rating. The graduates of these universities are in demand by the oil companies, and several of the professors who have abandoned the classroom for private enterprise have become wealthy. The American Association of Petroleum Geologists grew out of a conference called at Norman in 1916 by Professor Charles H. Taylor of the University of Oklahoma. At present this society has more than 5,000 members residing in forty-four states and forty foreign countries; and 678 members live in Oklahoma.

The Oklahoma Geological Survey was authorized by the constitution and established in 1908 by the first legislature. It has its offices in the Geology Building at the University of Oklahoma. At first it concentrated on the mapping of structures and published its findings in bulletins which proved valuable in locating oil. In recent years it has been more concerned with the chemical and manufacturing possibilities of petroleum and its by-products, and its publications are extensively used by the Planning and Resources Board to advertise the industrial potentialities of the state.

The United States Geological Survey is also working actively in Oklahoma. And the major petroleum and natural-gas experiment station of the United States Bureau of Mines is located at Bartlesville. With an investment in buildings and fixtures valued at more than two million dollars, it is the best-equipped public institution for petroleum research in the world. The register of visitors in one recent year carried the names of petroleum engineers and chemists from Mexico, Venezuela, Argentina, Canada, England, France, Romania, Russia, India, and Burma.

The University of Oklahoma Press has published a number of books dealing with the petroleum industry—well techniques, price stabilization, economic organization, and history. Several of these are widely used as texts in college classes. One of them—Gerald Forbes' *Flush Production*—is a colorful as well as accurate account of oil development in the Gulf Southwest. The Standard Oil Company of New Jersey made two grants of $15,000 each to the University for a more intensive study in the same field. The project was assigned to Carl Coke Rister, research professor of history. He spent three years to investigate prospecting, production, transportation, refining, and the emergence of company operations; and his *Oil! Titan of the Southwest,* thus becomes the newest contribution in the field of petroleum studies.

The International Petroleum Exposition held at Tulsa every even year attracts petroleum executives, technicians, and purchasing agents from all over the globe. In 1948 at its first postwar meeting, there were 301,307 visitors representing every one of the forty-eight states and thirty-three foreign countries. The *Oil and Gas Journal,* published since 1910 at Tulsa, is recognized as one of the two standard periodicals of the industry. With a circulation of more than eighteen thousand, it is read by oilmen everywhere. An oil page with an editor of highly specialized knowledge is a regular feature of Tulsa and Oklahoma City newspapers, and every little country weekly in a producing area reports local oil news with a high degree of technical understanding.

In Tulsa and other oil centers, even banking is largely geared to the petroleum industry. Men started banks and then found investment opportunities in oil. That was the way of Frank Phillips, head of the great Phillips Petroleum Corporation of Bartlesville, whose orange shield and cryptic "66" flash from filling stations everywhere. Other men succeeded in oil, and then purchased banks because they saw the need for specialized financing of the industry. That was the way of Harry Sinclair, Robert M. McFarlin, James J. McGraw, Harry H. Rogers, and the Exchange National Bank of Tulsa.

Philanthropy and civic spirit also flow out of the oil industry. Here is Frank Phillips paying off the debt on every church in Bartlesville; his brother, Waite Phillips of Tulsa, handing over Philbrook, his palatial residence, to the city as an art museum with an office building to pay its expenses, or giving the Boy Scouts a New Mexico ranch with a Tulsa skyscraper for its upkeep; Charles Page building an orphans' home and widows' colony at Sand Springs and establishing a vast network of industry to support them; E. W. Marland setting a heroic bronze statue by Bryant Baker on the highway to honor the pioneer woman; Lew Wentz with his student loans at state colleges and his glorified youth camp north of Ponca City. And besides spectacular donations such as these there is perhaps a little jewel of a church in some small town, the gift of a hard-working farm woman who got oil money. It is all a part of the exuberant spirit of Oklahoma. The people enjoy money, they like to build, and they want to invite the whole world in to share.

The signs of oil are not all in tall derricks or complex plants or vast tank farms. To one who knows the state, the record is there to read on every hand. Here is a new farmhouse too good for the surrounding acres. (A lease bonus.) Here is a city exquisite in its symmetry, a perfect thing, all built at once. (Built on oil.) Here is a substantial brick residence in a bare little town. (Oil royalty.) Or a tall office building looming above a modest sky line. (Oil profits.) A mansion in some rich suburb. (Home of an oil magnate.) And thus the plain fabric of Oklahoma life is shot through with gleams of splendor.

But the quiet life goes on, too. People were making a living from the soil before they even suspected the wealth that lay beneath it. Forty per cent of the population still lives on the land and about 30 per cent more lives in towns supported by farming. In

1940, before the war started the inflationary spiral, the total value of farm products was $215,000,000 compared with only $193,000,000 from oil and gas. And while agriculture may not sound as exciting as oil, its demise would cause vastly more excitement. There is no doubt about it—farming deserves some chapters, too.

VII

"Plowman's Folly"

IT WOULD BE PLEASANT to begin by pointing with pride. The wheat fields of the northwest—I'll tell that in the next chapter. The farm club boys and girls—No, it won't do. Those stories can wait. To the Oklahoman who loves his state, the salient agricultural fact is that much of it has already gone down to the Mississippi delta.

Oklahoma had a bad condition to start with: light, thin soil; large areas too rough for agriculture; and violent extremes of flood and drought. Then the method of settlement, although in the American tradition, was the worst possible method for the land. All the bad practices inaugurated at Jamestown and repeated on successive frontiers were intensified in Oklahoma.

Everybody knows the mighty force with which the tide of settlement flowed west. When it came to the Oklahoma border, it was stopped by the dyke of federal commitments to the Indians. (The figure belongs to the historian, Edward Everett Dale, and it is a most effective one.) It filtered through in places, but in the main it swirled around it and piled up in angry power against the barrier. Then on a certain day and a certain minute the dam was broken and the flood surged in.

This happened in every one of the land rushes. Every quarter-section became the farm of a settler. In the extreme western part the land was taken more slowly, but the result was the same. If the 160 acres was level and deeply fecund, it survived the shock. But if it was of rocks and blackjacks or of sand and sagebrush, it also went under the plow. The homesteader had no other way to live.

74

The thin soil was of virgin richness; it would produce for a few years. Then gullies streaked the hillsides or sand dunes drifted against the fence.

In the eastern half of the state the land rushes were of another kind. Here the "grafter"—the word was generally accepted and used with no unfavorable connotation—acquired Indian allotments by guardianships, fraudulent leases, or forgery—the method did not count—and leased his immense holdings to share-croppers. The ruthlessness of the "owner" and the needs of the tenant did the rest.

Then came oil. The producer fighting for his share of what lay beneath, never once thought of the surface. If the farmer felt a measure of compunction over the ruin of his familiar fields, he was consoled by his royalty; he knew he could buy good land else-where. The soil was soaked with oil and brine, and when the madness passed, nothing was left but naked "bad lands." There is no more desolate sight on earth than a played-out oil field.

Yes, it was a thoroughly bad system. But worse even than the system was the pioneer psychology behind it. For nine generations the process had been repeated in the United States, gaining momentum, gaining dignity by association with the noblest of human motives. To establish a family on the land, to build a new free society—this was the American ideal. And slashing the timber, destroying the grass, mining the soil—this was noble, too; this was a part of the process.

Now after sixty years the experts sum up what has happened to Oklahoma's forty-four million acres. One-third of the topsoil has been carried away, and the remainder has lost more than one-third of its nitrogen and organic matter and a varying amount of its minerals. More than two million acres of cultivated land have already been abandoned, and eight million more are on the margin. In spite of improved methods of farming, the average yield of corn has dropped 45 per cent, of cotton 32 per cent. (Wheat is more tenacious; corn is always the first crop to move out of a new country as fertility declines.) The experts also say that another fifty years like the first fifty will see agriculture in Oklahoma confined to a few isolated, protected valleys. A dreary prospect for Oklahoma? Yes, but much more dreary for the millions of people at home and abroad that Oklahoma helps to feed.

One does not have to be an expert to appraise this damage. Most Oklahomans past middle age can remember when the land was new. They remember when this network of gullies or that bed of sand bore grass and timber, when these roads, now so many hollow trenches, ran level with the fields. Perhaps for the very reason that Oklahoma lost its land more rapidly than any other state, it now is among the leaders in awareness of its problem.

Scientific agriculture had spoken since the beginning. An experiment station was started at Stillwater under federal funds as soon as the A. and M. College was opened. Tributary agricultural colleges were established at statehood, and these also conducted experimental farms. A college for Negroes was created at Langston by the territorial legislature in 1897, with one of its aims the training of Negro boys to be good farmers. The state constitution required the teaching of agriculture in the public schools. When the federal government initiated the county-agent system, Oklahoma was among the first states to make use of these facilities. About the same time (1914 and 1915) the federal service established stations at Woodward and Lawton for the study of dry-farming practices. Although all these were concerned mainly with crop production, soil saving also figured in their teaching. And during the whole period, farm journals originating in Oklahoma City and Guthrie as early as 1891, 1892, and 1893, warned against the dangers of soil depletion.

But it was not until about 1930 that the public became alarmed. And soon nature began to pile on the evidence in the "dust bowl" years. The "dust bowl," of course, comprised the whole High Plains area of the United States lying east of the Rocky Mountains. In Oklahoma it included only the Panhandle and the adjoining section, but the whole state was scorched with drought.

It was a fearful experience. Small wonder that the panic spread from the farmer, whose land was drifting over the fences, to the officials at Washington, who visioned the whole country turning into a desert. At first there was wild talk of setting up a hundred-mile-wide barrier of trees running from Canada to Texas to fence off the lost area and save the rest of the country. But the plan simmered down to individual strips along the windward side of blowing farms. First came a row of shrubs, then low-growing

76

trees and taller trees to form a sloping wall to catch the wind and lift it over the field. Native or proved varieties known to be adapted to the soil and climate were selected; and their growth and survival has been good. Some were planted where they are not needed, for in time of drought it is hard to look to green years ahead, but along sandy fields they have proved their worth.

Although the shelter-belt plantings represented a Washington policy more than an Oklahoma conviction, Oklahoma was developing its convictions, too. In 1935, when the desolation was at its worst, the University of Oklahoma Press published one of the most important books ever written on soil conservation. The author, Paul B. Sears, was only a temporary Oklahoman—he had come in 1927 to serve as head of the Botany Department at the University—and his *Deserts on the March* was not a regional book. But it was the sight of the dry wind scooping up the Oklahoma soil that drove his pen, and it was an Oklahoma institution that gave his warnings to the world.

This beautiful and terrifying book is still generally quoted wherever men are concerned at the prospect of an expiring race trapped on a dead planet. A Book-of-the-Month Club jury selected it as the most important book of science published that year, and awarded a $2,500 fellowship to the author. With his prize money he carried on the research for a companion volume, *This Is Our World*. It also was published by the University of Oklahoma Press just before Sears returned to his native Ohio.

Perhaps it was the success of *Deserts on the March* that caused the director of the University Press to investigate a startling manuscript that drifted to his desk in the early nineteen forties. Its author, Edward H. Faulkner, was another Ohioan, who had become acquainted with Sears through their common interests; and when his manuscript was rejected by an important Eastern publisher, it was Sears who advised him to send it to Oklahoma. But Faulkner's ideas were his own. The whole theory of agriculture and soil conservation, he said, had been based on the use of the plow; but *he* had discovered that "PLOWING IS WRONG," and thus the whole structure came toppling down.

The manuscript was submitted to seven readers—three farmers and four scientists. All concluded that its challenge had to be taken seriously. The Press accordingly published *Plowman's Folly* in 1943. At the present time 340,000 copies have been printed—of which 140,000 were in the Armed Services Edition. This volume has provoked more controversy than any other book ever written on agricultural practice. It may have inaugurated a revolution. Certain it is, that nobody can afford to disregard it; the one who fails to accept the methods it advocates must base his refusal on actual tests.

And in such tests Oklahoma again leads the nation. At the close of 1928, Congress made a small appropriation—of which $40,000 was immediately available—to establish ten experiment stations to discover principles of erosion control. Guthrie business-men went to work. The red hills that lay to the south and east of their city had once been a jungle of blackjacks, but in 1889 if any-body had dared to question the people's right to homestead them, he would have been classed as an enemy of "progress." The set-tlers cleared patches and planted crops, even laid out extensive commercial orchards, and for a time they prospered. Then the fields washed away and the farmers moved out. Poverty-stricken Negroes occupied the tumble-down houses, supplementing their meager income by labor in neighboring cities. And this situation was typical of millions of acres in the Cross Timbers country.

The Guthrie Chamber of Commerce leased a quarter-section from an absentee owner and persuaded the federal officials to establish the Red Plains Conservation Experiment Station there. This was in 1929, and the station was the first to be established in the United States to test methods of soil conservation. The A. and M. College co-operated in the management, and eventually took over the lease, adding an adjoining tract of 110 acres.

The land consisted of abandoned gully-scarred fields and virgin blackjack undamaged by erosion but almost worthless in its native state. The men in charge worked slowly and carefully. In the light of experiment, many of their guesses turned out to be wrong. They found that by no known system of cultivation could the land be cropped without damage. They smoothed the sides of the gullies and planted them to grass, trying out various kinds. The native varieties proved best except for the weeping love grass, re-cently brought in from Africa. The change from raw, red gullies to lush, grassy slopes is almost unbelievable. Erosion has completely stopped, and summer grazing experiments over a four-year period produced an average of thirty-nine pounds of beef an acre. The experimenters also found the most efficient method of killing the blackjack, and developed machinery for removing it. Nature did the rest in these undamaged areas, and the slopes are growing tall, dense bluestem. Here every acre will produce sixty-three pounds of beef a year.

The success of the project has attracted wide attention. Articles have been written about it in national magazines, and visitors have come even from foreign countries. Thousands of Oklahoma farmers have received demonstrations in methods of handling the most difficult kind of land in the state. The experts say that these findings promise the equivalent of seven million acres of new land in the Southwest capable of grazing one and one-half million additional cattle. It will take time to change concepts of land ownership and use, but eventually these rocky hills will be a ranch country. The sod was the right side up in the first place.

But obviously the human race will starve if the land is all given back to the cattle. For that reason the Wheatland Conservation Experiment Station was established at Cherokee, in the rich deep soil of the wheat belt. The work got under way in the fall of 1941. The studies include methods of tillage, terracing and contour farming, and crop rotation. The time has been too short for complete results, but it is plainly apparent that runoff was reduced more than 40 per cent, erosion was greatly checked, and wheat yields were increased by terracing and contour farming. Also, it appears that Faulkner was mistaken about the villainy of the plow when used in wheat growing. In a six-year period a "stubble mulch" method of tillage checked the runoff only slightly, but reduced the yield almost one-fourth, and encouraged weed, disease, and insect infestation.

During these same years the experiment station at Stillwater has branched out to establish ten special soil-improvement stations, located in different regions of the state to correspond with Oklahoma's varied land problems. All of them hold field tours, largely attended by dirt farmers owning similar land. And when Congress provided for systematic soil conservation by groups of farmers or-

OKLAHOMA

ganized into districts, the legislature of Oklahoma was the first
to implement the policy by state action. The first district was
formed January 28, 1938. At the present time these organized
units comprise more than 98 per cent of the area of the state. Only
Texas with its great acreage has a larger number.

Every farmer living in an organized district may enter into a
contract with the Soil Conservation Service of the United States
Department of Agriculture by which his needs are diagnosed and
a portion of the expense is borne by the federal government. Already more than four million acres of Oklahoma land has been
given an acre-by-acre treatment to reclaim it, and fifty-nine different conservation practices have been applied in various combinations. More than forty-six thousand miles of terraces have been
constructed and more than one and one-quarter million acres of
land placed under contour cultivation. Thousands of farm ponds
have been made, under this and other federal programs, to impound the water where it will do the most good. Trees have been
planted, worn-out land has been returned to grass, and overgrazed
pasture has been restored.

Negro farmers have also been enlisted in the movement. At
a South-wide meeting at Atlanta, Georgia, in 1947, Collin Johnson
from Choctaw County on the Red River was adjudged the outstanding Negro conservationist in Oklahoma. A former share-
cropper, in 1940 he purchased an eroded eighty-acre farm that
nobody else would have, for $1,500. Under the direction of the
Soil Conservation Service he constructed terraces and ponds,
planted legumes, and applied fertilizer. The first year his cotton
averaged 133 pounds and his corn 15 bushels to the acre, and his
thirty-nine acres of pasture grazed only four head of livestock.
Since then he has built up his cotton yield to 857 pounds and his
corn to 35 bushels an acre, and his pasture supports seventeen head
of stock besides a cutting of seven and one-half tons of hay. And
the family living in milk, butter, eggs, meat, fruit, and vegetables
comes from this same farm. Soil-saving, says Johnson, is "just like
having a good pocket to put your money in instead of a pocket
with a hole in it."

It is an impressive experience to take a plane trip over the red
hills of central Oklahoma. Here the pattern of large squares cut

80

in four pieces is a striking reminder of the day when every home-steader staked his quarter-section. A more sinister pattern is the ramiform tracery of gullies on abandoned fields. But here and there is a new pattern of curving terrace, gleaming pond, and green cover; and not a rivulet cuts across it to drain the very life of Oklahoma as it runs blood-red to the sea. In 1947 the federal government spent about seven and one-half million dollars on soil conservation in the state. It would have been cheaper to open up the country under scientific principles of land use, but such a policy could not have been suggested in those days of clamorous individualism. Much water has flowed under the bridge since 1889—and too much of it has been colored with Oklahoma soil.

The same practices that prevent runoff and check erosion also relieve the pressure on Oklahoma's rivers. But additional plans are afoot to curb those destructive streams. Since the first month of statehood, Oklahoma leaders have launched campaigns to persuade the federal government to control floods where they start instead of building futile levees along the lower Mississippi. Few officials listened until the need for relief "projects" arose in the nineteen thirties. Now eighteen great dams have already been constructed or are in process of construction (all but three with federal funds), nine more have been authorized, and many others have been recommended by army engineers. Some of these, notably the Grand River Dam and the Denison Dam, are designed to furnish power, with flood control a secondary—and not always apparent—feature. Others on the watersheds have already had a noticeable effect in taming the streams. An example is the dam that forms Lake Carl Blackwell, now leased to the A. and M. College. By blocking a high watercourse among blackjack hills, it protects the whole rich lower valley of Stillwater Creek. A few more such dams on the creeks should soon begin to show on the rivers. Still other dams impound the water for irrigation. One important irrigation work is already in operation—the 70,000-acre W. C. Austin Project of the United States Bureau of Reclamation on the North Fork of Red River. Its first crop (1946) averaged returns of better than two hundred dollars an acre; it ranked among the first eight of all reclamation projects in the United States. And the water used in bringing these arid acres into fruitage will not tear out the soil farther down the stream.

During this decade of the forties, Oklahoma is in fact becoming a land of lakes—almost half a million acres in total extent, with four thousand miles of shore line. A map of the state is beginning to look like a map of Minnesota or of Maine. Ten years ago the people in the western part had seldom seen any water except mirages or any waves except waves of wheat; it was even averred that the frogs had never learned to swim. Now every family knows where to drive to find a cool, wet place on a hot day.

If Oklahomans take as ducks to water, they plunge even more avidly into conservation discussions. In 1944, Governor Kerr and the Oklahoma City Chamber of Commerce inaugurated an annual "Save the Soil Clinic" at Oklahoma City. At the 1947 meeting, Secretary of Agriculture Clinton P. Anderson was one of the speakers, and the sessions included a field trip to an outlying farm. Of the 1,131 registrants, 844 were farmers; the rest were professional and business leaders of the state. Following—or sometimes preceding—this statewide gathering are sectional clinics held in farm communities, where soil conservation experts demonstrate their methods to deeply interested groups of neighborhood farmers.

One Sunday in the summer of 1946 from almost every pulpit in Oklahoma, the minister, at the suggestion of Governor Kerr and the Board of Agriculture, preached a sermon on man's sacred obligation to hold God's earth in trust for the future. This also became an annual custom, with an even greater interest shown in succeeding years. And at least one bank—in Miami, as it happens, where the wealth from lead and zinc mines for a time obscured the importance of the soil—employs an A. and M. graduate in a full-time job of running terrace lines, helping farmers select good livestock and seed, and working with farm clubs. He also makes recommendations on farm loans, but his agricultural work is so much extra service, for the president believes that his bank and everything else in the long run is dependent on the land. At the other side of the state Lloyd Noble, oilman of Ardmore, has recently established a foundation for soil conservation as a memorial to his pioneer father. A distinguished agricultural chemist has been placed in charge of a soils laboratory, and contests in good farming practices have been inaugurated throughout a four-county area.

All this is written on the landscape. As one drives through Oklahoma he still sees appalling damage, but on every hand are encouraging signs that the damage is being checked. The weakest spot of all is highway maintenance. Dirt roads—and this means most of the roads in Oklahoma—are worked by state and county alike with no regard for soil conservation. Ditches approaching the dimensions of canyons are already undermining the fence posts and cutting into the sides of the fields.

Even the farmers' efforts to save the soil have not gone far enough to show appreciably in land-use statistics. True, the total farm and ranch acreage increased almost one and one-half million acres during the first half of the present decade, but this increase has been rather constant throughout the state's agricultural history; for worn-out land retired from crops is still included in some sort of farm or ranch acreage, and more and more submarginal areas have been added. But apparently the war and postwar demand for wheat did not tempt Oklahoma farmers to build up conditions for another "dust bowl." When the United States Conservation Service started worrying in 1947 about more than one and one-quarter million acres of sod unwisely broken in the Great Plains region the previous year, only 8,880 acres were in the Oklahoma portion— probably fewer than the number returned to grass.

It is also true that conservation practices do not yet show appreciably in increased total production. Production, in fact, had never declined except temporarily in drought years; for soil depletion was more than balanced by better seed, better livestock, and improved machinery. Now, under the incentive of good prices and war needs, the output of the farms and ranches during the present decade has reached an all-time high.

VIII

The Land Still Produces

OKLAHOMA RANKS EIGHTEENTH in farm income, which is a fairly good indication of its comparative production. This places it about the average in acreage yield, for, as has been pointed out, it ranks seventeenth in size. About thirty-six million of its forty-four million acres are in farms and ranches. The remainder belongs to lumber companies or is used by the oil industry; it is still held by Indian allottees, and not counted in farm statistics; or it is included in parks, cities, and highways.

There is little subsistence farming; the Census Bureau classes only about one-fourth of the farms as self-sufficing. Each region has its own specialization depending on its particular kind of soil and climate. And although in the "west side" the fences may mark the original 160-acre homesteads, the amount of land each farmer tills is now based on more efficient land management. The average grades rather evenly from 1,847.4 acres in the western end of the Panhandle to less than 100 acres along the eastern border. But the increase in the west more than balances the decrease in the east. In 1920 there were 191,988 farms in Oklahoma with a population of 1,015,899; in 1940 the figures were 179,687 farms and 926,741 people. And this trend continues. The agricultural census of 1945 showed a further decline to 164,790 farms. The average size of farm was then 219.4 acres.

This is the modicum of truth in *Grapes of Wrath*. No corporate owner ever literally pushed aside the houses and plowed through the dooryards with a tractor, but mechanized farming has decreased the rural population. The people who quit the farm were often the most ambitious—most of the state's industrial and professional leaders and skilled laborers are of this type—and the ones who stayed increased their holdings and adopted a higher standard of living than the smaller unit could supply. But many farms are still too small for successful full-time operation; for it should be borne in mind that large ranches in sections too rough for any type of agriculture are included in this 219-acre average.

The largest single item in Oklahoma's farm income is cattle. The bovine population runs from two and one-half million to three million head; in some years it goes above the latter figure. Probably there are almost twice as many as grazed over the same prairies in the storied days of the "cow country." The state now ranks ninth or tenth in cattle production.

The largest unspoiled ranching area is found in the vast rolling hills of Osage County. About one-third of this one and one-half million acres is still owned by Indians and leased to cattlemen; the rest has been purchased outright. The ranches vary in size from a few hundred to over one hundred thousand acres. More than two hundred thousand Herefords graze there every summer: probably two-thirds native, the remainder shipped from Texas or southern Oklahoma for "finishing" on the rich bluestem.

The wild, beautiful country stretches for mile on vacant mile, the western part a sea of grass, the eastern diversified by groves of blackjacks and post oaks. Only rarely is the view broken by a distant ranch house, or a few dots of cattle dwarfed to insignificance by the immensity of hills and sky. Early in the morning from the middle of June on, horsemen may be seen cutting out beeves and trailing them to some loading pen beside an empty railroad.

Every June the Osage County Cattlemen's Association holds a convention at Pawhuska. Here large, booted men still bearing the unmistakable imprint of the "cow country" come from a dozen states to discuss federal legislation, market trends, and the efficacy of DDT; and to tour the area, inspecting herds and joining in the barbecue dinner at a hospitable ranch. Let nobody think that the ways of the cattle kingdom have vanished from the West, for he can still find the real thing at Pawhuska. The A. and M. College has recently purchased a nine-hundred-acre ranch here to study diseases of range cattle. Just across the river from the Osage country at Cleveland a drugstore has a frieze of well-known brands running around the wall as a decorative motif.

Another important ranching area covers a still larger acreage of the broken buttes and scarps in the northwestern part of the state and the rugged portions of the Panhandle. The grass here is "short grass," and much of the land is relatively barren, but the feed is supplemented by sorghum crops grown on the level places. The cattle add up to almost a half-million—good ones, all beef breeds with Herefords leading. The ranchmen of the ten counties of the area have organized the Northwest Oklahoma Cattlemen's Association with more than one thousand members, meeting annually at Woodward. Here they discuss the complexities of brands and the problem of feed; attend a feeder show, where cattle in carload and half-carload lots are judged by experts from the A. and M. College; and watch demonstrations of range rehabilitation by the United States experiment station. Here again is the real thing, where ranching is not a synthetic "Western" but a way of making a living.

A more publicized cattle country comprises about one and one-half million acres surrounding the Arbuckle Mountains. Here, where bluestem grown on limestone makes good bones, and fancy prices paid for breeding stock make good blood lines, some of the finest cattle in the world are raised. The owners are wealthy oilmen who have not forgotten a farm or ranching boyhood; but they make their hobby pay, and royal blood from these fabulous herds is improving the general quality of Oklahoma cattle. Every ranch has its brand, which adorns the gates and buildings, but is never burned on the silken sides of the cattle; nothing harsher than a comb and brush ever touches these curled darlings of the stock shows.

Fine Aberdeen Angus cattle are raised on some of the ranches; but the most famous herds are Herefords, and the region has been organized as "Hereford Heaven," with main offices at Ada. The visitor should not be surprised at the scrawny cows of doubtful ancestry he sees in the pastures. These are the "nurses" of the royal calves; the mothers find their time too filled with hairdressing appointments and personal appearances to bother about their off-spring. When the most famous bull of all—Governor Turner's "Old

81"—was mercifully put to death in his rheumatic old age and buried in a tile-lined vault with a concrete-and-stone marker after siring more than a million dollars' worth of sons and daughters, the event made front-page news and later a whole-page spread in the Sunday *Daily Oklahoman.*

Several of these ranchmen—Turner, in particular—sell good nonbreeding stock at fifty dollars a head to young people in the farm clubs. But several world's records in price have been established in the sale of the best cattle: $25,000 for a bull is not uncommon, and some prices have reached more than $50,000. Each of the important ranches holds an annual sale of young stock in January or February. In 1947, Turner's sale brought $125,105 for fifty head.

In the rough wooded section of the southeast the cattle are not combed and manicured, and they are frequently consigned to a place other than "Heaven." Here are large areas of mountain range that have never been fenced, and the cattle drift during the summer. The cattlemen's associations organize autumn roundups, where cowhands comb the brush in the old-time way, cut out the separate brands, and move each herd to its own winter range. McAlester is the economic center of this region.

In spite of these specialized ranching areas, most of Oklahoma's three million cattle are raised on farms. Almost one million, in the vicinity of cities, are dairy cattle. Even Ada and Woodward, in the heart of the beef country, are also dairy centers.

In the northeastern part of the state are the most celebrated Aberdeen Angus herds. The Sunbeam Farm near Miami has even surpassed Hereford Heaven price records and set new world's figures: at the February sale in 1946 the $280,700 total for fifty head was the highest for any cattle auction, and the $21,000 paid for a heifer was the record price for a female; a few months later a buyer from Virginia set a new mark of $60,000 for a ten-months-old bull. Other breeders in that part of the state argue earnestly that these jet-black, hornless cattle are superior to the more generally known Herefords. Tulsa, a cow town in the old days, is now becoming a center of Aberdeen Angus breeding. The ranches occupy broken sections of the surrounding farmland; some are in the eroded hills of the Cross Timbers.

But Oklahoma's most famous beef animals of recent years were of neither Hereford nor Angus breed. For two years running —1946 and 1947—the state won the grand championship of the International Livestock Show at Chicago, both times with Shorthorns. The first year the winner was Royal Jupiter, a steer raised on the A. and M. College farm. He was purchased by the Firestone Rubber Company for exhibition purposes at a record price of $10.50 for each of his 1,370 pounds; but before he was taken on tour a reception was held in his honor at the college with Governor Kerr and Governor-elect Turner making speeches. In 1947 it was Big Boy, raised by eighteen-year-old Claude Millwee of Fort Cobb. The little town declared a holiday, with a parade, a tour of the Shorthorn farms in the area, a barbecue for five thousand visitors from over the state and Shorthorn breeders from over the nation, and speeches by the Governor and the presidents of A. and M. and the University.

With so much interest in cattle it is inevitable that Oklahomans should still be interested in riding. Even a mechanized wheat farm usually has a pony or two, and farm boys more used to handling tractors than reins like to teeter around on high-heeled boots. Here one often sees the beautiful Palomino—"the color of new-minted gold." In the ranching sections the breeding and showing of that glorified cow pony known as the "quarter horse" has become a cult. Nobody knows much about the ancestry of these tough heavy-set creatures—they are like their fellow Oklahomans in that—but they got their name from the quarter-mile races upon which the cowboys and Indians in the old days used to bet their all. They are smarter than any human at cutting and roping; they will "turn on a dime and give a nickel in change"; and they can jog tirelessly uphill and down all day and all night, or skim over the ground like a swallow when speed counts. After a quarter-horse show held at Ada recently, thirty-nine of these animals sold for a total of $31,510.

Most Oklahoma towns have "roundup clubs" of amateur riders —it is said that there are nearly two hundred such clubs in the state. It is a poor community that cannot afford some anniversary for a pioneer celebration, with neighboring roundup clubs in the parade and a rodeo in the afternoon. According to a rather careful count made by the *Daily Oklahoman* in 1946, about forty Oklahoma cities held rodeos during the year, and the spectators added up to more than 333,095. The rodeos at Woodward and Ada are the most notable. Ada's five-day celebration approaches the nationally known rodeo at Cheyenne, Wyoming, in interest and attendance. And Oklahoma riders take their share of the prizes in out-of-state contests. Jim Shoulders of Tulsa and young Todd Whatley of Bethel in the southeastern mountains won the top honors at Madison Square Garden in 1947; and Whatley was later named world champion of the year by the Rodeo Cowboys Association on the basis of points piled up at rodeos across the country. Horse races are popular, also, especially in the small towns of the west; these are "brush circuit" races, with the quarter horse a favorite, but they are well organized, and they have all the color and interest of big-time racing.

Next to cattle in the Oklahoma farm income is wheat. The state usually ranks fifth in production (in 1944 it ranked third, and in 1947, with an all-time record yield of 104,734,000 bushels, it ranked fourth); and the quality regularly wins prizes at the hay and grain show held in connection with the International Livestock Exposition. Under the stimulus of world demands about half of the entire crop area of the state is now planted to wheat— 6,825,000 harvested acres in 1948, with a total yield slightly below that of 1947. This makes wheat raising important through all the western half; but the old-established wheat counties are in the north end of the Red Beds and (skipping the eroded margins) in the High Plains of the Panhandle.

In these rich counties the prairie rolls for mile on mile of living green in winter, billowing waves rising ever higher through the spring, then hot, golden stubble, and smooth red-brown soil. Little towns far in the distance can be marked by their towering elevators —usually owned by farmers' co-operatives—and the cities are overshadowed by row on row of the great massed bins. Every activity of life is geared to the rhythm of wheat. In the summer and early fall the tractors crisscross the fields with their plows and harrows and drills. Winter is a long, golden time of leisure while the wheat grows and the farmers come to town. Spring is preparation. Then comes the sweat and strain of harvest, when the great combines march across the land, and the roads and the towns are crowded with loaded trucks. At the same time the railroads are blocked with cars hauling from the receiving elevators to the terminals. Enid, with a terminal elevator capacity of 22,000,000 bushels—and an additional 4,000,000 bushels under construction at this writing—regularly checks in 600 to 800 carloads a day through the rush weeks of June and early July.

Most of the wheat farmers live in large, comfortable houses in the midst of their fields and supplement their income with livestock and chickens. But a good many live in town, driving out to take care of their crop; and these work most of the year at other employment.

Cotton once ranked above wheat as Oklahoma's cash crop. It was grown throughout the southern half of the state, but the southwest was the real cotton section. In some of these rich Red River and Washita Valley counties the economy was geared to cotton as that of the northwest is geared to wheat. Rural schools were open in summer and winter with a fall vacation for picking, and the season when the great white loads moved to the gins was the time of financial ingathering. On "Sat'dys" during this season the towns were filled with happy Negroes rich with picking wages.

But the acreage has been going down steadily since the middle nineteen twenties, and recently the total income dropped below that from wheat. The yearly planting now runs close to one million acres, with a total production of about 300,000 bales. The southwest especially has gone into the wheat business. For example Tillman County's 300,000 acres of cultivated land was once planted to 240,000 acres of cotton, with possibly 60,000 acres of wheat; now 75 per cent is in wheat, only about 30,000 acres in cotton, and as much or more in alfalfa. War conditions accelerated this shift, but as a long-time trend it is an evidence of soil depletion.

If cotton ever comes back to this part of Oklahoma, it will come through mechanization. Raising it has always been a thirteen-months-a-year job requiring the labor of children and Negroes. Now a few farmers are beginning to plow, plant, and cultivate with tractors; then when the bolls are well opened, they apply a de-foliant to destroy the leaves, and gather the cotton with a mechanical picker. One farmer near Hobart thus produced fifty-eight bales from 145 acres with no help except from his wife, who hauled the loads to market.

Corn ranks next to cotton in the Oklahoma farm income. In the early years of statehood the acreage was more than twice the combined acreage of wheat and cotton. Then wheat and cotton moved in on the corn land as wheat is now moving in on the cotton; and corn planting dropped from nearly 6,000,000 to less than 2,000,000 acres. There were only 1,336,000 acres in 1948. One can run a finger down the columns of acreage and production statistics since statehood and spot the two great drought cycles: the first year the yield drops; then the acreage goes down, and is never regained. The western half of the state was lost to corn after 1910; the eastern part was struck in the thirties. The distribution now follows the stream valleys in the eastern half of the state. Hogs— about one million a year—are concentrated mainly in the corn sections.

Oklahoma ranks third among the states in the production of grain sorghums. They are grown most extensively in the Panhandle and other western counties, where they are cut for feed or threshed for grain. At the International Exposition in 1946 the state won both the grand championship and the reserve championship, besides a number of first prizes in the various kinds. Oklahoma is also the largest producer of broomcorn in the United States. It is grown in the western half, with the greatest concentration around Lindsay.

Oats are raised extensively in all sections except the northwest and the southeast. Alfalfa is grown in every county: for hay, it makes three to five cuttings a year; in seed, the state ranks as one of the top producers—sometimes the top producer—in the nation. Peanuts are rapidly becoming important in the south-central section. Bryan County on the Red River harvests almost one and one-quarter million bushels a year, plus about sixty-five thousand tons of peanut hay. A few such counties bring the state up to sixth rank in peanut production. For many years Oklahoma has ranked second in pecans gathered. Most of the nuts come from native groves along the creeks through the southern and eastern portions of the state, but some orchards of the papershell variety have been planted.

Peaches, pears, and apples are grown commercially in the

Ozarks and in the valleys and the belts of sand along the rivers. Stilwell, in the "flint hills," is the center of the strawberry section; the fruit is all processed in town and shipped frozen or canned to wholesale buyers. The blackberry business around McLoud is one of the best examples of specialized farming and co-operative marketing in the state. Every grower hauls his morning's picking to a central shed in town; then each afternoon an auction is held for buyers waiting with trucks from Kansas City, Denver, St. Louis, and other distant points. Solid truck-gardening farms line the lower Canadian and the Arkansas from Tulsa down. Hundreds of acres of commercial tomatoes are raised along the lower Red River, and the fruit is shipped in refrigerator cars to Eastern markets. Widely separated sandy areas—Rush Springs, Cleo Springs, Lamont, Weleetka, and Crescent—specialize in watermelon growing, shipping their product even to foreign countries.

Thus the visitor may be pardoned for assuming that Oklahoma is a flat land growing nothing but wheat, or one vast ranching area, or a berry patch, or a fruit orchard. And when the products of the different sections are added together, they feed a goodly number of people. But the state exports not only agricultural products but agricultural (and pastoral) ideas.

This traffic began rather naturally with histories of the fabled cattle kingdom. Edward Everett Dale, of the History Department at the University of Oklahoma, knew from experience the duties of a line rider, the equipment of a chuck wagon, and the handling of a trail herd. He knew also how to disguise scholarship under a literary style as effortless as sunshine on new grass. When the University "print shop" branched out as the University of Oklahoma Press just before 1930, his *Range Cattle Industry* was one of its very first books. Twelve years later the same organization published his *Cow Country*. Shortly thereafter it published equally interesting books by J. Evetts Haley and Laura V. Hamner, both of the Texas Panhandle. Its most recent publication in this field, John L. McCarty's *Maverick Town*—another Texas Panhandle book—approached the dimensions of a "best seller."

But little had been published about the lowly sheep; for the man who dealt with cattle had become the spokesman of the West, and the things he said about "woolies" were not fit to print.

The Land Still Produces

The University Press broke this taboo in 1945 with *Shepherd's Empire* by Charles Wayland Towne and Edward Norris Wentworth. In a style as lively as any cow talk this book gives the past and present of an American industry much older than Plymouth Rock. Strangely enough, it did not appear alone. Although the story had been there for centuries, the idea of using it struck in two places at once. *The Golden Hoof* is as interesting and authentic as its twin. It was not published by the University of Oklahoma Press, but it had an Oklahoma motivation: Winifred Kupper, the author, was a student in Walter S. Campbell's professional writing courses at the University. None of these three writers is an Oklahoman; neither has sheep raising ever been very important here; but the production of their books under Oklahoma influences is typical of the state's intellectual leadership.

Other University Press books in the general field of agriculture have to do with farming practices and the present overshadowing influence of the United States Department of Agriculture. Elmer Peterson, a critic of the New Deal's interference with supply and demand, argues for a living direct from the soil in *Forward to the Land* and *Cities Are Abnormal,* the latter a symposium which he edited. Ferdie Deering in *USDA, Manager of American Agriculture,* is sympathetic with the aims of the Department of Agriculture, but intolerant of its bungling, overlapping organization. Both of these writers are connected with the Oklahoma Publishing Company of Oklahoma City: Peterson writes articles for the firm's two daily newspapers, the *Daily Oklahoman* and the *Oklahoma City Times;* and Deering is the editor of the influential *Farmer-Stockman.* On the other side of the fence is T. Swann Harding, veteran employee of the Department of Agriculture. His *Two Blades of Grass* reads like a romance as it recounts the amazing achievements of quiet government research workers, which in some cases have returned a profit of 10,000 per cent on the public money invested.

After the remarkable success of Sears' two books and *Plowman's Folly,* the University Press found itself the chief spokesman of soil conservationists throughout the country. And it has continued to be heard. Joseph A. Cocannouer's *Trampling out the Vintage* is the agricultural pilgrimage of an Oklahoman who grew up in pioneer days in the red hills, and it tells with circumstantial detail what happened to the land and its people. Faulkner came back in *A Second Look* to maintain his stand against the plow, and to argue further that soil-building by adding minerals and fertilizers and planting legumes is expensive and unnecessary if the land is allowed to recuperate naturally through proper tillage. In 1946, George F. Hellick, Pennsylvania industrialist and lover of the land, made a gift to the Press to be used in furthering its conservation work. The money is being spent in printing more books to reach more readers and make more converts. Meanwhile, Angus McDonald in *Old McDonald Had a Farm*—released by an Eastern publisher—told how his shrewd, hard-working father reclaimed one eroded piece of Oklahoma land.

All this writing springs from the essential rural-mindedness of the whole population. For even the nonfarming Oklahoman is close to the soil. Once in a while one meets an exception. Thus Sam Schneider, director of the farm bureau of Tulsa's KVOO radio station, found people measuring food "in terms of how many canned peas a barrel of oil or a chunk of moulded iron will buy"; and he reminded them that "*milk doesn't come from bottles*—but . . . from cows and cows eat grass and grass grows in the soil." I myself recently heard a man say—in Stillwater of all places—"Yes, I suppose the farmers do need rain, but none of the rest of us do." In general, however, the average Oklahoman's thought is set to the rhythm of seedtime and harvest.

The work of the junior farm clubs grows out of this same ruralism of spirit. Here are the elements: united adult support, whether by farmers, small-town businessmen, or wealthy industrialists; and a genuine love of the farm on the part of the young people. Added to this is the unfailing leadership of the A. and M. College, which in all its scientific studies has never neglected the point of view of the dirt farmer.

In March every little community in the land has its exhibit, to which the boys bring their livestock and the girls their garments and foods; and all the adults, whether parents or neighbors, come to beam approval. Then come the county shows, and the district shows, and the state shows. And the men go along, and when a boy (or girl) at any stage decides to quit exhibiting and sell, they bid fancy prices for his calf or pig. The whole set-up is a blaze of rural glory in which everybody shares and nobody is disappointed.

The big-time competition comes in the fall. And here a sober summary of the youngsters' achievements sounds like wild boasting. No other state in the Union has such an astounding record. The year 1946 was typical.

In September the Future Farmers of America entered sixty-five hogs in the National Barrow Show at Austin, Minnesota. They had often won prizes at Fort Worth, San Francisco, Denver, and Kansas City, but this was their first large-scale invasion of the corn belt. They were competing against adult and junior exhibitors from thirty states, but they captured so many purple and blue ribbons that they practically took the show. And Oklahoma is not a hog state; most of the purebred business is in the hands of the club boys and girls.

The next month came the American Royal Livestock Exposition in Kansas City. Boys from sixteen Oklahoma high schools entered the FFA division; on their fat calves they won seven out of twelve class firsts, three out of six breed championships, and the championship and the reserve championship of the division, besides winning most of the lesser prizes. In the same way they took the lead in the FFA swine show. And the Stockyards Challenge Trophy for the best three steers, three lambs, and three barrows from a single chapter went to an Oklahoma community—Garber, in the wheat belt—that had won it for ten consecutive years. This was the way it looked to a Kansas City market journal: "For all practical purposes in reporting winnings in the FFA division it might be assumed that the exhibitor was from Oklahoma unless otherwise specified." The 4-H boys and girls did almost as well in their division; in cattle they won two class firsts, the championship of the show, and a great number of lower places; and they dominated the fat-lamb show. In addition, an Oklahoma girl was chosen to be princess of the exposition.

It was the same story over again at the national 4-H Club Congress held in connection with the International Livestock Show in Chicago. The young people won five national titles besides a long list of firsts where the contests were not narrowed down to a national championship; a three-boy team won first place in live-stock judging; and the state placed both a boy and a girl among the eight national health champions of the meet. A boy from Maryland ruefully commented, "You gotta beat Oklahoma if you win up here."

The year 1947 was remarkable even for Oklahoma. First the FFA boys repeated their previous year's performance at the national swine show. Then at the National Dairy Congress held in Waterloo, Iowa, early in the fall, they won eight gold medals, the highest awards given at this meet. Next, at the Royal, Oklahoma FFA and 4-H young people took one-third of all the prize money in the junior steer division, and more than 85 per cent of the prize money on hogs and lambs; and Ray Gene Cinnamon of Garber was named the FFA's Star Farmer of America. Even in the rodeo contests the boys won first and second in calf roping and first in bareback riding. At the International, Oklahoma again dominated the junior exhibits. Then the FFA for the first time entered the "open" division—competing with the best adult stock raisers of the United States and foreign countries—and here Claude Millwee won the most coveted award of the whole show with his grand-champion steer. At the same time, in the 4-H Congress, Oklahoma club members won more achievement awards than any other state; and here Lavona Thorndyke, from a farm near Lambert, was adjudged the outstanding 4-H girl in the United States.

The record was repeated in 1948. And here one sees the scientific leadership that trains the champions. In the International show that year A. and M. College teams won four out of five first places: Saddle and Sirloin essay contest (second consecutive year), crop judging (second consecutive year), livestock judging, and meat judging (permanent possession of trophy through three victories), leaving only poultry judging for the rest of the country. This is the know-how that sifts down to the farm children.

When the youngsters come back from these meets with their trophies, their home communities fairly explode into parades and banquets and bronze plaques. But the children bear themselves soberly as befits men and women of affairs. Some of them have already accumulated property worth several thousand dollars. Most of them plan to attend the A. and M. College, and all of them are looking forward to a dirt farming or a professional farming career.

The national winnings tell only a small part of the story. In my little home town of Marshall, I have seen these long-legged farm boys and these pretty farm girls tear into the hard work of their projects. I have watched their pleasure, entirely disassociated from ribbons, in the local exhibit, and their serious and responsible demeanor at the county fair. They seldom go farther; but they represent the tens of thousands of average young people from whom the champions emerge. And there is no reckoning the influence they have had on the farming practices and farming ideals of the adult generation. It was these children under eighteen who carried the burden when their older brothers went to war and their sisters went to work in war plants. Girls drove tractors in the fields and hauled the loads to market, and boys did men's work at home or rented land and branched out into independent farming.

The challenge of war needs was accepted vigorously by Oklahoma farmers. In the early thirties when prices were driven down by surpluses, they accepted the government's crop-reduction plan as a desperate expedient, but their hearts were not in it. Now they dread the time when surpluses will mount again. Some leaders in the state are trying to find uses for farm products through chemurgy. In 1947 they brought the National Chemurgic Conference to Oklahoma City.

Inflationary prices for their products have made Oklahoma farmers more prosperous than ever before in their history. The average cash income of 1944, as shown in the mid-decade agricultural census, was $2,620; it was probably twice that figure in 1948. And this was in addition to the farm family's own living—and better living than any other part of the population had in those days of scarcity.

Much of the extra income has gone to pay farm loans. Oklahoma land has always been thickly plastered with mortgages. The original homesteader, who got his farm free by living on it, was so hard run by the drought and depression of the nineties that on the very day he received his patent he usually slapped on a mortgage for buildings and equipment. The settler who came later and bought a farm always had to mortgage it for part of the pur-

chase price. More land is clear now than at any other time since
title passed from the government. In 1948 the total farm-mortgage
debt stood at $112,963,000—a reduction of $46,000,000 since 1942.
But too much of the present load represents new debt for recent
purchases of land at inflated values. When the price drops again,
the buyer's equity will disappear and the mortgage will loom higher than the farm. Oklahoma saw this happen after World War I.

One must be very careful in writing of farm ownership in
Oklahoma. Even sincere scholars unfamiliar with the history of
the state draw false conclusions from farm statistics that are not
parallel. It was not until 1907 that "Oklahoma" covered its present
area; and even then, land tenure in the eastern half was in transition from Indian to white ownership. I have told this complicated
story elsewhere.[1] Here I can only say briefly that no farm-tenancy
statistics carry their present meaning before the census of 1920.

In 1920 slightly more than half the farmers—51 per cent, to
be exact—were tenants; and an additional 12 per cent owned the
"home farm" and rented another "quarter" or two. The number of
tenants jumped to 58.6 per cent during the postwar bankruptcies
of the early nineteen twenties, and continued climbing to 61.5 per
cent by the end of the decade. At the last date only 26.3 per cent
of the farmers owned all the land they tilled. Probably tenancy
went still higher during the terrible drought and depression years
that followed. But the farm census of 1935 showed that the trend
had been checked; there was, in fact, a decrease of .3 per cent.
During the next five years the percentage went down to 54.4. By
1945 it had decreased to 40 per cent; 43 per cent of the farmers
were full owners, and 17 per cent more rented only part of their
land. The same trends are reflected in the acreage; at present almost exactly half the land in Oklahoma is owned by the man who
farms it.

The state helped to bring about this change by the Homestead Tax Exemption Law of the Marland era; one thousand dollars of assessed valuation—which means two or three thousand of
real valuation—of the home-owner is free from all taxes except
previous bonded commitments. The federal government helped
more by its loan policy. Since 1935 almost two thousand tenant

[1] Angie Debo, *And Still the Waters Run* (Princeton, 1940).

farmers became owners through forty-year loans. These have now cleared off 82 per cent more than their required payments on this debt. (The national average is 75.7 per cent.) Almost 10 per cent of the borrowers have paid in full.

Most of the rented land is owned by individuals. A large percentage belongs to retired pioneers or heirs of deceased pioneers; in these cases the tenant is usually a member of the family. There is some corporate ownership, but it is rapidly decreasing. Loan companies that became the unwilling owners of farms by mortgage foreclosure during the depression are selling them in this time of boom prices.

But no matter who owns the land, there is not enough agriculture in Oklahoma to furnish work for 2,336,434 people. Kansas, with 18 per cent more land—and better land—has only 1,801,028. (Incidentally, during the "dust-bowl" years that state lost 4.3 per cent of its population in comparison with Oklahoma's 2.5 per cent.) It was at first the land rushes and then the oil booms that attracted so many people to Oklahoma. But the land is no longer free or even cheap, and the oil business is steadying down. The state's leaders, therefore, are working earnestly to discover unused natural resources and develop new industries.

IX

Why Not Try Something New?

OKLAHOMA HAS FLOUR MILLS, packing plants, canning factories, butter and cheese plants, pecan-shelling plants, cottonseed mills, and one great cotton mill (at Sand Springs)—but the bulk of its farm products are shipped outside the state for processing. It has been shown that even in the oil and gas industry the state's refining lags behind production. Who makes the money from Oklahoma's farm crops and minerals? Here are some statistics worked out by the Geological Survey:

In 1939, before the war upset the normal course of economic life, the manufactured goods of the United States were worth twice as much as its combined agricultural and mineral products. To say the same thing in figures, agricultural products were worth eight and one-half billion, minerals five billion, and manufacturing twenty-five billion dollars. In other words, the producers of raw materials received only half as much as the manufacturers.

Contrast this national average with conditions in Oklahoma. Here agricultural and mineral production in 1939 added up to 80 per cent of the state's income, manufacturing only 20 per cent. Better than average in agriculture, near the top in minerals, it stood thirty-third in manufacturing. This is the real story behind *Grapes of Wrath*. The cold fact is less moving than the imaginary sorrows of the Joads, but it has its pathos: people left Oklahoma—whether by jalopy or Pullman—to go where the jobs were. And here is a surprising revelation. Rank the states in two columns according to income per square mile from agriculture and from manufacturing. With a few exceptions the columns are almost identical. Translated in terms of making a living, this means that farmers make more where they have industrial workers to feed. There would be a more intensive agriculture in Oklahoma—less wheat and beef, more dairy products and fruit and truck gardening—if there were a home market.

The war, of course, changed this situation temporarily. Oklahoma offered a good climate, cheap fuel, some hydroelectric power, a protected location, and a mechanically-minded population. Thus it won eighteenth rank in war contracts and facilities; in expansion of employment, Tulsa ranked third and Oklahoma City sixth among cities of the United States. The most spectacular of the government plants were the great bomber assembly plant at Tulsa for the use of the Douglas Aircraft Company; the army Air Depot at Tinker Field, Oklahoma City, where the great Flying Fortresses and Super-Forts came limping home for repairs from their missions over Europe and the Pacific; the Naval Ammunition Depot at McAlester, which brought a business boom to all the "Little Dixie" area of the southeast; the smokeless powder plant at Chouteau, near Tulsa, for the E. I. Du Pont de Nemours and Company; and the tire plant at Miami for the B. F. Goodrich Company. The last one is permanent; it was made possible through the power generated by the Grand River Dam, which had been constructed at a fortunate time. The Ammunition Depot at McAlester has become a naval arsenal, storing, reconditioning, and adding to the stocks in its vast underground rooms; and the huge Tinker Field Air Depot has become the repair and overhaul base for all jet engines used by the United States Army.

Perhaps it was the experience of going after this business that started Oklahoma leaders out to stalk industry to its Eastern lair and bring it home. They had agencies already at hand. The Geological Survey had long been arguing against excessive preoccupation with oil and collecting data on the location and uses of lesser minerals; and since 1940, it has sponsored an annual Mineral Industries Conference, where first by charts and diagrams, then by tours, the experts show the visitors the possibilities in Oklahoma's neglected minerals. Then in 1943 the legislature authorized the Planning and Resources Board to collect and distribute information about the state's industrial potentialities. Kerr, who was governor when the

101

act was passed, and Governor Turner have both been active in "selling" the state to outside investors. Remember when the governor's chief employment was fighting the legislature or the federal government? Murray even vetoed the appropriation for the Geological Survey, so that it was dormant all through his term; to his agrarian mind it was merely wasting the people's money.

Once before—in the early years of the century—Oklahoma worked systematically at self-advertising, urging the world at large to join homeseekers' excursions, buy cheap land, and speculate in townsites. Brash little Tulsa even sent out "booster" trains to visit Eastern cities. They took along young Will Rogers to show off his fancy rope twirling. A newspaper of the time reported: "He is the center of attraction, and when dressed in his cowboy outfit creates a sensation."

Now it is a steadier Oklahoma offering statistics rather than "sensation," and industrial opportunities instead of a lucky gamble in oil or town lots. And this time the cities are surrendering old rivalries to a new discovery that "anything we can locate in Oklahoma will help the whole state." Again a quantity of paid advertising has gone out and the movement has reached the fervor of a crusade with the Planning and Resources Board in the forefront hurling the statistics. The culmination was the industrial tour of 1947.

At first it was a Tulsa project, but other cities—sixty-two in all —fell in so enthusiastically that its base was broadened to include the state. Even Oklahoma City, Tulsa's one-time deadly rival, joined in as loyally as little Wakita in the wheat belt, where a blacksmith with an idea for keeping plow shares sharp built up a business employing one hundred men. They prepared a train with four carloads of exhibits and took it to specially-invited industrial leaders in eleven major cities of the North and East; then they turned the material over to the Planning and Resources Board, and it was taken over the state to educate the home folks. They made an impression; I happened to be in Chicago when they stopped there, and I was surprised at the interest they aroused. Their arguments were bare of adjectives, but embellished with graphs and tables. And they did have some convincing facts about the state's unused resources.

102

Why Not Try Something New?

There is coal, for example. The reserve is estimated at fifty-five billion tons. It is found throughout a huge L-shaped area dropping down from the Kansas border west of the Ozarks, with its extended arm touching the Arkansas line south of the center of the state. The most important mining districts at present are near Henryetta, in northern Le Flore County, in scattered places radiating east and northeast of Tulsa, and in the towns centering around McAlester.

Coal production is not new in Oklahoma. It began in the Choctaw country in 1872, and increased steadily until it reached three and one-half million tons in 1903; it sagged a little with the use of oil and gas, but World War I boosted it to nearly five million tons in the peak year of 1920. From that time on, it declined and coal mining became a very sick industry during the thirties. The average miner worked only 120 days in 1939. Then came the recent war, lifting production up again to about three million tons. Both pit and strip mining are employed.

Most of the pit operators are small capitalists, usually—but not always—with a mining background in older states. Their relations with their employees are personal and friendly. The miners form a specialized labor group strangely static in the fluid economic life of Oklahoma. Most of them are American-born descendants of British, Italian, or French miners who came to the Indian Territory by way of Pennsylvania. They are intelligent, steady people, living in neat, modest houses, which they usually own; attending Protestant or Catholic churches; and sending their children to the public schools. They labor mightily in their dark burrows, and they keep their own counsel. When John L. Lewis calls a strike, they quit; and nobody knows their private reaction. And nobody knows how they live when the mines shut down. Some of the Italians around McAlester have branched out into farming, and there is a tendency for sons to drift away into other industry; but the average miner sticks to his hard job through fat years and lean.

Strip mining has been practiced a long time in Oklahoma. Even before the Civil War in the Choctaw country a little coal was dug out and used in houses and blacksmith shops, and commercial mining began in the vicinity of Tulsa almost as soon as the railroad came through. Now under the stimulus of war industry and postwar strikes these shallow seams are producing

103

about half the state's coal output. The most important operations are at Broken Arrow, Catoosa, and Talala in the Tulsa area, and at Morris and other places near Henryetta. Huge shovels taking twenty square yards at a gulp bite into the covering layer of earth and rock to form a long ditch sixty feet wide with a coal floor. When this strip of coal is removed, the trench is filled as the next one is made, so that the worked-over area with its succession of filled strips looks like a giant's plowed field. The laborers are not coal miners, but mine-run Oklahomans, who worked yesterday on a farm and will work tomorrow in the oil field.

Most of the Oklahoma coal is shipped north to domestic consumers or south to Gulf ports and overseas. But the most important use of coal—for which there is no substitute—is in the making of coke for the steel industry; and Oklahoma coal did not qualify for this purpose. Recently the state Geological Survey with the help of the United States Bureau of Mines found a way of blending two grades of coal to produce a coke better than any other outside the Appalachian region. This made it possible for the first time to establish the steel industry in the Southwest. Oklahoma coal is now being shipped to coke ovens at the new blast and steel furnaces in Daingerfield, Marshall, and Houston, Texas. But the Geological Survey is still seeking an Oklahoma industry that will use coal as a raw product—for instance, the manufacturing of chemicals or plastics.

The northeastern corner of Oklahoma forms a part of the famous Tri-State (Oklahoma, Missouri, and Kansas) lead- and zinc-mining area, for many years the richest in the world. Oklahoma's segment was the best—good enough to rank the state first in the Union in zinc and fourth in lead production. This remote little corner has a life of its own centering around its metropolis, Miami, and its mining towns, Quapaw, Commerce, Cardin, and Picher; and its capital is not Oklahoma City or Tulsa, but Joplin, Missouri. It has had its own kind of boom years as dramatic as the oil booms, when mining stock was a favorite gamble; and it has had its own heart-breaking depressions. It has its own Indian tribes, fragments of once-powerful groups whose names are written on the whole early history of the United States; and they, like their brethren of the oil fields, had their sudden wealth, their guardians, and their wrongs.

The region is a prairie-dog town of shafts and mounds. The ore is brought to the surface and crushed in great mills; and huge piles of the refuse (chat) rise above the mines. Most of the operators are Eastern capitalists, who work mines in other states and even in foreign countries. Here is the flaw in the present picture. The ore is so nearly worked out that it required government subsidies on the production of critical metals to make mining profitable even during the war years. When these premiums were withdrawn in the middle of 1947, zinc production dropped 50 per cent and a black depression settled on the mining towns. No wonder an intelligent bank president in Miami began in time to look to agriculture. It is indeed fortunate that the community has its tire factory and its other hydroelectric possibilities.

The lead is sent across the line to Kansas and Missouri, but much of the zinc is smelted in Oklahoma—at Henryetta, Bartlesville, and Blackwell. These smelters take ore not only from the Tri-State area, but from company mines in the Rocky Mountains and Old Mexico; and they send out great trainloads of molded zinc—150,000 tons a year. They employ more than two thousand laborers and technicians, average Oklahomans with no industrial tradition. They burn Oklahoma gas as fuel; but they use a high-grade Missouri coal to mix with the ore during the smelting process, and they make their pottery for the retorts from clay bought in St. Louis markets. Probably the Geological Survey worries about the source of these two minerals.

The state is largely made of clay—every home gardener knows that—and much of it is of good quality (for non-gardening uses). Long before the Civil War when the Five Tribes established their great schools, the bricks for the buildings were made on the grounds. In Oklahoma Territory after the land rushes, the industry branched out to commercial proportions. There are now several brick and tile plants in Oklahoma, but they supply only a fraction of the material used in the state's own buildings.

In one notable respect Oklahoma clay has turned out to be "pay dirt." John N. Frank, a young Chicagoan, came to the Art Department of the University of Oklahoma to teach its first classes in ceramics. He succeeded so well with a clay he found near Ada that he launched the Frankhoma Pottery as a side line. The talented Joseph R. Taylor, a faculty colleague and sculptor, created spirited designs for his use; and Mrs. Frank was his production engineer. His early "plant" on the outskirts of Norman would not have housed a self-respecting hen; but his business grew until he resigned his teaching and moved to Sapulpa. He now has a modern plant with seventy employees, whom he has trained from scratch; and through his ware of warm color and daring line he tries consciously to interpret the Oklahoma spirit.

One of Frank's student assistants at the University was young Oklahoma-born Keating R. Donahoe, gifted in ceramic sculpture. After four years spent in war plants, Donahoe set up a studio on the Edmond road north of Oklahoma City, where he makes exquisite Dresden-like figures and art objects of intricate design— all of Oklahoma clay. He is teaching his techniques to forty students, and he envisions a ceramic center where individual artists will work on special orders. A very different product is made by two young World War II veterans at Perry. They created their heavy, handy Tamac ware for buffet suppers and lawn parties. Their workshop has grown from a backyard garage to a modern plant beside the highway, and their pottery is finding an extensive market.

Glass also is an Oklahoma product. The industry started more than a generation ago, but now it is growing very rapidly. High-grade sand is found in several places—in abundance in the Arbuckles. It is loosened from the pits with streams of water and a little blasting, sifted and washed until it is as pure and appetizing-looking as powdered sugar, and shipped to factories in Oklahoma and North Texas. The Oklahoma plants are located at Ada, Blackwell, Sand Springs, Sapulpa, Okmulgee, Henryetta and Muskogee. They use gas for fuel, but the availability of coal as a possible substitute was often a factor in choosing the location. The owners are large Eastern companies, and each plant has its own speciality— window glass, plate glass, milk and beverage bottles, tableware, large jars and containers, and industrial glass. The products are shipped throughout the two Americas, and the biggest problem is to fill the orders that are pouring in.

Why Not Try Something New?

Some local men are employed in packing and loading, but the manufacturing and cutting are performed by Belgians, Frenchmen, and Italians with a tradition going back many generations. These workmen train their sons to follow them—with an output strictly limited during a three-year apprenticeship—and they permit no outsider to enter. Men without sons have been known to adopt heirs to whom they can bequeath their skills. This in Oklahoma, where the average man has worked at half a dozen trades or businesses in his one lifetime!

The very first mineral industry in Oklahoma was the making of salt. In the northwest are two immense glistening plains, where the wild Indians met for councils, hunting, and trading as well as salt-gathering. In the northeast are salt springs discovered and worked commercially, first by pioneering white men, then by the immigrant Cherokees. Grant Foreman, the state's most diligent historian, has written at length of this early business.[1] He believes that a salt works near present Mazie operated at least as early as 1815 was more potent in the history of Oklahoma than the greatest oil well ever discovered here. Wells one hundred feet or more deep were drilled at these springs, and cased with reamed-out tree trunks; and the water was pumped out and evaporated in shallow kettles over a wood-burning furnace. The salt was hauled by ox team to distant points in Missouri and Arkansas or shipped down the rivers to New Orleans.

Besides these early sources of salt, Oklahoma now has the brine unwillingly produced by the oil industry. The public has become squeamish about letting it spray over the land; and so the oil companies now construct expensive disposal plants for forcing it back into the earth. It contains from forty-five to fifty-five pounds of salt in every barrel. There is a salt spring in Blaine County in western Oklahoma that runs seventy-seven pounds a barrel. Sea water contains nine pounds. Yet San Francisco has an important industry of evaporating sea water for salt, and this salt appears on grocery shelves in Oklahoma. Perhaps it is being made by the very "Okies" who went there for the jobs they failed to find at home.

There is enough gypsum in western Oklahoma to plaster the earth. The homesteaders not only saw it striping the red banks,

[1] Grant Foreman, *A History of Oklahoma* (Norman, 1942), 55–58.

107

but tasted it in their drinking water; and gypsum mills were important before statehood. The largest ones now are at Southard and at a place south of Hitchcock—both in the gyp hills of Blaine County—but most of the gypsum used in the state's own building industry is imported. Beautiful alabaster art objects have been made experimentally of fine-grained Oklahoma gypsum from Freedom and Clinton. This seems to indicate another undeveloped industry.

Oklahoma limestone is crushed for concrete work and road surfacing, ground and mixed with shale for cement (with dry ice as a by-product), "burned" for lime, and quarried for building stone; but these industries also are relatively undeveloped. Dolomite—impure limestone containing magnesium—is also widely distributed, and has long been used as a building stone. In the late nineteen thirties the Geological Survey began laboratory experiments to turn it into rock wool. It was melted at high temperature, and blown with jets of steam into fine, soft fibers; and a gas-burning furnace was designed and used, in order to adapt the process to Oklahoma. Then the Survey issued a bulletin on the subject and sent it out to sell the industry. The project succeeded; a plant was built in Sand Springs in 1940 and a second was started at Ada in 1946. The fluffy product is used for insulation in dwellings and factories. And now the Survey is working to make tough, porous building blocks by melting and baking the volcanic ash which is found in extensive deposits over the state.

Rock from the molten core of the earth forms granite masses in the Wichita Mountains, at various places in the Arbuckle uplift, and at one small outcrop in the Ozarks. It occurs in all colors—bright red, pink, gray, blue, and black—and is fine in quality. In 1941 an Oklahoma stone won first prize at the convention of the Monument Builders of America. The state ranks sixth in granite production, with an annual output worth nearly one-half million dollars. Some is shipped as far as New England for monumental purposes. But even so, most of Oklahoma's dead sleep under Minnesota or Pennsylvania stones, and most of the granite used in buildings comes from distant states.

There is one industry, however, that developed too soon and too fast. "Stealing" is an ugly word, but it was largely by this means, not only in a technical but in an actual sense, that lumbering developed. First it was the railroads that took out timbers not only for construction in the Indian Territory, but to ship to other parts of their systems. Then the Kansans came down and stripped the cedar from the western canyons to be used as fence posts. At the same time the great walnuts were cut from the river valleys throughout the eastern section and shipped to furniture factories in the East or even to Europe. The Indians fought the whole process with growing despair; they could not cope with the innocent persistence of pioneers who thought all virgin resources belonged to them, or the ruthlessness of the great lumber companies.

When the land was allotted, the method became legal. The lumber interests helped full bloods select land in the pine belt, acquired guardianships by the hundreds, and sold the timber to themselves through the probate courts. Secretary of the Interior Hitchcock withheld from allotment one and one-third million acres of the best pine in the Ouachita Mountain area, hoping to create a forest reserve; but Congress never gave him the authority. Timber thieves worked there almost at will until 1914, when the Department of the Interior began selling it at auction, dividing the money among the tribal citizens. Probably these above-board sales stimulated lumbering, for 1916 with 236,000,000 board feet was Oklahoma's year of peak production.

Obviously there was no place in this early system for conservation. But now the United States, the state, and the lumber companies are all working together to protect the remaining timber. The federal government is buying up the cutover land for reforestation. The tract now contains about 165,000 acres. It is located in Le Flore County, and with a larger area on the Arkansas side of the line, it forms the Ouachita National Forest. A few miles away in McCurtain County the Oklahoma Game and Fish Commission has acquired about 16,000 acres of virgin timber, which is used as a refuge for deer and wild turkey. The United States Soil Conservation Service also maintains a demonstration area of about 30,000 acres in McCurtain County to show owners of timberland how to manage and harvest their product. In 1925 the state established a forestry service, which is now in the Division of Forestry and State Parks of the Planning and Resources Board. With some

109

financial help from private owners and the federal government, it furnishes fire protection to about one and one-quarter million acres of pine and hardwood in southeastern Oklahoma. Workers in CCC camps built watchtowers and constructed truck trails and telephone lines through this almost inaccessible region, and the rangers and tower men are equipped with two-way radio sets to keep in touch with each other and volunteer fire fighters. In 1946 the A. and M. College established a department of forestry, and the college is rapidly assuming the same influence in scientific forest development that it has long exerted in agriculture.

Logging and lumbering even now rank seventh in the state's industries, with a total production of about 140,000,000 board feet a year. Broken Bow and Wright City each has a mill with a daily capacity of more than 80,000 board feet—enough to build seven five-room houses. These two mills account for almost half of the lumber output. The rest is sawed by "ground-hog" mills that are moved from place to place following the loggers.

Many sportsmen visit this country, but its real economic and social life is almost unknown to the rest of the state. It is a wild, beautiful region with clear, rushing streams, verdant shade, and wooded ridges rising beyond each other in the blue distance. It is all open range, where a few lean cattle and razorback hogs run in the woods and the small fields are protected with worm fences. (The way to tell when these hogs are fat is to hold them up by the ears; if the body overbalances the snout, they are ready to butcher.) Here are remote little towns built on lumbering, and once in a while an isolated farm dwelling—a double log cabin with a dog-trot through the middle, surrounded by a fence of hand-split palings. The tall, rangy men shoot squirrels with uncanny accuracy, raise a little corn and cotton, and work most of the time logging or at the mills. The women dip snuff, cook hog jowl and poke greens, and plant old-fashioned flowers around their clean-swept dooryards. Sturdy, tow-headed boys and little girls of wild-flower beauty grow up almost without school privileges. A number of Choctaws also live in this region, a bright-brown, soft-spoken people, making a precarious living on their denuded land.

This large section of commercial timber does not tell the whole story. More than ten million acres—about one-fourth the state's

110

area—is woodland. The best timber is gone from the Ozark region, although the Cherokee and white hill dwellers still eke out their incomes by cutting hickory for implement handles and oak for railroad crossties. In the Cross Timbers the post oak furnishes mine props, fence posts, and firewood. Most of this region is in farms of a sort. Probably the blackjack will eventually be removed, leaving good grassland. But Oklahoma once had six million acres of commercial timber, and all this area should be brought back into production.

I have told in a previous chapter how the oil industry followed a similar policy of ruthless waste and belated conservation. Now branching off from oil are several industries that seem destined to grow. Heavy industry and precision manufacturing both came to Oklahoma when Tulsa began to make oil-field equipment. These plants impress out-of-state observers by their ingenuity of tool design—improvements installed by restless Oklahomans with a passion for new ways of doing things. This resourcefulness brought the state's production very high in the war plants. The same skills are still available, and the whole state is stirring with new industry. The greatest concentration is around Tulsa—with its industrial suburb of Sand Springs—and Oklahoma City; but every smaller city has its speciality. "Decentralization" seems to be the present shibboleth of industrial planners; but Oklahoma discovered the fact long before heavy thinkers advanced the theory. It is characteristic that the National Decentralization Conference, launched at Notre Dame University in 1945, met two years later at Norman.

There is the matter of transportation. Oklahoma has an old grievance in the discriminatory freight rates fixed by the Interstate Commerce Commission against the South and the Southwest. But the wall is breaking down; in 1945 a new order was issued requiring uniform rates for class freight through all the area east of the Rocky Mountains. Meanwhile, Oklahoma and Arkansas, with Tulsa in the lead, have about convinced the federal government that the Arkansas River should be improved for navigation.

Oklahoma highways are not the best—too much rugged terrain, with rugged politics not entirely absent—but the people give

111

them maximum use. Most of the local freight is hauled by truck; and as for automobile travel, the family that does not own a car is almost unheard of. In the rural neighborhoods even the children, with the consent of their parents, drive for business or pleasure—some even own cars—in complete disregard of licensing laws.

Oklahomans as a matter of course are air minded. They have plenty of space for landing strips, a year-round flying climate, and an urge to go places in a hurry. There is, moreover, a natural affinity between aviation and oil. I have said elsewhere: "Both industries are new; both appeal to the same qualities of youthful daring, initiative, and creative imagination."[2]

The airplane-manufacturing industry began in Tulsa. It was in 1928, when Lindbergh's trans-Atlantic flight was fresh news, that a Tulsa oilman formed the Spartan Aircraft Company to build light planes and the Spartan School of Aeronautics to train pilots. The firm prospered during the thirties, boomed during the war, and settled back to civilian manufacturing with mass production of house trailers taking up the reconversion slack.

Oklahoma ranks twelfth among the states in the number of privately owned planes, fifth in per capita ownership. Tulsa County leads with 341, but only four counties are not represented. More than two hundred farmers and ranchmen operating in rough terrain have discovered the convenience of planes in managing their far-flung acres. Their work includes everything from shooting coyotes to seeding denuded grassland from the air; and their pleasures range from calling on a neighbor to seeing a show in the city. In 1944 they met at the A. and M. College and organized the Flying Farmers Association, which now has branches in thirty-two states. At the same time several publishers have instituted an aerial delivery service for dropping the morning newspaper at the farmers' front doors.

Oklahoma City and Tulsa are on the main routes of commercial air lines, north and south, east and west. American Airlines is rapidly centering its activities in the state: its pilots are trained at Ardmore; its auditing and treasury departments, its stewardship training school, and its main overhaul base are at Tulsa.

[2] Angie Debo, *Tulsa: From Creek Town to Oil Capital* (Norman, 1943), 109.

Why Not Try Something New?

In 1943 when civil aviation was at a low ebb, Oklahoma City invited President Roosevelt and the National Aeronautical Association to call an aviation clinic to meet there. Four annual meetings were held, growing all the while in attendance and interest. Then the Oklahoma City leaders decided to release the clinic and concentrate on save-the-soil, decentralization, and chemurgic conferences, which promise more in the development of the state.

For as this chapter has shown, Oklahoma's industrial development represents a wish more than a fulfillment. But in other respects the people have made their dreams come true. In the final analysis the future is dependent upon the strength and the intelligence of those who plan it. Just what kind of people are these Oklahomans?

X

Sooners or Okies?

EVERYBODY KNOWS ABOUT OKIES. They are shiftless people with many children, who wander about in wretched jalopies, speak bad English, and enjoy public handouts. And Oklahomans are sure they know the characteristics of the Sooner, the energetic individual who travels ahead of the human procession. Can the same people be both? Suppose we look at the conditions that produced them.

Let me illustrate by a story, a true story. It happened in the Cheyenne and Arapaho country, in the county laid out as "D" ("Dewey" since Manila Bay). Although the land had been opened in the Run of 1892, this part was too far west to fill up rapidly. But a few hardy souls braved the drought—anything to own a farm.

Here a homesteader staked a claim, and brought his wife and four children—the youngest a baby—in a covered wagon. He moved their few possessions into a crude dugout he built, plowed some land, and even set out a small orchard. Then he took the extra team and went back to Kansas to earn a little money shucking corn, leaving his family to hold down the claim.

Soon after he left, the baby became sick in the night. The next morning it seemed sluggish and feverish. The mother watched it through the day with increasing uneasiness. By evening a second child was ill. The next day the other two were stricken. The mother had to have help—but she could not leave the children. She remembered how they had traveled on the way to the claim. Working desperately she threw the cover over the wagon bows and fastened it down; she carried out a straw mattress and made a comfortable

114

bed in the box, and placed the sick children inside; then she hitched up the team and started out.

She knew of only one other homesteader's dwelling in that whole barren land. She drove up to the place. She would not endanger another family, but she knocked at the door and asked for advice. The man came out to the wagon and looked at the children. He said, "Of course I don't know anything about medicine—I don't know what's the matter with them—but I know they're awful sick children. They ought to have a doctor." Then he told her that a doctor lived about a day's journey away, where there was also a little store and a post office. She had to follow a dim trail, and cross the wide, sandy Canadian, but he gave her minute directions.

It was morning when she left. The weather turned cold, but the children lay in a stupor and gave her no trouble. She reached the little settlement after dark. The doctor came out to the wagon and looked at his patients; then he pronounced the dread word "diphtheria." He was afraid to take them into his house, for he also had children, but he brought them medicine. Antitoxin, of course, was unknown. Then he took care of the tired team, and brought out hot food to the mother. She wrote a letter to her husband and mailed it, and the next morning she started her desolate journey back. The children seemed to grow worse as the day advanced.

Once more she drove up to the neighbor's house. In a few words she told what the doctor had said. The man looked at his wife. Their youngest child was a nursing baby. He said, "You can't leave, and she's got to have someone. There's nothing for us to do, but for me to go." Both knew it was a risk, for he might carry the contagion home, but a neighbor's need was greater than their fear. He went along and helped.

The baby died that night. The man made a coffin out of a box, and the mother covered it with some scraps of finery she had in the house. Another child was so near death that he made the coffin large. The child seemed to rally for a while, but it soon grew worse, and died before the day was over. They placed it in the coffin with the baby. The man dug a grave in the orchard, and while they stood beside it briefly, he read a chapter from the Bible and prayed. Then he filled in the earth and mounded it up.

The next day a third child died. They made another coffin and

115

buried that child in another grave beside the first. They were almost sure they would lose the fourth child, too, but he passed the crisis and began to mend. He was the oldest—a boy named Charlie.

At last the father drove into the yard. He had started home as soon as he received the letter, driving as hard as he could make his horses go, but they had to have rest at night, and feed. His wife ran out sobbing wildly. He asked, "Are they all gone?" She told him Charlie was living, and apparently better. He said, "I knew it. Last night it came to me as plain as though I'd seen it that all the children were gone but Charlie, and that Charlie would live."

Here enters the narrator—Mrs. C. C. Rogers of Canton. As a young girl she came to Dewey County with her parents shortly after the turn of the century when the land was finally filling with settlers.

"Charlie was about twelve years old when I knew the family. And they had another child born after the three died. Their orchard was growing, and they were getting property ahead. One day the mother told me they were trying to sell their farm. I said, 'Why do you want to leave when you are getting along so well? You've passed the hard years.' Then she showed me the graves and told me the story. She said, 'We've paid too much for our start in a new country.' After the children died, everything she saw was hateful to her. Every time she stepped out, there were the graves in the orchard. And always in her mind was that terrible drive in the covered wagon to the doctor's. Her husband told her that time would heal her, but it didn't. He told her another child would take away the loneliness, but that didn't help either. And shortly after she talked with me, they did sell out and move away and I never heard from them again."

Now here is the point I want to make. Mrs. Rogers is a typical Oklahoman, the wife and office assistant of a successful country doctor; she works hard, reads books, and keeps abreast of modern thought. Outwardly she might be a citizen of any state. But this pioneer experience, although received at second hand, is not fictitious embroidery but the fabric of her life. Such memories form the solid background of all the variegated tapestry of Oklahoma character.

No wonder Oklahomans never see a stranger. Along the highway, on busses, sitting at lunch counters, they enter into immediate conversation. And out of their instantly shared experiences there emerges a common pattern of "Why I knew your uncle in—" or "Why I married a girl from your town; did you know—" They help each other on the road. People everywhere help their friends, and in Oklahoma almost all are friends. And there are few class distinctions except in the minds of the very young, who have not had time to move up and down the social and economic scale.

Only the Negroes are held outside this general neighborliness. The state has a "Jim Crow" law, which theoretically provides segregation with equal accommodations for members of both races. Actually it often works to the Negroes' disadvantage. This is apparent in public conveyances, in parks and other recreational facilities, and in financial support for separate schools.

At present the Negroes are fighting the whole segregation policy; and for their point of attack they have chosen the absence of graduate and professional schools at Langston University, their only state college. The state had been paying tuition and transportation to outside colleges for Negroes studying in these specialized fields; but in January, 1948, the National Association for the Advancement of Colored People, using the case of a young Negro student denied admittance to the University of Oklahoma School of Law, won a United States Supreme Court decision that this practice violated the Fourteenth Amendment. This left the state the alternatives of establishing a complete system of graduate and professional schools for its colored citizens, or of modifying its segregation policy. The Negroes are very much in earnest about the matter, and a few white leaders of Oklahoma have spoken out in their behalf. But one wonders if they realize the emptiness of their victory. For there is little place for a Negro educator in a nonsegregated school system; and this extralegal barrier exists not only in Oklahoma but throughout the United States. The "Jim Crow" law is only the outward expression of a feeling not confined to one section.

There are signs that this feeling is abating in Oklahoma. No respectable editor would now place the story of a fatal accident to a Negro citizen under the heading "Another Dead Nigger," which I found in a county-seat newspaper of about the time of statehood. No corporation involved in a gasoline explosion would now make a death settlement of $7,500 each for white victims, $2,500 for Negroes; as happened in a disaster that shattered Ardmore in 1915. For more than twenty-five years there has been not even a sign of racial violence; and this was once a general threat, culminating in one destructive riot at Tulsa, after World War I. In the summer of 1947 the powerful WKY radio station of Oklahoma City and Kenneth Johnson, a gifted Langston senior, launched a Sunday morning program high-lighting instances of progress in race relations. The following February it received one of the ten citations for "distinguished merit" awarded by the National Conference of Christians and Jews.

Oklahoma Negroes have their own business and professional leaders, their churches, their chambers of commerce, and their newspapers. They even have their all-colored towns.

Langston (population, 514) is strictly a college town; it has no business section and its houses have that indefinable professorial look. Taft is a straggling settlement with a population of 772, supported mainly by the state pay roll for a children's home, a reform school, and a mental hospital. Boley (population, 942) follows the pattern of white farm centers; it has substantial brick buildings along a paved Main Street, and a spreading circle of residences dotted with churches. In the surrounding country are prosperous—even wealthy—Negro farmers. Just now the Chamber of Commerce is working hard to bring in more. Its advertising makes this revealing appeal: "Have you ever experienced complete freedom? . . . A place where your supreme thoughts can be put into action without any fear or hesitancy?" If a white visitor shows a tendency to linger in these Negro towns, he is told courteously but firmly that only colored people live there. There is plenty of precedent, for a good many Oklahoma towns forbid any Negro to remain "after sundown."

The Negroes form 7.2 per cent of the total population of Oklahoma—a proportion that has remained almost constant since the first census. Indians constitute another strongly marked racial element, but their influence has been so great that they deserve special chapters. And there was once a small foreign-born element; besides the industrial groups previously mentioned, there were rural settlements of Germans and Czechs, and a few Irish and Swedish homesteaders. But the foreign-born members of these groups are largely dying out. They now comprise less than 1 per cent of the population.

This leaves almost 90 per cent of the people American-born whites. More than any other American population they came from all sections of the United States. In the early years, "What state are you from?" was the first topic of conversation among new acquaintances. The census of 1890 showed that 97.8 per cent of the native-American white population had been born in other areas of the United States. The 2.2 per cent, of course, represented the first baby crop grown on the new soil. The percentage of outside-born dropped steadily, reaching 40.6 in the last census, the first time it had fallen below one-half. It is no longer the highest in the United States—Florida, for example, has 45.8 per cent, California 48.7, and Nevada 57—but it is twice as high as the national average.

There would be more Oklahoma-born Oklahomans if they would stay in the state. The last census showed 33.7 per cent of the people born in Oklahoma are now living elsewhere. And even the ones who stay do not stay in one place. Their fixity is not that of the bump on the log but of the popcorn in the skillet. And through all this jumping about and mixing, the whole population has become acquainted with each other or each other's relatives.

Out of this contact of North and South, East and West, and its medley of dialects, an Oklahoma language is forming. It is hard to describe—by one who speaks it—but easy to recognize. Its rhythm is essentially Southern—lazy, even, drawling. To an Oklahoman the Northern, Eastern, or West Coast talk seems to run in waves. Its vowels, however, are not the rich vowels of the South, but flattened after the Midwestern manner except for a softening of long "i's" that probably came over the hills from Arkansas. Its consonants are indistinct—"r's" and "l's" blurred, and a good many others dropped from the beginnings and endings of words. There is a tendency to move all accents to the first syllable, leaving the rest of the word to follow as best it can.

Most Oklahomans avoid the ambiguity of the second person pronoun by distinguishing the singular "you" from the plural "you all" with its possessive "you all's." (*You Alls Doins* was the expressive title of an early-day newspaper.) In their grammar they have a tendency to use obsolete inflections. Thus they like an "a" with their present participle "a-goin'" and "a-comin'." They have accumulated more kinds of bad grammar than a people of less varied origins; a single individual may use both the Northern "had ought" and the Southern "might could."

Lynn Riggs' plays probably show a more accurate understanding of rural Oklahoma speech than any other published work. He learned it growing up in Will Rogers' neighborhood about the time of statehood. And although education and modern living have sharpened some of the lazy accents and tightened up the grammar, its basic rhythms still flow through informal conversations and its earthy color gives richness to commonplace expressions.

Oklahoma humor is as elemental as its speech. Like all Western humor, it uses exaggeration, and it springs up according to the need. I know a farm boy who is inclined to "blow." Once in a group of men he boasted of work he had done. Another boy spoke up unsmiling, "That reminds me of the hardest job I ever did. My dad sent me to the river after sand with just the running gears of the wagon. I tied the load on with baling wire and I got home all right, but it was sure hard work tying down every grain of that sand." The men all laughed, the "windy" one most of all, but he understood the rebuke.

Oklahomans like to talk. They know few occasions for silence. Also they are a restless breed. They like to lay pavement and tear it up, erect buildings and raze them, establish "annual" celebrations and abandon them. They look with disfavor at anything that has stood in the same place for ten years. Their highways are in a perpetual state of re-routing. They even move trees.

It is with an instinctive sense of its appropriateness that they have accepted the name "Sooner." It was a fighting word at first. No honest homesteader or city builder would be classed with those who got an unfair start and tried to hold it, when challenged, by perjury. For ten years they called themselves "Boomers"—which certainly described their activities. But the students at the University of Oklahoma with youthful nonconformity embraced the opprobrious title, and eventually the whole state accepted it. For in a profound sense it is true.

120

This quality was recognized early. In 1903 a man came from somewhere to my home town to edit the weekly newspaper. He was one of a series whose names flashed on and off the masthead, but during his brief stay he tried to define the spirit that had dominated the fourteen lusty years of Oklahoma's life.

"The Oklahoman's main characteristic is to be previous. The trait may have originated in the days of soonerism, but it is getting stronger every year. It is in the very air. Our wheat goes first to market, our cattle mature earlier than others, our hens lay before they are half feathered, our children graduate from high school at fifteen. . . . Our motto is 'Get there first.'"

One may skip the freaks of nature; the insight is sure. Oklahomans *are* energetic. And probably for this reason: they are primarily a happy people. They have always been happy. In the days of their greatest pioneering hardships if they lost any sleep, it was not from worry; it was because they had gathered to dance all night in some neighbor's sod house. They made a joke of the scarcity of food; and when real tragedy came to the community, they fell to and helped. Hard times, yes—but always new sod to turn, a railroad to build, or an oil field to bring in. It was not until the nineteen thirties that they felt the pressure of a shrinking economy.

Once I went into the county records and traced the land history of a good prairie township opened in the Run of 1889. About half the original homesteaders left before the required five years' residence; of the ones who "proved up" and received a patent to their farms, more than two-thirds sold out before 1902. During the first months a man might relinquish his claim for ten dollars or a scrawny pony; after a year or two it required five hundred dollars or more; after the land was patented, it sold for about a thousand dollars; and by 1902 the price had gone up to three, four, or even five thousand. It was not the hardships but the lure of these rising prices that proved too much for the settlers.

Many of these former homesteaders remained in Oklahoma. With the stake they had acquired from their free land they went into business in some of the growing towns. Many prospered, and became the business leaders in their communities. More failed, and tried something else. Finally these became old and penniless. But there had to be another pot of gold at the end of a new rainbow.

121

They turned to Townsendism. They did not win their crusade, but they did receive the Social Security Act. Then they hastened to claim their old age "pensions."

Thus a psychological factor enters into the cause of Oklahoma's large old-age-assistance roll. People with prosperous sons and daughters or with valuable property of their own sometimes apply for aid as a natural right, and it is hard for the case workers to resist the pressure of public sentiment. Thus the percentage receiving old-age assistance has been the highest in the United States ever since the law was passed. In December, 1948, the number stood at 98,692, which is 58 per cent of all the population past sixty-five. The national average is 21 per cent.

In the size of the monthly check the state stands close to the top. The maximum is fifty-eight dollars a month, with the average running about fifty-two dollars. The state's share of the payment comes from a 2 per cent sales tax. Of the amount collected through this tax, 72.5 per cent is apportioned for old-age assistance, 17 per cent for dependent children, 7.5 per cent for administration, and the remaining 3 per cent for crippled children, child welfare, and the blind. The maximum aid for dependent children is $27 a month for one child, with $15 for each additional child in a family. Thus a widow with seven growing children to feed, clothe, and educate receives about the same as one elderly couple. The reason for this disparity is obvious; the children do not vote. But here also the number receiving assistance is abnormally high; once—in the fall of 1948—it stood at 59,470, or 7.5 per cent of all the children under eighteen in the state, three times the national average.

A still more helpless nonvoting group could be put out of sight and forgotten. Oklahoma has about ten thousand mentally ill or feeble-minded people confined in institutions. In the past, the management of these so-called hospitals was honest and humane for the most part, but the state simply did not supply enough money for adequate care. Bad as conditions were in the rest of the United States, Oklahoma at the beginning of 1947 ranked near the bottom in the care of mental patients: in proportion to the number of patients, forty-fifth in expenditures (twenty cents a day for food), forty-third in number of doctors (one doctor to seven hundred patients in the largest mental hospital in the state), and forty-fifth in number of nurses. The salaries of employees were so low that certain types of patients were generally used as attendants; and the crowded, cheerless wards and ragged inmates presented a picture of complete desolation.

Then a leading bishop of the state, who had visited a relative confined in one of these institutions, requested the *Daily Oklahoman* to give publicity to prevailing conditions. The assignment went to young Mike Gorman, a former New Yorker who had elected to become an Oklahoman after his war service at Tinker Field. He visited the hospitals and described what he saw in plain language; then the newspaper published his reports as a series of full-page feature articles reinforced with frightful photographs. The public response amazed the writer, to whom "Oklahomans will always be a strange and wonderful breed of people . . . ; they want to do everything—but now." The legislature then in session passed a comprehensive mental health act, and virtually doubled the hospital appropriation for the 1947–49 biennium. Gorman received a special award of the Lasker Foundation for "public information leading to public action" in the field of mental hygiene; and there is every prospect that his forthcoming book, *Oklahoma Attacks its Snake Pits,* will stimulate similar reforms in other states. As he looks back on his newspaper's crusade, he concludes: "I have heard a great deal in my time about government by the people, but this is the first time I ever actually saw it happen."[1] Oklahoma still has far to go in solving the problem of mental disease, but at present it is energetically on the way.

The state is less seriously short, but still short, of medical care for the general population. Worst of all, the doctors are not evenly distributed. According to a recent survey Cimarron County had only one medical doctor for the 3,654 people scattered over the 1,800 square miles of its great farms and ranches; other rural counties had only four or five each; but Oklahoma City and its suburbs had 465, or one for every 552 inhabitants, all living on pavement. The state ranks forty-sixth in approved hospitals; in about half the counties there is no hospital at all. And there are plenty of chances to get sick, for Oklahoma ranks forty-third in sanitation. More than

[1] A condensation of this book appeared in *The Reader's Digest,* September, 1948.

half the counties have no public health service, and provision in most of the others is very meager.

The state ranked thirty-second in draft rejections during the war. Probably this was due to defects that would have been corrected with more general medical care, for in spite of everything the people are healthy. The death rate has always been 20 per cent or more below the national average. The birth rate, which of course depends on other factors than health, usually runs about 10 per cent above the average for the United States.

Probably there are no statistics to prove it, but it seems to me that Oklahoma men are tall, and growing taller with every generation. And they are tanned—deeply, darkly tanned. They dress informally: the coat is generally discarded in hot weather, and sometimes the shirt goes, too.

The slender strength and sensitive beauty of one Oklahoma girl is familiar to Americans throughout the world. In James Montgomery Flagg's Red Cross poster released the spring after Pearl Harbor, it was Georgia McDonald, born in Texas and reared in Oklahoma City, who stood out in her nurse's uniform against the storm clouds and the troubled face of Uncle Sam as the symbol of a compassion that transcends disaster.

Of course not all Oklahoma girls reach this idealization. Many lack dignity and polish. But a selected group—say the girls on the University campus—are so pretty that one casts about for the reason. I am seeing this through the appraising eyes of women who come to the state to teach college classes in home economics or physical education. They explain it in various ways. Some say it is sunshine and clean atmosphere, or the fact that the minerals are not yet all leached out of the soil. Others think it is clothes and grooming, because of an exuberance of spirit that makes a girl dress up every day, or a frank preoccupation with matrimony that makes looks more important than lessons or a career.

Courting is rampant in Oklahoma, and early marriage is the rule. Some of these unions do not last; at present Oklahoma City has the highest divorce rate in proportion to its marriages of any city in the United States. But to offset this trend—golden wedding celebrations are common in these later years. They correspond roughly to the waves of settlement, for many of the young pioneers started their two ventures at once. These anniversaries, held on the old farm with all the children and grandchildren present for the occasion, show the essential steadiness beneath the changing surface of Oklahoma life.

The moralist cannot take refuge in the "good old days" in Oklahoma. One who reads—as I have read—the old newspaper files finds overwhelming evidence that sexual immorality, juvenile delinquency, drunkenness, and crime were more common in early times than now. But the people have always been too lively to bother about their neighbors' conduct. They forget lapses before they have time to forgive them. No wonder it is hard for them to keep their criminals in prison. But although this tolerance does not reform those who are really depraved, it apparently does not encourage general moral laxity. At least the majority of people do right from conviction, and not from fear of what others might say. Such crime as exists seems to spring from the isolated, underprivileged life of the hill country, or the swift undisciplined living of certain groups in the cities.

In one notable respect Oklahoma has made a serious attempt to reform the conduct of its people. Its legal prohibition of the liquor traffic adopted at statehood has been endorsed repeatedly by popular vote, even when it was abandoned by the nation and all but two or three of the individual states. This is not to say that there is no drinking in Oklahoma; bootlegging is so generally recognized that the metropolitian newspapers identify members of that profession as casually as they class other men as farmers, doctors, or oil-field workers. But so far nobody has ever made a careful and dispassionate study of the total effect—whether beneficial or harmful—of the prohibition policy.

As to why Oklahoma clings to prohibition, one may find an answer suggested in the Yale alcohol studies. These investigations reveal a drinking pattern differing according to social and economic class: at the top is an almost universal acceptance of moderate drinking; at the bottom, drunkenness is rather common; and in the middle is a general principle of teetotalism. Since Oklahoma has not had time to build social classes, most of its citizenship falls in this middle group. At least its ideals are the ideals of this group. Its people may break over and drink, but its pattern is that of total abstinence. This is the way it votes. This is the standard set by its newspapers, which regularly refuse liquor advertisements. This is the policy followed by its political leaders.

In its church preferences Oklahoma follows the same middle-class pattern. Its favorite denominations are informal in ritual and fellowship. Baptists, Disciples (universally called "Christians"), and Methodists are the most numerous. Their congregations once dotted the state—town and country—but they have shifted their interest with the shift of population to the cities; and their ministers now commonly regard a village pastorate as a steppingstone to "advancement." Also in the cities—usually in the poorer sections—are the serious-minded, plain-living Nazarenes. Their work is centered at Bethany, just west of Oklahoma City, where they are valiantly trying to maintain a blue-law community against encroaching oil wells and industrial suburbs.

Several small denominations like the Christian Union and the United Brethren maintain flourishing country churches, religious and social centers for a whole farm community. The Evangelical and Reformed and the Lutheran churches perform a like service for the grandsons of German pioneers. The Roman Catholics, always numerically weak in Oklahoma, have recently become actively interested in the rural field. In the western part of the state are several prosperous farm settlements of Mennonites. They retain their quaint customs in dress and manners, but they are the most active people in Oklahoma in sending help to the outside world. They haul their wheat to the mills and ship flour by the carload to Europe, and they have a mobile canning unit traveling by trailer from church to church, where the whole congregation cans beeves by wholesale to be sent abroad with the label, "Food FOR RELIEF, In the Name of Christ."

Where the cities thin out into modest suburbs or the plains tangle up into blackjack hills, anyone familiar with the signs will begin to look for the big, barnlike pavilions of the "Holy Rollers." (That is not the name painted in black letters along the front.) The barbaric rhythm of their music and the declaiming in "unknown tongues" can be heard for blocks. Here is rich material for a sociological and psychological study; but although it has been exploited by fiction writers, it has been avoided by serious scholars leaning over backward in deference to "religious tolerance." The whole movement is a contemporary manifestation of the emotional revivals that swept the frontiers of America in past generations.

Other frustrated Oklahomans find comfort in predicting the end of the world. But most of them are too optimistic to act on their own belief. I remember a state convention they held one time in Guthrie. They spent several days working themselves up to the certainty that the end was here, now, without delay. Then they calmly decided on the place for their next yearly meeting.

Thus Oklahomans find various expressions of a deep and instinctive religious feeling. There are many who seldom go to church—the state is somewhat below the national average in per capita church membership—but there are few, if any, without this basic reverence. Religious faith was a powerful sustaining influence in the hard, early years; and the people have never got away from its fundamental concepts. This does not mean that they make good churchmen. Sunday may be used for visiting, fishing, or even working; and as for following what the preacher says, they have their own thoughts on the subject.

Oklahomans, in fact, have no strong group loyalties of any kind. For in spite of their friendly habits they are individualists. They are incapable of group thinking. This is apparent in committee meetings. When Texans, for example, meet to work out a plan, one holds up an idea and another trims it and a third nails it down until no one can distinguish his own part in the finished structure. When Oklahomans meet, they have as many plans as there are people and one wins out to adoption. Again—comparing them with their neighbors across the river—it has been said that Oklahomans have no state pride. This is not true; they have a fierce state pride, but it centers in some particular section. All this makes for brilliant personal achievements. This book has not interpreted the spirit of Oklahoma if it has not shown on every page the originality, the initiative, the creative genius of its people. On the other hand it contributes to the bad politics, the economic instability, and other collective failures.

This same individualism is shown in the attitude of Oklahomans toward labor organization. Unions do exist, but they are not generally approved. Some of this hostility is created by employers, who know how to "divide and rule," but more comes from the plain man's belief that he is the arbiter of his own destiny. If the depression years showed him he was not free to make his economic choices, he has forgotten the experience.

The terrible Woodward tornado of 1947 came in the midst of the nationwide telephone strike. All through that blustery April day, whiteclad girls had been strolling their beats as usual on the picket lines around the exchange; the rest of the operators were relaxing at home or enjoying the social activities of their enforced leisure. Then suddenly the pitch of the High Plains wind rose to a howl, there was a feeling of intolerable suction, and in a great crash of sound the city collapsed in shredded wreckage. Several of the forty-nine telephone girls were injured and homeless, but through some strange chance none was killed. The first thought of every one was to pick her way through the ruined streets to her post of duty; within two hours all had reported. At the same time the repairmen, also on strike, went to work as quickly to put the tangled lines back in operation. Meanwhile distant union and company officials tried to effect a truce to aid the stricken city, but they failed to agree on terms; and the labor leaders sent a telegram to the chairman of the Woodward operators: "Do not permit union members to report to work. . . . This is no time to weaken." She answered: "Girls refuse to stop work. Will work as long as needed. Have you seen this place?" Many stayed on the job for thirty-six hours without rest. When the union condemned their stand, they said only: "We hope they would do the same thing we did if it had been their home town."

Thus I have tried to describe that distinctive type of American who lives in Oklahoma. Probably these traits are shared to a certain extent by his compatriots; but in Oklahoma they are more strongly marked, for every force that has shaped the American spirit since Jamestown has molded the character of one still-living generation. Even so, it is hard to make generalizations. Perhaps the reader would prefer to meet some representative Oklahomans.

"The High Plains are deeply eroded along the streams"
Between the Cimarron River and Carizzo Creek, in the western
end of the Panhandle

Courtesy Gilbert Hill

"The mountainous east end of the state is heavily forested"
Ozark scene near Grand Lake

Photograph by Bob McCormack
Courtesy Tulsa Chamber of Commerce

"Young, beautiful oil-built Tulsa"

"The greatest oil pool of all lay beneath Oklahoma City's busy streets"

"A hard-working farm couple begins to think in seven figures"

"The practiced rhythm of the drilling crew"
Courtesy Claude V. Barrow

Demonstrating brush eradication
at Red Plains Conservation Experiment Station

Courtesy Extension Division
Oklahoma A. and M. College

"The prairie is an ocean of wheat"
Farm scene in Grant County

Courtesy Extension Division
Oklahoma A. and M. College

"Oklahoma ranks third in the production of grain sorghums"
Small fields on an Arkansas Valley farm near Tulsa

Photograph by Bob McCormack
Courtesy Tulsa Chamber of Commerce

"Fancy prices paid for breeding stock make good blood lines"
Watering calves on Flying L Ranch in Hereford Heaven

Courtesy Bill Likins

Dewey County team with champion calves at Junior Livestock
Show, Oklahoma City

Courtesy Extension Division
Oklahoma A. and M. College

"Some say it is the sunshine and clear atmosphere"
Blue ribbon health group, 4-H roundup at the A. and M. College

Courtesy Extension Division
Oklahoma A. and M. College

"You were born inside the fence like my own grandchildren"
Kiowa girls at Riverside Boarding School, near Anadarko

Courtesy U. S. Indian Service

"They wear their native garments on ceremonial occasions"
Winnifred Ellis, Cheyenne girl of Clinton, as queen of a Ponca
celebration at White Eagle

"Rock from the molten core of the earth
forms granite masses in the Wichita Mountains"
View from the top of Mount Scott

Buffalo herd in Wichita Mountains Wildlife Refuge

Turner Falls

"He paints animals with loving interpretation"
Woodrow Crumbo and his mural, "Wild Horses," in Interior
Building, Washington, D. C.

Courtesy U. S. Indian Service

XI

We Meet Some Oklahomans

WHEN I GO DOWN THE STREET a few blocks in my home town, I come to the snug little house of Billy and Cora Fox.[1] Here is an active elderly couple stirring about the yard, holding open house for children and grandchildren, joining in church and neighborhood gatherings; but in their memories is the history of the state.

Mr. Fox was eighteen years old in 1876 when he came out from his native Kentucky to the buffalo plains. So far as I know, he is the last of that hardy breed who swept the great herds from the path of settlement. He had a gusty zest for life that even in old age keeps his spirits high; but his story is not one of adventure, but of a job.

"We hunted in the Texas Panhandle. The man I worked for did the killing, and I was one of the skinners. A hunter could keep just about two skinners busy. He used a Sharps rifle with black powder. It would kill at three to four hundred yards. When a buffalo was hit, the others would mill around it, and if there was a hundred or so in the bunch, the hunter could get nearly all of them.

"The skinner used a straight knife for slitting the hide, and a special kind of crooked one for stripping it off. His knives were razor sharp. He carried a whole box of them and ground them up every night. Also he kept a steel stuck in his belt to whet them. Buffaloes wallow in mudholes like hogs and hook muddy banks till their hair is so full of sand and dirt it soon dulls the knife.

[1] The sketch of Billy and Cora Fox is adapted from Angie Debo, "Buffalo Hunter," *The Daily Oklahoman,* January 17, 1943, and is used with the courteous permission of the Oklahoma Publishing Company.

129

"We staked the hides out on the prairie to dry. When they got hard, we 'broke' them down the back and folded the hair in and stacked them. Freighters would pick them up and haul them to Fort Griffin, Texas. It took us only a week or ten days to get enough for a big load, like a load of hay."

After two seasons of this, Billy went to work as a cowboy. During the next ten years the brands he worked and the trails he followed mark an odyssey of the range country. Wide distances—New Mexico, the Chickasaw Nation, the Cherokee Strip, Colorado, and Wyoming; fabulous cow towns—Tascosa, Cheyenne, Sundance, and Hunnewell. In 1888 he bought a gorgeous saddle in Cheyenne. It had long tapaderas and black llama-hair pockets. Then in all this splendor he came back to Hunnewell on the Kansas line to see Cora Brewster. He had first danced with her when she was twelve or thirteen years old.

Cora now was a tall, vital girl with "a skin like milk" and beautiful red hair. She had grown up in that border town where her father taught school, practiced medicine, and ran a drugstore. Behind her were traditions of culture and education, but before her was the lure of the wild Indian Territory. The cowboys of the Cherokee Strip were her friends. Indians from the reservations across the line often came to her father's store. Once when she was a little girl they fingered her shining curls and offered many ponies for her. And she knew and sympathized with the Boomers.

"I knew David L. Payne and admired him very much. He was a big man, and handsome. I was sixteen years old when he started a settlement on the Chikaskia. We used to go down there to dances. Once I danced with Captain Payne himself! When the soldiers burned his settlement, we could see the fire from Hunnewell. I stood at my father's door and watched it and cried."

But Cora and Billy were soon establishing their own home in the Territory—this time with the blessing of the government. It was in November of 1888 that they were married. The following January the Indians agreed to cede the "Oklahoma Lands," and the President set the date for the opening. The Foxes prepared to join the homeseekers. In their party were several of Billy's cowboy friends—one, just married, with his bride.

The Foxes have never forgotten the freshness of those spring days when they drove their covered wagons across the swollen rivers and the wide grasslands of the Cherokee Strip. Cora, youngster that she was, had brought fishing lines and hooks and she looked longingly at every creek they crossed. On the night of April 21 they took their station on the border of the tract to be opened. The next day is history: noon, the starting gun, and the furious race. Cora waited at the line and guarded the wagons while the men rode in. Billy knew every foot of the land from working cattle over it; it was not difficult for him to find a rich quarter-section on the Skeleton bottom. He came back to the line about three o'clock. He was wildly exultant.

"Well, Cora, I got us a farm; it's about four or five miles south."

"Is there a creek on it?"

"Yes, it's on the Skeleton."

Cora got her lines ready, and cut salt pork in pieces for bait. By this time the rest of their party had assembled. The friends had been able to stake claims close together in the same valley. They were all in high spirits, laughing and talking excitedly. The men hitched the teams to the wagons, and all drove in and camped together in a bend of the creek on the Foxes' claim.

While the men were caring for their horses and making camp, Cora hurried down to the stream. Before they got the teams unharnessed, she had caught five fish that filled her big iron skillet. She spread a tablecloth on the clean prairie grass and all gathered around to eat. It was the Foxes' first meal on the spot that was to be their home for fifty-three years. "I always used to think of that when I was plowing," says Mr. Fox, "when I came to the place in the field where we slept that first night."

They stayed there several days. The men rode to the land office, thirty miles away, to file on their claims, leaving the girls at the camp. Each also plowed a few furrows or did some other brief work on his land as evidence of possession. Then they turned their wagons north. They all had much to do in the six months the government allowed them to establish a residence.

The Cherokee Strip was still a cow country. Billy Fox's friend, Ike Clubb, was foreman of a ranch on the Black Bear. It was easy for him to get a job riding the fences, and Cora cooked for the outfit. The boys appreciated her good meals. They gave her a pig that had been lost from the covered wagon of some passing settler; she named it "Boomer" and fed it from a bottle. They also gave her five dogies, and she raised them all, and Ike gave her a cow and calf. She and Billy took a trip to Hunnewell and brought back ten hens and a rooster; and she raised 102 chickens in dugout shelters, for her start on the claim. Somehow they got another pig.

When the boys were away from the camp, Cora worked happily at another task. "The coming of our first baby was such an eventful thing," she says, "that I made a nice layette. My sister sent me material, really fine material. I put silk lace on every one of the little shirts. And you know how I still do all kinds of fancy work—" well do I know that her whole house drips with crocheting —"and I made everything just as nice as I knew how."

About the first of October the Foxes moved down to their claim, with their summer wages in their pockets, their two shoats, their chickens, and their start in cattle. The bluestem was growing so tall in their valley that only the top of Billy's hat showed when he rode through on horseback. He hauled lumber from the railroad, eighteen miles away, to finish their dwelling. "We had the best dugout in the whole country," says Mrs. Fox proudly. "It was ten by eighteen feet, and it had a shingled roof and a board floor and three half-windows." The walls, of course were of the bare earth, but she put curtains at the windows and a rag carpet on the floor, and divided the dugout into two rooms with a cloth partition.

They had to work fast, for their baby was born on October 17. They got a doctor who had settled on a claim across the Skeleton, and Billy rode to a tent on a claim two miles away for a neighbor's wife. She proved to be a good friend; every day she made the four-mile walk through the tall grass to wash and dress the baby until Cora was able to take care of it.

That winter Billy fenced five or six acres for pasture and made a pen for the hogs. He made eight trips to Hunnewell for corn and supplies. Cora always stayed alone until after the night the baby got a choking spell; then she got little Myrtie Rutherford from the adjoining claim to stay with her. Boomer grew to weigh four hundred pounds, and was butchered. The other pig had five pigs of her own; the coyotes came around and snapped at them until the young pioneers had to tend a fire all night to keep them off. The wild turkeys came from the timber and stole the corn from Cora's chickens. Once Billy stood on the roof of their dugout and shot a deer. The former cowboy made his ultimate sacrifice to the ways of the homesteader when he sold his cherished saddle because the mice and rats came into the dugout and chewed up the llama hair for their nests.

But Billy was a good farmer, and they prospered. They built a comfortable house, and planted a big orchard. And the years rolled on. In 1941 Mrs. Fox still raised a big flock of turkeys and lived the life of a busy farm woman, and Mr. Fox still plowed his land, and milked his cows, and harvested his wheat. At the end of that year they retired and moved to town. But when they get in their car and drive out to the farm, there they are really at home.

They show how dear the past is to them by their interest in pioneers' activities—eighty-niners' meetings, the Cherokee Strip Cow Punchers Association, and reunions of old neighbors. They read every book they can find that gives an authentic account of ranching and homesteading, but they have a vast scorn for "Wild West" sensationalism. Where except in Oklahoma can one find a hale and active couple whose life spans so great an area of human expedience—from the hunting stage through the pastoral to the agricultural, and on to the complexity of modern times?

But not all Oklahomans came with the land rushes. It was a small quantum of Indian blood that enabled Dr. Fred S. Clinton to be born in the state, although his blue eyes and blond complexion as well as his ambitions place him among the white pioneers.[2]

Charles Clinton, his father, was a Georgian, who had migrated to Texas, and discovered the Indian Territory by way of a trail herd. Here he met and married Louise Atkins, a one-eighth Creek girl, a teacher in the tribal schools; and he established the Half Circle S Ranch. Fred, born in 1874, was the oldest child. He says, "We lived in a world of sweeping prairies, grazed by fine horses and cattle." Charles Clinton died before the boy was fourteen, but the widow and her sons managed all the extensive ranching interests. They lived in a large, ornate house on a hilltop, aristocrats

[2] Some of the material in this sketch was used in Angie Debo, "Jane Heard Clinton," *Chronicles of Oklahoma*, Vol. XXIV (1946), 20.

in the best traditions of two races. The three sons and their sister attended the tribal schools, and then went East to college.

Fred S. Clinton completed his studies for a degree in medicine in 1897. The same year he married Jane Heard, whom he had met while at college in Georgia. She was a talented musician, a high-spirited, radiant girl with a gift for friendship, and she came from a family distinguished in Georgia history since the Revolution. It was a brilliant wedding: a spacious plantation house crowded with guests; a small niece and nephew holding white satin ribbons, and brothers and sisters and cousins as attendants; the mockingbirds singing outside; and the bride sweeping down the wide stairway in her misty veil. A far cry, all this, from the life that lay ahead in the Indian Territory.

The doctor opened his office in Tulsa. The place probably had a population of five hundred; it consisted principally of corrals and loading chutes, and a straggling line of buildings along a "Main Street" cutting at right angles across the railroad tracks. He drove to see his patients if the trails were passable. Also, he says, the Frisco "was very accommodating," allowing him to ride passenger and freight trains and handcars to make calls along the line. But sometimes in bad weather he walked four or five miles to attend seriously sick people. If the river was low, he forded by buggy or on horseback. Years later, Mrs. Clinton used to laugh about the time the buggy stuck in the quicksand, the horse jerked loose and reached the bank, and the young couple remained marooned in the middle of the current until help came, fearful of ruining the doctor's new suit.

He had a partnership with Dr. J. C. W. Bland of Red Fork. Mrs. Bland was a Creek citizen, who held land under the occupancy title of tribal law, but had not yet applied to the Dawes Commission for her allotment. One day the two men happened to notice an oil-drilling rig that had been shipped into the territory by some promoters and was standing on the siding at Red Fork; and they managed to have a test started on Mrs. Bland's land. The location was just outside the townsite, in a wheat field not far from the Bland house.

Thus came the Red Fork strike, and the wild excitement that followed it. While promoters rushed to the well to pick up leases

134

or form companies and sell shares, the partners worked as feverishly to confirm Mrs. Bland's title. It would have been inconvenient
if some other Creek had filed on her land! Dr. Bland had taken that
day of all others to be stricken with acute appendicitis, but Dr.
Clinton secured a power of attorney from Mrs. Bland and took the
train for Muskogee, headquarters of the Dawes Commission. He
carried along a quart bottle of the liquid that spurted from the
hole. He had to be sure—he had never seen any crude oil before.
Reaching Muskogee after dusk, he went to the home of another
doctor friend, and the two went out to the woodshed. In dark
secrecy they soaked a few shavings and struck a match. The blaze
lighted up the yard. Then they tried the liquid in a lantern, and
it burned with a clear, steady flame. It was oil all right—good oil
with plenty of kerosene. The next morning long before the land
office was opened, Dr. Clinton made the head of the line. The rest
was pure formality. The land became Mrs. Bland's allotment, and
the No. 1 Sue A. Bland was the oil well that started Tulsa on its way.

Soon after they settled in Tulsa, the Clintons became active
members of the Methodist Episcopal Church, South. This little
congregation had been organized in 1893 with seven members,
and had progressed through a brush arbor meeting place to a one-
room shack with a door in one end and the pulpit in the other, and
three windows on a side. When the congregation outgrew these
quarters, Dr. Clinton served on the three successive building committees, which planned the neat brick structure occupied from
1901 to 1907, the large, pillared, strictly utilitarian building used
from 1907 to 1928, and the glorious edifice that now dominates
Boston Avenue with the light of a modern faith. At the same time
Mrs. Clinton played first the small reed organ, then the piano for
the growing congregation, and was active in securing the first pipe
organ.

Dr. Clinton became very active in civic affairs. He became a
charter member and a director of the Tulsa Commercial Club,
which by a series of daring coups grasped for the ambitious little
town the leadership of the oil industry; he was one of the organ-
izers and an officer of the company that gave the young city its
streetcars; and he established the first hospital and nurses' training
school in Tulsa. He was chairman of the committee that reorgan-

ized the Indian Territory Medical Association to conform to national standards, and later served as president; then he was active in the Oklahoma State Medical Association formed by the union of the two territorial societies. He initiated the Indian Territory branch of the American Red Cross, and led in the merger after statehood. He organized the Oklahoma State Hospital Association, and was annually elected president until 1927, when he became honorary president for life; he was one of the founders of the Midwest Hospital Association, and served two terms as president. He read papers before medical meetings in the days when Indian Territory physicians were far removed from outside professional contacts; and published them in national journals.

Some of these articles throw as much light on the society of the time as on medical techniques. An article published in the *American Journal of Surgery and Gynecology* describes in learned terms how he patched up the abdomens of two patients shot at different times in 1904. But along with "the anterior superior spinous process of the illium" and "a continuous sero-muscular suture" is the laconic "We did not find this bullet, nor do we ever waste any precious time hunting them." One of the operations—on a young Negro woman—"was performed in an old soot-stained tent 10x12 feet in size, with no light except thru the flaps and holes, and no floor except Mother Earth, and no heat except by a small cook-stove, and no nurse except a Negro man, whose recently invited guest she was when shot by a jealous lover." Then he details her care during convalescence—"on the fifth day, water and beef-juice (the latter obtained by permitting her to chew rare steak at two-hour intervals, swallowing the juice only)." Six weeks later she was disporting herself at a dance. Such were the practical skills developed by the young Indian Territory physician.

Meanwhile Mrs. Clinton was finding a place for all her gracious gifts on this same raw frontier. When the first Parent-Teachers' Association was organized, she became a charter member and at one time served as president. She was one of the founders of the public library. The Y. W. C. A. was organized in her home, and she was chairman of the social committee when the present building was opened. When Girl Scout troops were formed, she helped with their music and their programs. She was a charter member of the Ruskin Art Club, out of which grew the Philbrook Art Center. She was one of the founders, and for the rest of her life the only president of the Hyechka Club, which made Tulsa a musical center even during the stress of its early growth.

Mrs. Clinton carried on her many responsibilities until her death, at the age of seventy, in 1945. Dr. Clinton has retired from active practice, but he marshals his failing strength to contribute articles to the quarterly of the Oklahoma Historical Society. He lives in a big house (he has since remarried), which is almost a museum of accumulated living, and welcomes all visitors with the old unstudied friendliness. Where except in Oklahoma of the past half-century could two joined lives have accomplished so much in shaping the soul of a city?

Such are the people who lived this history. It remained for Edward Everett Dale to become their spokesman. He was born in Texas of pioneer stock in 1879. When he was nine years old, his father moved to old Greer County and started a small ranch. There the boy learned to ride and work cattle; he made friends with the Indians as he hunted and fished and trapped on the neighboring Kiowa-Comanche Reservation; he attended an occasional three- or four-months' term of school; and he read every book he could lay his hands on. When he was seventeen years old, Texas lost the Greer County case. Thus by judicial decision he became an Oklahoman.

Young Dale and his brother borrowed money and went into the ranching business. "Handling a trail herd was very much like teaching school," Dr. Dale now tells his students; "you had your fast cattle at the point, then your average strung out following, and your slow ones at the drag. And no cowboy ever liked to ride the drag." But the range days were about over in western Oklahoma with the homesteaders taking up the land; and the brothers' venture ended in disaster.

Dale tried picking cotton, then went to teaching school. For preparation he had a four weeks' "summer normal" at the little new town of Cloud Chief—then the county seat of Washita County —where he slept on the prairie and took his meals at a near-by house. The year after he started teaching, the Kiowa-Comanche Reservation was opened; and he taught there the following winter.

137

He lived with a homesteader's family in a one-room sod dugout, where he managed his dressing under an improvised tent of bedclothes while his hostess was preparing breakfast in the opposite corner. His account of the opening of this school shows the familiar Oklahoma pattern of an event that will hardly occur again in American history.

The settlers had built a real schoolhouse—one of the first in that area. It was of rough, unpainted boards, and inside was not a single stick of furniture. Dale got there early the first morning, and waited for the children to appear. Soon they came from all directions across the prairie, carrying boxes, benches, chairs, some large empty powder cans left by road builders—anything that would serve as a seat. By nine o'clock about thirty had assembled. They settled down to work with no sense of discomfort; most of them lived in dugouts or rough cabins and sat on trunks and boxes at home.

Their books were from many states. The blackboard was a large scratch tablet nailed to the wall; the teacher wrote the exercises on the top sheet and tore it off when he changed the assignment. The children brought their lunches in tin pails. They carried their drinking water half a mile from the home of a settler. But they were so eager to learn that they made remarkable progress.

Dale taught this school for two years. Then he was elected principal of the six-teacher school in one of the new towns of the community. Such a promotion involved more academic preparation; and so in 1906, at the age of twenty-seven, he began to attend summer sessions at the territorial normal school at Edmond. Here, as he says, he "paid ten dollars a month for bed and board and could hardly tell which was which." As he had never been to high school, he was enrolled "in what was very appropriately called 'the sub-normal department.'" He has never forgotten his impression of the "magnificent" building of brick, made near the campus, and native red sandstone, the "great" library of more than one hundred volumes, the "scholarly" faculty, some of whom even had college degrees.

Horatio Alger could take the story on from here. Dale graduated from the University of Oklahoma in 1911. He entered Harvard in 1913 and received his master's degree the following spring.

We Meet Some Oklahomans

He then came back to the University as an instructor in the History Department. Later he returned to Harvard for his doctorate. There the history faculty, especially Frederick Jackson Turner, encouraged him to carry out his studies in his own way without trying to prune his individuality into a standard form.

For many years Dr. Dale served as head of the History Department at the University of Oklahoma; and he has lectured as a visiting professor in various colleges—from William and Mary to the universities of Texas and Wyoming. It is impossible to describe the power of his classroom lectures. His first word sweeps his hearers into a land of wild and virgin beauty as it lay brooding through the centuries. Over it moves the soft-footed native with his loves and hates and problems, the cowboy watching his herd beneath the lonely splendor of the stars, the ragged settler with the bare poverty around him and the light of the future in his eyes. Throughout is a sparkling humor that differs from the professorial "joke" as the spring rain differs from the fireplug.

Almost as important as his lectures are his individual contacts. All kinds of people stream into his office: youngsters in trouble, returned alumni, important-looking official delegations, Indians, and graduate students in grim pursuit of knowledge. And Oklahoman that he is, he nearly always finds some common ground of "Of course I remember your mother; she used to live in—" or "And so you came from Blair; do you remember Old Man—"

A few years ago I was working in his seminar room when he brought in a full-blood Kiowa couple: a very pretty woman, who spoke good English, and her older husband, who sat impassive, apparently not understanding a word. Dr. Dale and the woman fell to talking about Indian costumes. He showed her a photograph he had used in one of his books—a beautiful graceful girl with rich fringe and beadwork dripping from her buckskin dress. The tears rushed into her black eyes; she cried, "That's my picture. Where did you get it?" The professor was almost as excited as she. He had picked it up somewhere and had never expected to meet the original. He carefully autographed a copy of his book and courteously presented it. One knew she would treasure it. Then other Kiowas drifted in and they began to talk of Satank, the proud old war chief who raided in Texas back in 1871 and then chose death to

139

captivity. The old man still sat propped against the wall. Suddenly his voice boomed out in a wild chant. He was singing Satank's death song! The very song the old leader had used just before he forced his captors to kill him! The others translated it excitedly. It went something like this:

> "O sun, you remain forever;
> O earth, you remain forever;
> But I must die."

In spite of his busy life with people, Dr. Dale has always found time to write. Recently he has been made a research professor and relieved of administrative duties and most of his teaching load so that he can devote more time to authorship. In his books as well as his lectures he has become the spokesman of the frontier. His philosophy of history may be summed up in the one word: Progress. The material forces have been conquered; the dream of the pioneer has been realized; it is the next task to make similar conquests in the realm of culture, the kingdom of the spirit. The hardihood developed in taming the wilderness will win this greater battle, and he has full faith in its ultimate triumph. He knows that dreams come true; in his own career and in the life of his state he has seen the dramatic power of their fulfillment. And so he goes blithely on his way in an age of disillusionment. A story so fascinating has to have a happy ending. Doubt is nothing new to him; there were homesteaders who feared that a living could never be wrested from the tough Oklahoma sod, but the optimists proved to be the better prophets. And as even an uncritical faith is more potent than doubt, and movements are mightier than those who would define them, this homespun Oklahoman may have sensed more truly than the despairing intellectual the course of history. But whether his philosophy be true or false, he voices the deepest feelings of the strong young state from which he sprang.

XII

Oklahoma Accepts the Indians

OKLAHOMA HAS ALMOST ONE-THIRD of all the Indians in the United States. The Indian Office knows and serves 110,503,[1] most of whom are half-bloods or over. This is almost 5 per cent of the people of the state. The greatest concentration is in Adair County, where the Cherokees living in remote hill cabins form one-third of the population. But the Indians' real importance is not numerical but cultural. Somehow this minority has captured the thought of the whole people.

Oklahoma did not deliberately select Indians to represent it in Statuary Hall of the national capitol. It chose its best-loved citizens; it was only incidental that both were Cherokees. Sequoyah was chosen less than four years after statehood. The other place remained vacant until Will Rogers died.

Sequoyah, like many white Oklahoma leaders, was not born in the state; the site of his native village is now inside the boundaries of Tennessee. His father was probably a wandering white man who married an Indian girl and then forgot her, but his rearing was all Cherokee. He taught himself to work in silver, using coins that came to hand, and with native paints or charcoal he became an artist. With other Cherokee warriors he served briefly under Andrew Jackson in the War of 1812. In 1818 he came West with about one-third of his tribe to a tract of land the Cherokees bought in what is now the state of Arkansas.

He had no knowledge of written—or even spoken—English;

[1] Census Bureau figures are inaccurate in enumerating Indians. For example, the number jumped from 57,000 in 1920 to 92,000 in 1930, and then fell back to 63,000 in the next decade. The Indian Office statistics seem entirely reliable, except that I am inclined to question one roll—the Cherokee—as too large.

141

but he knew white men used "talking leaves" to fix their speech in permanent form, which seemed to him "like catching a wild animal and taming it." He began to experiment with writing in Cherokee, making a character for each word. When his characters became too numerous, he discovered that all language is made up of repeated sounds. Then he made a character for every syllable. While he was inventing his symbols, he found a scrap of printed matter and appropriated some of the letters—upside down perhaps, and with no relationship to their English usage.

He worked about twelve years, neglecting his hunting and farming. His wife thought he was wasting his time, and other Cherokees began to fear him as one who dealt in magic; but his little daughter helped. In 1821 he got the last sound "caught" and "tamed"—eighty-six characters in all. He returned East to show his invention. The tribe appointed a committee to investigate and perhaps to punish, and he taught the new art to the committee. Then the Eastern Cherokee council formally adopted the system, and within a year Sequoyah returned to Arkansas. From that time on, the divided portions of the tribe corresponded with each other in the characters he had taught them.

There were no spelling worries; anybody who would spend a few days memorizing the sound symbols could read and write anything in the Cherokee language. And the Indians broke into spontaneous practice, scratching the characters on trees, fences, houses, and pieces of bark. Christian missionaries who had been working in the Eastern Cherokee country since 1802, had been trying without much success to reduce their difficult language to writing. Now suddenly they found the whole tribe a literate people. They were inclined at first to distrust the native movement, but it was already out of their hands. In 1824 a young Cherokee convert made hundreds of manuscript copies of a portion of St. John's gospel and distributed it to eager readers; the next year another Cherokee finished translating the New Testament. At the same time the council voted a medal to Sequoyah; employed two tribesmen to make eight manuscript copies of the laws and one New Testament for the use of the council (labor bill, $72); and authorized the building of a chinked-log office (cost, $250) and the purchase of a printing press to start a national newspaper. The influence of the

142

great missionary, Samuel Austin Worchester, is apparent in the last of these acts; he came to the Eastern Cherokee country in 1825, sensed the importance of what was happening, and spent the rest of his life helping the Indians in publication.

Soon white settlers crowded the Western Cherokees out of Arkansas, and they removed to present northeastern Oklahoma. Sequoyah built a stanch little cabin near a stream in the hills of what is now Sequoyah County.[2] Here he farmed a little, raised some ponies, cattle, and hogs, and operated a salt works, while his thrifty wife, Sally, kept the cabin neat and made the family clothing from her own spinning and weaving. Occasionally they took a trip to Fort Smith to exchange their honey, butter, eggs, chickens, and deer and raccoon skins for a few necessary supplies. Sequoyah always wore a homespun hunting shirt trimmed with fringe and held down by a beaded belt, buckskin leggings and moccasins, a bright-colored cloth wound around his head for a turban, and his medal fastened by a ribbon around his neck.

It was here that the Western Cherokee council passed its school law, making Sequoyah a teacher at large with a salary of four hundred dollars a year. This was more of a literary pension than a salary, for Sequoyah never had to be paid for the privilege of sharing his discovery. Grant Foreman has painted an unforgettable picture of his method with the visitors who came to his salt works. "Taking a charred stick from the fire and a piece of smooth bark from his wood pile, he would sit down on a log and patiently explain to his listeners gathered round, the principles of his alphabet, simultaneously making sounds of Cherokee syllables and marks on the bark that represented them." One of his greatest pleasures was in reading the tribal newspaper that came to him regularly from the East.

White travelers sought him out and talked with him through an interpreter. His conversation was eager, ardent, and rapid, and his thin, sensitive face glowed with animation as he talked. It would have surprised him to know that his fame had traveled across the sea; even now there are copies of the tribal newspaper in the British Museum.

[2] It is still standing; a few years ago the Oklahoma Historical Society sponsored a WPA project enclosing it with a stone building to preserve it.

Soon the Cherokees that had remained in the East were driven out of their country and forced to join their kinsmen in Oklahoma. The tribe was torn by feuds growing out of the sufferings of the Removal, and Sequoyah was very active in the councils that united all the factions under one government. Next he heard of a band of dispossessed Cherokees that had sought refuge in Old Mexico, and with his son and several other men he started out to find them—probably to teach them his alphabet and join them to the tribe by the magic symbols. After many hardships he reached a Cherokee village beyond the Río Grande; but the trip had been too much for the old man, and he died there, far from home, but among the friends he seemed to make wherever he went. This was in 1843. When he failed to return, the tribe prepared to finance a search for him; and when his companions finally came back with their sorrowful story, the national newspaper, now published by the Cherokees in their Western home, carried a full account of his death and a tribute to his services. Such was the first man that the state of Oklahoma chose to honor.[3]

As for the second, all the world knows Will Rogers. But he belongs to Oklahoma in a special way. Clem V. Rogers, his father, was a leading mixed blood, prominent in Cherokee affairs; he ran the C V brand, served as roundup captain of his district, and built a commodious log ranch house (later covered with siding and painted white) in the valley of the Verdigris to which people from distant states now make pilgrimage. When the state of Oklahoma was formed, he served in the Constitutional Convention—he was an old man, then—and the present Rogers County carries his name. Mary Schrimsher Rogers, Will's mother, also came from a prominent mixed-blood family; and she had the combination of refinement and sturdiness that characterized the well-educated Cherokee woman of that time.

Will, born in 1879, grew up in the careless security of a society where everybody had all the land and cows he wanted, every big house was practically a hotel, and all the neighbors were related to each other. He raced his pony over the ranch, attended the rural school his brother-in-law started, was sent to a "college" at the

[3] The standard biography of this Indian genius is Grant Foreman, *Sequoyah* (Norman, 1938).

little railroad town of Vinita and to military school in "the States." Through his skill with the lasso he wandered to far places; and then through his wisdom he became a teacher of the world. In his later years his house was in California, but Oklahoma was always his home and he never forgot that his "folks way back didn't come over on the Mayflower; they was just standing there when it docked." He owned a piece of land near Claremore, to which he planned to retire some day; his body rests there now, close to the rambling stone building erected by the state as his memorial. Reverent visitors pass all day through the rooms, and out in front are cars with licenses from many states. His relatives still live around the Claremore and Oologah country, charming, friendly people with the unconscious grace of a natural aristocracy.

All through Oklahoma society are such aristocrats of the Five Tribes, more or less Indian in blood, perhaps even blond in coloring, but never forgetting the days when they were citizens of a republic so small and so closely integrated that anybody could attain his ambitions. No wonder they became leaders of the state. They were the old settlers; the struggling homesteader or the febrile city builder was a newcomer without roots. It is difficult even to guess how many there are—their white blood eliminates them from census statistics and Indian Office records—but they are very numerous, and it is through their influence that the whole state has appropriated Indian history and tradition.

This is hard for outsiders to understand. A college professor recently imported from Texas, where even the historians think of Indians as painted fiends slipping up in the night to murder settlers from sheer malevolence, was lecturing about the War of 1812. "What military leader gained the most fame from this war?" he asked a member of the class, meaning, of course, Andrew Jackson. Without an instant's hesitation she answered, "Tecumseh." She was not an Indian, and every book she had read told the white man's story; but instinctively she chose the Indians' side. In my own college teaching of Oklahoma history I have had out-of-state students say something like this: "You have a new concept of history here. In my state we start with the first white settlers and tell how they drove out the Indians; here you tell what the Indians built and how the white people came and joined them."

145

The first little grade-school Oklahoma history text introduced immediately after statehood followed this sequence. The story has been enlarged since by the researches of scholars, but the point of view has not changed. Oklahoma writers have no noble red men nor red devils—they write of the Indians critically and objectively, just as they would deal with any human beings—and their findings have become internationally known through the Civilization of the American Indian Series of the University of Oklahoma Press. (Characteristically the Press colophon is an Indian design by the Kiowa artist, Monroe Tsa-to-ke.) Twenty-seven volumes have been released since this series was launched in 1932.

Third in appearance, and one of the finest in literary merit, is *Wah'Kon-Tah,* by John Joseph Mathews. The author is an almost-white Osage, an Indian only in his sensitive perceptions; an Oxonian and a cosmopolite, he and Mrs. Mathews choose to live in a remote cabin swallowed in the vast emptiness of his native hills. His book is a prose poem of Osage feeling set against this noble background of sweeping distances and sheltered hollows, as it traces the progress of the tribe on the White Man's Road. It was a Book-of-the-Month Club selection, the first publication of any university press to achieve this popular recognition.

Fully as beautiful are the writings of Alice Marriott, an ethnologist trained at the University of Oklahoma, who contributed the two latest books in the series. The first one, *The Ten Grandmothers,* takes its title from the sacred medicine bundles of the Kiowas. Here the stories of the old people are woven into a connected account of the Kiowa way of life from the happy buffalo-hunting days through defeat and hunger to the education and new skills of the younger generation. To my mind it is among the great books of all literature. Its meaning is not Kiowa alone, but universal; in a style as simple as setting up a tepee by a stream, it covers the whole range of human experience. One reviewer has used the word "Homeric"; it seems the only adequate appraisal. The second book, *María: The Potter of San Ildefonso,* is a biography of María Martínez, notable among the Pueblos for her craftmanship. It shows all the intimate human relationships within one compact little Indian community.

In the series are several books by Grant Foreman and his

equally gifted wife. Foreman as a young lawyer came from Illinois about the turn of the century to work with the Dawes Commission. He met and married Carolyn Thomas, an Illinois girl, whose father had come to the Indian Territory to serve as a federal judge. After several years of successful private practice, Foreman retired, and the pair devoted their time to the writing of Oklahoma history, especially the history of the Five Civilized Tribes. They do their writing in their quiet home at Muskogee, but to collect their material they travel a great deal, visiting the great libraries and archival collections of the world. They find clues everywhere— even in India in a forgotten pile of rubbish they discovered material that fitted into a gap they had been trying to fill.

Then there is *The Cheyenne Way* by Karl N. Llewellyn of the Columbia University law faculty and E. Adamson Hoebel, an anthropologist of New York University. This is a case study of primitive jurisprudence, not only showing the complex structure of Cheyenne law, but aiding the white man to understand his own legal origins. There is *Civilization,* as told to a white scribe by Thomas Wildcat Alford, a Shawnee, the great-grandson of Tecumseh. His reminiscences cover a long life in Oklahoma from primitive tribal ways through an English education to an old age as a respected member of the white man's society. Stanley Vestal (Walter S. Campbell), whose brilliant books on the Plains Indians have appeared under other imprints, contributed two volumes to the series. Knowing a good yarn when he sees one, he edited the lively memoirs of John H. Seger, a great educator, in *Early Days among the Cheyenne and Arapahoe Indians;* and he published some first-hand Sioux experiences in *New Sources of Indian History.* There is a symposium on present Indian Office policy in *The Changing Indian;* Oliver La Farge is editor, and the contributors are specialists in many fields. And so the volumes run. It is impossible to name them all here. Through such publications Oklahoma has righted one of the Indians' greatest wrongs: the bias that has colored nearly all the books that have been written since the two races started fighting each other across the first frontier.

More recently the Thomas Gilcrease Foundation of Tulsa— to be opened to the public in 1949—promises to be a great international center of Indian study and culture. It was made possible through a gift of Thomas Gilcrease, Tulsan of Creek descent, who prospered in the oil business from Glenn Pool on. The building was erected on an eminence at the northwestern edge of the city, where it commands a magnificent view of the distant sky line and the changeless Osage hills. It is of sandstone, quarried in the locality and dressed by all-Indian labor.

Its library contains valuable first editions, relating the experiences of travelers in the Indian country from Columbus on. Among its manuscripts are unpublished documents dating back to the sixteenth century—even a copy of Sequoyah's alphabet drawn by the Cherokee Cadmus himself. Here are the sources of many books on Indian history. The director of the Foundation, Georgia-born Lester Hargrett, is himself a scholar in this field. His useful *Bibliography of the Constitutions and Laws of the American Indians* was released by the Harvard University Press shortly after he assumed his duties at Gilcrease.

But if Oklahoma does give the Indians an equal hearing before the bar of history, the same equality did not work so well before the bar of justice. It sounded noble—"abolish their petty nationalities and grant them United States citizenship with the equal protection of the laws." I have told how they were stripped of their property through these legal forms; very few people even in Oklahoma know what the process did to their spirit. The hardest hit were the full bloods of the Five Civilized Tribes. The most fortunate of all were the hunters of the Southwest.

One of John H. Seger's stories deserves to be retold here. The agency people managed to interest Black Kettle in hog raising. He took a hog to his tepee and made a pet of it. The little children rode it, and in cold weather it lay by the fire. But in spring it rooted up the agency gardens. Black Kettle ignored all complaints, and so it was finally caught and penned. When he "missed his hog from the family circle"—to quote Seger—he went to inquire, "Why has my hog been put in the guard house? I am sure he has not done anything wrong intentionally." The agent told him that it had rooted up the potatoes. Then Black Kettle argued very earnestly that his hog was not to blame, for it was a hog's nature to root. The fault was with the person who had carelessly placed the potatoes in its reach. Now in *his* camp they always put things in the forks of a tree or on a pole out of the hog's way. As Seger said, "All of which, spoken seriously, shows how primitive they were in the business of raising poultry and pork. Hunting buffalo was an industry—raising potatoes was an illogical sort of amusement."[4]

Nobody could demand that Indians like this should at once be made the "equal" of white men. And nobody was greatly interested in making such a demand anyhow, for these tribes had no oil money and their allotments were not sufficient for wholesale exploitation. As a result, the restrictions remained on their land and the Indian Service continued its educational work; and the Indians were elevated rather than degraded. The progress made by the Kiowas, in particular, is notable. Take my friends, the Pauahtys.

Reverend Linn Pauahty is a full blood. He came from a family of native priests. Even now he is the keeper of the sacred Buffalo Medicine Bag, which he inherited from his father, and from his grandfather, Tone-zion-day-ah, still remembered as the greatest of Buffalo medicine men. His aunt was until her death the keeper of one of the Ten Grandmothers. As he says, "I had the good fortune to sleep many years in my boyhood under this sacred object, and was taught all of the religious observances within the premises of the sacred tepee." Thus he still speaks with reverent understanding of the native religion, but he found Christianity better suited to his changing concepts. He graduated from the junior agricultural college at Lawton, went on to A. and M., and then took his divinity degree from Southern Methodist University. Now he is a Methodist minister serving Indian churches, a cultured gentleman meeting Indian or white on equal terms.

Mrs. Pauahty (Edna Hokeah) is not quite a full blood, but her family background is all Kiowa. Her great-granduncle was Kicking Bird, the great Kiowa war chief who first saw the necessity of co-operating with the white man and left this dying message to his tribe: "I have taken the white man's road. I am not sorry for it. Tell my people to keep in the good path." She is a charming woman, capable and intelligent, with her Indian shyness throwing a veil over her smile. Once I saw her, modest but unabashed, explaining

[4] John H. Seger, *Early Days among the Cheyenne and Arapahoe Indians* (Norman, 1934), 26–27.

Indian cookery to an audience of white women. And yet when she entered a government school she spoke no word but Kiowa.

Here is Tsa-to-ke or Hunting Horse, whose life threads through the episodes of *The Ten Grandmothers*. As a young man he established himself in the tribe by raiding the Texas frontier. Then when the buffalo were killed and the soldiers came and the spirit of the Indians was broken, he enlisted as a government scout to go out on the Texas plains and persuade the straggling bands of fugitives to come in to the reservation. (He still wears his army uniform on grand occasions.) When his wife was selected as one of the helpers in a desperate ceremony to bring back the buffalo and restore the old ways, he encouraged her to act; but after the pathetic failure he accepted her conclusion that the "old-time power" was dead. "The buffalo took it away when they went. . . . But I think there is a new kind of life starting now. I think we will need a new kind of power to live in it."

When he was more than fifty years old, he went to listen to a missionary preach, and found it was "like listening to the old people talk in the old times. That used to make us feel good, too." And thus he became a Christian. There was tragedy here, for a cruel edict forced him to give up one of his wives. But his children and grandchildren learned the new ways. Two of his sons, Cecil and Albert Horse, are Christian ministers among the Kiowas. Another, Monroe Tsa-to-ke, a son of his old age, studied art at the University and won international fame as a painter of Indian subjects. Hunting Horse himself has become a sort of institution. When he reached his one-hundredth birthday in 1946 a Methodist bishop was among the relatives and friends who came to help him celebrate. The Wichita Mountains Wildlife Refuge regularly donates a buffalo to be barbecued at these birthday feasts.

To such older Indians the shape of the virgin land is still reality; the cities, plowed fields, and fences are only a transparent film over camp site and hunting ground. A wizened little Sac and Fox grandmother was in the hospital at Cushing with a broken leg. Her bright-eyed vivacity made her a pet of the nurses. One day they asked her if she had ever eaten buffalo meat. She answered, "Oh yes; and I remember the hunts too, out on the prairie where they put Guthrie."

150

XIII

Where Can One See Some Indians?

THE VISITOR TO OKLAHOMA always wants to know where he can find Indians. Perhaps his best bet if he is in Tulsa or Muskogee or any of the "east side" cities is to look at the filling station attendant or the girl behind the counter or the senior member of the law firm. Also he is sure to find Indians on any college campus. "How do they dress when they go to college?" "Well," says Dr. Dale reflectively, "they paint their faces." This never fails to create excitement. "That is, I mean the girls do," explains the professor.

But that is less than the whole story. Deep in the Cherokee hills is a sacred fire that has never been allowed to die out since it was brought over the "Trail of Tears" from the Eastern home. Here every year the Kee-Too-Wah Society, claiming six thousand full-blood members, carries out its rituals in the name of the seven ancient clans of the Cherokees. Then in the midst of an Osage village of neat frame dwellings stands the huge barnlike ceremonial house with its sixteen sides and its high-pointed roof. Or driving along a country road one glimpses through some distant vista what looks like a little town—the small houses built over the graves of a Creek cemetery.

The Creeks, living on wheat bread purchased at the grocer's, still celebrate their thanksgiving for the corn. More than a century ago they lived in compact villages centered around a square with imposing public buildings. The square survives in some out-of-the-way place in the timber, and the people, scattered as they are through the farms and cities of Oklahoma, remember their ancestral "town." When the corn is in roasting ear, they gather there for their ancient harvest festival.

151

Recently with some friends I visited Arbeka Square south of Henryetta. We parked on a country road and walked a few rods in a pasture through hickory and oak trees to the top of a low, sandy hill. Here, enclosed on three sides by brush arbors, is a hard-packed plot of earth with dead ashes in the center and a circular path made by the feet of dancers around the fire. Just beyond the unenclosed side is a tall pole with a wooden carving of a cow skull on top, which forms the goal of a scrambling, hilarious ball game played by the Creeks from time immemorial. Scattered through the surrounding timber are other brush arbors, apparently used as camps, and off to one side is a rough storehouse with a cookstove, a refrigerator, and a few bed springs. These are the only visible remains of a town that was important in the powerful Creek Confederacy of the Gulf region centuries before the white man laid out his states there; but the spirit lives on.

The Osages in their wild days had elaborate burial ceremonies: painting and dressing of the body, three days of dancing and mourning culminating in the capture of an enemy scalp, the placing of presents at a rock-piled burial place on a hilltop, and general feasting. A modern Osage funeral is a strange modification of these native rites blended with Christian customs. Here is an account given me by a white couple related by marriage to an Osage family.

A three-year-old boy had died at Pawhuska. He lay in his coffin at the house, dressed in store-bought clothes and over all a loose native garment of buckskin. Very inconspicuous on his forehead and in the parting of his hair were lines of paint applied by Fred Lookout, venerable chief of the tribe.

When the time came for the burial, the body was taken to the church for the regular Catholic mass for the dead; and there was also a Catholic service in the cemetery. Then relatives brought forward a large pot with partitions in which they had placed the child's favorite food—barbecued meat, a gelatin dessert, and some custard. Also they had a thermos bottle filled with water, and a toy airplane he had played with during his illness. After the coffin was lowered, these were placed on top and the grave was filled. Then the relatives and friends left the cemetery for the funeral feast.

The meal was served in the large arbor built by the Osages in the midst of their village as a community meeting place. The child's parents furnished the food, and friends of the family had worked through all the previous night to prepare it. A whole beef and hog had been barbecued; and there were homemade hominy, beautifully baked squash, fruit salad and vegetable salad, and the inevitable Indian fried bread made of flour, salt, baking powder, and water and fried in chunks in deep fat. Of course there was coffee.

The table was already set, Osage style. At each place were a tablespoon, a shallow bowl-like plate, and a handleless bowl-like cup; also a boiled egg, an apple, a pear, and an orange, which the guests were supposed to wrap up and carry away after the meal. Friends waited on the table and placed generous servings directly on the plates. The two white relatives sat with the boy's parents, and everybody in their circle was careful to speak in English, although Osage conversations broke out in older groups around the table. The people were no more and no less cheerful than white neighbors and friends relaxing in mutual fellowship after a funeral.

The killing and scalping of an enemy was the burial custom hardest for the Osages to adapt to civilized ways. They gradually toned it down to a tuft of hair (without skin) cut from the head of a hired "enemy"; then their white teachers finally persuaded them to plant instead a United States flag at the grave. Now their cemeteries are gay with fluttering flags. Their monuments—expensive as befits their wealth—are carved with names like 'Wah-tsa-me" or "Tom Big Chief," and ornamented with photographs of strong, massive-looking people dressed in fringed buckskin.

The Five Civilized Tribes have long forgotten their native garments, and the Plains tribes wear them only on ceremonial or dress-up occasions. Thus garbed, they are a familiar feature of the parades and historical celebrations in Oklahoma City, Guthrie, Enid, and other western Oklahoma cities. They have an elaborate celebration of their own in the Indian Fair held every August at Anadarko. Here the Plains tribes of Oklahoma and visitors from New Mexico and Arizona meet for four or five days of pageantry, dances, and a display of arts and crafts and agricultural products. Their tepees, carefully saved for such occasions, are set up all over the grounds, and the whole encampment throbs with the care-

153

less fellowship of the old time. Probably sixty thousand persons—two-thirds of them white spectators—attend this celebration. A permanent building to house the exhibits was erected by joint state and federal funds and dedicated in December, 1948.

There is nothing to hinder Indians from attending any Oklahoma church, but they prefer to form separate congregations. Most of their buildings are in rural neighborhoods, built like the white man's churches, but surrounded with cabins and brush arbors. They like to join in inter-church meetings, camping on the grounds, eating at a common table, and visiting together in the friendly Indian way. When different tribes are represented, they conduct their services in English or in the native tongues through interpreters, and each group usually contributes some of its own hymns. They love to sing. The Five Tribes have hymnbooks printed in their own languages; the others make up songs of their own, wild and sad as the dawn of human consciousness. And all sing together in English, reading from the regular church hymnals.

Some Indians find in "Father Peyote" a more indigenous religion than the white man's expression of Christianity. This small "button" of cactus was used ritually by the tribes of Old Mexico at least four centuries ago. The cult reached the Comanches and Kiowas about 1880, and spread tribe by tribe through the western half of the Indian Territory. The government tried to stamp it out, and so in 1918 the Indians—advised, it is said, by a distinguished ethnologist—incorporated the Native American Church under Oklahoma law in order to claim the protection of the statutes for religious freedom.

The worshipers meet in a ceremonial lodge for an all-night session of prayers, exhortations, and ceremonial eating of the peyote—all in an atmosphere of peace and fraternity, with liberal borrowings from Christian and native ideology. The drug can bring nausea, anxiety, terrifying hallucinations, and a frightening disintegration of personality "as if I could throw my arms out and my arms left me, went off in the air, and I felt I was going all to pieces." But in this religious atmosphere it brings flowing sensations of color, beatific visions, and a mystical sense of union with the Infinite. It never incites to violence, it is not habit forming, and it seems to have few, if any, damaging aftereffects.

154

Where Can One See Some Indians?

The peyote religion is the Indians' relief from frustration—the despair of the hunting tribes over the extinction of the buffalo, the losses of the agricultural tribes under the allotment system, the bewilderment of all Indians forced into an alien mold. The government no longer tries to suppress it forcibly. Probably the suppression policy was unconstitutional. Certainly it is wiser to try to remove the cause.

It is undeniable that the Indians needed guidance into the new way of life, but too often the "civilizing" agencies tried to destroy every native trait. (When Mrs. Pauahty went to boarding school, she was given a dose of castor oil if she spoke a word of Kiowa; this meant that the lonely child had to live without speaking until she acquired the use of English.) In 1933 the United States Indian Service reversed this policy, and now the Indians are encouraged to take pride in their race and develop their distinctive gifts.

The Indian Service is limited by law to half-bloods or over of the Five Tribes, quarter-bloods or over in all others. This eliminates practically all of the white "Indians," for the Plains tribes have little white blood except that which came through the adoption of young children captured in early-day raids on the frontier. The work is centered in six agencies—at Anadarko, Concho, Shawnee, Pawnee, Pawhuska, and Muskogee. The government also maintains eleven boarding schools and eight Indian hospitals in the state.

The service of the boarding schools is confined to orphans, children with a bad home environment, or children living remote from public schools. Others of this needy class are educated by churches. But the great majority of all Indian children in the state attend the public schools. This is unquestionably the most desirable way to educate them so far as possible. The state receives financial assistance from the federal government for their training. This is a just claim on the United States because the Indians' restricted land is exempt from taxation. In the first years of statehood the amount of nontaxable land on the "east side" was so great as almost to paralyze the services of the local government. Then as the allotments passed from Indian ownership, this tax exemption declined. Probably at present the government contribution balances the losses. The aid to the public schools has run close to $400,000 annually

155

since 1931; and to this, one must add all sums expended for boarding schools, hospitals, and social and economic rehabilitation of Oklahoma Indians.

There are no available statistics on college enrollment of Indians, but their influence on campus life is plainly apparent. They are fine athletes, and more gifted in art, music, and literature than in science and business administration. Most of them attend state-supported schools, but Bacone College, a Baptist institution at Muskogee, has an all-Indian student body. Opened first at Tahlequah but moved to its present location in 1885, it has long held a unique place in Indian education. Its library contains a fine collection of Indian material, its art department and museum display native crafts and teach modern adaptations, and its vocational work is geared to Indian needs.

The language and literary achievements of Oklahoma Indians have become an influence in teaching primitive races in distant lands. A summer Institute of Linguistics was located on the campus of the University of Oklahoma in 1942 because—as its director decided—"this state is the best linguistic laboratory in the world." Its courses deal with fundamental principles of human speech, and Oklahoma Indians are brought in to give the students practice in analyzing aboriginal languages. It trains Wycliffe Bible Translators—missionaries who go to primitive tribes in remote enclaves throughout the world to learn their languages and reduce these languages to writing in order to give their converts the Bible in permanent form. Unreckoned benefits are: the beginning of a tribal literature and the development of a written history. All this will help them to adjust to any future white invasion of their homeland. The Institute has now had more than a thousand graduates. One has only to recall the influence of Sequoyah's great invention on the Cherokees to visualize what this can mean.

These Oklahoma studies received recognition at the Navajo Institute held in New York in 1947 by civic and philanthropic organizations interested in that great Arizona and New Mexico tribe. For it happens that the government is now helping the Navajos to start on the road over which the Oklahoma Indians have come: they are being taught to read and write their own language, while at the same time they are receiving their initial training in English.

Where Can One See Some Indians?

In the fall of 1947, 150 of their young people were brought to Oklahoma and placed in the boarding school at Chilocco; and the course of study, formerly of high-school rank only, was dropped back to the first grade for the newcomers. The experiment proved so successful that the number was increased to 250, and at the same time 50 were placed in the Cheyenne and Arapaho school at Concho, near Oklahoma City. Navajo interpreters are brought along to help them through their language difficulties, and the teachers and students are aiding them to a friendly adjustment. At Christmas time in 1948 Indian families of Oklahoma City united in providing a gala holiday for the young Arizona and New Mexico strangers at Concho.

But while the Oklahoma Indians' educational problem is largely solved or in process of solution, the Indians have a more serious economic problem. About 1930 the public first became concerned about the poverty of those who had lost their allotments. During the ensuing depression years some of the Five Tribes Indians in the hill settlements actually died from malnutrition. Then after the passage of the Oklahoma Indian Welfare Act in 1936, the Indian Service took over the task of rehabilitating them.

They were assisted to form Indian Credit Associations, which borrowed money from the government at 1 per cent interest and loaned it to the members at 3 per cent. Most of these loans were for agricultural purposes. The record of repayment has been very good—more than one and one-half million dollars borrowed, of which about half is already repaid, and less than three thousand dollars lost. Then four or five tracts of submarginal land in the Five Tribes area were purchased, houses were built, and the Indians were encouraged to settle there under the system of small individual plantings and range livestock that worked so well for them in territorial days. But this plan did not succeed: for one thing the land was too poor to support anybody; then the Indians apparently had forgotten their old techniques even though they had failed to acquire the new ones. The government will lose a little money on this experiment, which was never attempted except on a small scale.

Courses in weaving were introduced in the Sequoyah boarding school near Tahlequah, and adult Choctaw and Cherokee women were encouraged to revive their almost forgotten skills in

157

spinning and weaving and their native basketry. They have formed six crafts co-operatives centering in the hill settlements, with a total of 325 members. One Choctaw association buys, cards, and spins the wool, and Cherokee associations do the weaving. Still other groups specialize in baskets and Indian dolls. Individuals from a number of other tribes have joined the enterprise. Their woven products attracted much attention in the International Textile Exhibition held in New York in 1947, and their sales are reaching profitable proportions. Recently they bought a building from an abandoned army camp to set up as a market center on Highway 62 east of Tahlequah. Almost all the material they use in their crafts is Oklahoma-grown.

Oklahoma Indians still own 2,800,000 acres of land under restricted tenure. About 90 per cent of it represents what is left of their original allotments. Most of this is hills and cutover timber entirely worthless for agriculture, but it includes some good land still owned by the "wild" tribes of the west. The remaining 10 per cent was purchased with government loans, and each owner will receive an unrestricted title when the loan is paid out. Of course, any Indian who buys a farm through his own efforts holds it without restrictions; it is not even classed as "Indian land." As for the allotments, the restrictions are still needed; and the Indians themselves desire this protection.

This does not mean that the Indians are thereby tied to the soil. But it gives them something to fall back on. Although it is desirable for them to find a place in industry or business, it is not always possible. A young Indian from a remote full-blood settlement seeking work in a city is held back by his innate reserve, which forbids him to push and crowd; even worse, he has no "pull" —his father does not play golf with the boss. The recent war furnished many Indians with their first employment opportunities. They did good work in war plants, especially precision work, where they used the skills they had learned in school. They also found in the armed services of both wars an opportunity they had lacked in peace.

In World War I alert young Choctaws set up a communications system in their native language, which the wire-tapping Germans found impossible to decode. Oklahoma's Alvin York was

158

Where Can One See Some Indians?

Private Joseph Oklahombi, a full-blood Choctaw; he captured 171 prisoners singlehanded, storming a strongly held outpost containing more than fifty machine guns and a number of trench mortars, and holding the position for four days in the face of an incessant barrage. When the French government decided to place a painting of a typical American soldier in the Federal Building at Paris, Otis W. Leader, an Oklahoma Chickasaw, was selected as the model.

In the recent war the Southwest's famed Forty-fifth Division fittingly wore the Indian thunderbird as its insigne. The insigne had been the swastika, but Hitler spoiled that Indian symbol, and so it was discarded in 1938. Two of Oklahoma's seventeen Congressional Medals of Honor went to Indians, both members of the Forty-fifth, who won battlefield commissions in Italy. Lieutenant Ernest Childers, a Creek, was born and reared at Broken Arrow and attended the government school at Chilocco. When he returned home after receiving his decoration, the schools and business houses were closed for a grand parade and the whole town and countryside turned out to do him honor. Lieutenant Jack C. Montgomery, Cherokee of Sallisaw, also attended school at Chilocco, worked his way through Bacone College, and continued his education at Redlands University in California. Near Padiglione, Italy, he took three strong enemy positions singlehanded, killing eleven men, wounding an unknown number, and capturing thirty-two prisoners.

Indian girls also served as WACs and WAVES and nurses. Carrie Mae Downing, an Oklahoma Cherokee serving in a veterans' hospital, received one of the ten national awards of the American Nurses' Association in the search for the "typical American nurse" of 1946. Miss Downing is classed as a full blood, though quantum-of-blood classifications are only approximate in tribes like the Cherokee with centuries of white intercourse. Lieutenant James Colling Ottipoby, a Comanche from southwestern Oklahoma, was the first Indian in the United States to receive a chaplain's commission. His grandparents lived in tepees, followed the buffalo herds, and raided the frontiers.

Major General Clarence L. Tinker of the Army Air Force, who was lost in the Battle of Midway, was part Osage. He was born

159

on the reservation in 1887, sent to military school, entered the regular army, and worked his way up through military aviation. Oklahoma is proud of him, and Tinker Field in Oklahoma City is named in his honor. But his tribe claims him, too; and when the war ended, the victory dance was dedicated to his memory.

Indians like General Tinker never constituted a problem. And of the full bloods who found a place for their courage and loyalty in the army or for their manual skills in war industry, some probably gained a permanent toehold on the economic ladder. But when general unemployment comes again, most of them will be pushed out. Too many people are forgetting this. The danger now is that the very achievements of the Indians will be used against them. They had a chance to use their training and they used it well; therefore give them no more. They showed they could work at varied trades; therefore remove their restrictions and strip them of their land. Indian education at its best is a slow and patient process. So is any education. What of the white younger generation in Oklahoma?

XIV

Tomorrow's Oklahomans

ALL THROUGH THIS CHAPTER one must bear in mind that Oklahomans believe in schools more than scholarship. They started their schools early and courageously; scholarship is something they have not yet attained—nor apparently do they care to attain it.

Looking back on the history of Oklahoma education, one finds a dominant tendency toward centralization. Once each two- or three-mile-square rural "deestrict" laid its own taxes, made its own policy, and hired its own teacher—possibly with a little unregarded advice from an elected county superintendent. An active community life also centered in these one-room buildings, with "literaries," Sunday schools, and farmers' organizations—all the pleasant reasons early-day Oklahomans could think up for meeting. Meanwhile the towns slowly built up graded systems, and even more slowly worked up to high schools. People began to reason that by joining with the towns or by joining several rural districts together, the country children might have these same advantages. Thus was born "consolidation" and the transportation of pupils.

The oldest consolidated school district in the state centers around the little town of Quay. It was started in territorial days in 1903, and the children were picked up along the roads in horse-drawn vehicles. Other communities slowly followed, and the "kid wagon" with its homemade, roofed-over body became a familiar sight in the prairie sections. Then came the automobile. This made transportation of the children easier at the same time that it destroyed the social life of the little rural district—it was pleasanter to drive to town for a picture show than to work up a box supper at the schoolhouse.

Consolidation is now the rule except in the hills. The motor busses go out in all directions through an area probably fifteen miles square. (The largest district in the state takes in the whole west end of the Panhandle; it is thirty-five miles north and south, and thirty-seven miles east and west, and is bordered by Colorado, Texas, and New Mexico.) The school buildings loom up rather impressively in tiny villages or out in the midst of fields and ranches. Here, along with some sketchily taught academic subjects, center the farm clubs, the bands, the athletic contests, and the plays and programs that train the young Oklahoman more in leadership than in learning. Here also centers the social life of the community, built around many things, but most of all around an overmastering pride in the children.

This makes only for larger units. These units in turn have been brought together through state control. First came standards set up by the state superintendent of schools and the state Department of Education. Now comes financing.

Once each district was virtually on its own. The homesteader paid no tax on his land until he received a patent. But he paid on everything else: cash, if he had any; notes and all debts from solvent debtors, no matter where they lived; his team and wagon and plow; the two chairs and cookstove in his dugout; and every improvement on his claim. Even so, all the taxable property in a district might not add up to five hundred dollars. Happy was the one crossed by a railroad; and how they did sock it to those railroads! More fortunate also was the city school, with values other than land, or even the rural district with a little town in one corner. This was the first inequality. Then the farms became patented and the tax base varied with the value of the land; or one town grew and another died, with more variation. Next came oil, and the inequality became fantastic. Here was local democracy: one school showered—literally and greasily—with wealth, another comfortably supported by good farms or city property, a third starved for funds as its children were starved for opportunity.

True, there was from the very first a common-school endowment. Two sections in each township were saved out from homesteading in each of the "west side" land rushes, and at statehood Congress appropriated five million dollars in lieu of land in the unhomesteaded Five Tribes area. The state soon sold most of the "school land" to farmers on long-term credits, and the cash endowment now adds up to $46,000,000—plus about $22,000,000 more from land set aside for colleges and public buildings. The income from this common-school property, distributed on the basis of scholastic population, was the first supplement to local taxes. Then the state began to make small appropriations from time to time to aid the poorer districts. But no serious attempt was made at equalization until the Marland administration in 1935. State aid has been continued in one way or another ever since. The metropolitan newspapers complain a little and so do the prosperous farm communities; but the state seems to have accepted the principle that the hill child in McCurtain County deserves an equal chance with the city child of Tulsa—where the superb school system has developed many of the state's most brilliant leaders—or with the farm boy of Garber, nationally known for the achievements of its FFA. The present law does not go so far as that, for it lays down minimum requirements in local effort—and some backward communities make little local effort—but this might be classed as adult education as essential as helping the children.

All in all, whether in the three months' term of early days or the present system of state aid, Oklahoma has given loyal support to schools. The present problem grows out of a high population—plus a healthy birth rate—and low industrial development. This means many children to educate on a low state income. Thus, according to a very careful study of American education completed in 1946 by two scholars of Iowa State College, Oklahoma—dividing total income by scholastic population—ranks thirty-seventh in ability to finance its schools. At the same time they found that it ranks sixth in effort and seventh in efficiency, pulling itself up to twelfth rank in general educational performance and twenty-second in accomplishment—a record "in every sense creditable."[1]

Instead of the usual literacy statistics the federal census of 1940 shows the amount of schooling received by all the people

[1] Raymond M. Hughes and William H. Lancelot, *Education—America's Magic* (Ames, Iowa, 1946), 35–36.

twenty-five years old or older. By this standard Oklahoma, in spite of its difficult beginning days, exactly strikes the national level, a median of 8.4 years. But in people who have not completed even one year of school, it is below the national average—2.5 per cent in Oklahoma, 3.7 per cent in the United States as a whole. Also it ranks better than average in college-trained people: 6.7 per cent with one to three years of college, 4.7 with four or more, contrasted with 5.4 and 4.6 respectively for the whole country.

Probably Oklahoma has too many state colleges. In the early days when they were established, statesmen making history could not always be distinguished from politicians making hay. But the attendance figures show a remarkable educational interest. In the fall of 1947 there were 45,175 students in Oklahoma colleges, of which 34,510 attended state-supported institutions. This placed Oklahoma fourteenth among the states in total enrollment, about ninth in enrollment in state-supported schools, although it ranks only twenty-second in population.

At the head of the educational system are the University of Oklahoma and the Oklahoma A. and M. College, equal in importance, but very different in essence. Their rivalry is deeper than school spirit, for it grows out of the particularism of Oklahoma life. One cannot even compare them objectively, giving each its place in the scheme of things, without offending two sets of partisans. Their combined war-swollen enrollment for the first semester of 1947–48 was 23,388. Another excellent school is the Oklahoma College for Women at Chickasha. It has a small enrollment (less than 800), but high educational standards and studious, serious-minded girls. Its graduates are notable for their scholarship.

Colleges for the training of teachers increased with the territorial expansion of "Oklahoma." To the original school at Edmond was added one at Alva after the opening of the Cherokee Strip and another at Weatherford in the Cheyenne and Arapaho country; then after statehood, three to balance these were established at Ada, Durant, and Tahlequah on the "east side." Their influence on education has been very great; for whatever the students learned they carried out immediately to some little struggling school in the hinterland. Their curriculums have expanded through the years and their original purpose has even been dropped from their names, but they all maintain demonstration schools and their primary function is still the training of teachers. They have a combined enrollment of about 3,500 students.

Oklahoma also has a military academy at Claremore, training mainly high-school boys, with a few on the junior-college level. It also has six junior colleges, all but one specializing in agriculture. Their enrollment is small, and they serve mainly their local communities. The Murray school at Tishomingo has a number of Chickasaw and other Five Tribes Indians among its students, and Cameron at Lawton enrolls many young people of the Plains tribes. The Panhandle A. and M. College at Goodwell has advanced to a senior college; and it has become the educational center of that sparsely settled region cut off by geography and history from the rest of the state. Langston University for Negroes specializes in teacher training and agriculture. It enrolls about five hundred students, and about three hundred additional Negroes have been going outside the state for advanced training.

Because Oklahoma established colleges at the very beginning of its public-school system, church colleges have always been relatively unimportant. But they have their place; they furnish a more religious atmosphere than the state schools and they train the ministers and other full-time workers of their denominations. Five are of senior-college rank: the University of Tulsa, supported mainly by endowment—gifts of oilmen—but still remotely connected with the Presbyterian church; Oklahoma City University, a Methodist school; Phillips University at Enid, maintained by the Disciples; the Baptist University at Shawnee; and Bethany-Peniel College at Bethany, supported by the Nazarenes.

The average grade-school, high-school, or college student in Oklahoma does not rank high in scholarship. The young people and their parents in country and city alike care more for "activities" than for study. But the state unites in a great pride of its schools and its children. Here is something more than parental love. The young generation represents the future in which Oklahoma fervently believes.

We have seen how farmers, small-town businessmen, and industrial leaders of the state support the farm clubs. Athletics are so important that they deserve a special chapter. The band craze, which struck in the mid-thirties, has lasted longer than any other Oklahoma enthusiasm. Enid's Tri-State Band Festival is a truly exciting spectacle, with bands from seventy schools marching around the square along sidewalks packed to suffocation. Even Marshall (population, 382) has its Little Town Band Festival, where small bands loaded into their school busses drive all the way across the state to compete. The evening before, the businessmen turn out with shovels and brooms to sweep the pavement as clean as a floor; every organization in town sets up a lunchroom to feed the thousands of visitors; and all through the bright afternoon one uniformed group after another prances and twirls and twists its way back and forth through the wide Main Street.

One of the first Boy Scout troops in the United States was organized in Oklahoma—at Pawhuska in 1909. The Order of the Rainbow, girls' society sponsored by the Eastern Star, was founded at McAlester in 1922. There are now 1,695 chapters with 135,000 active members in forty-five states and several foreign countries; but the Supreme Office of the order is still at McAlester, where it owns a beautifully landscaped seventy-five acre tract with a symbolic path of initiation and substantial stone buildings for the girls and their supervisors.

Growing up in this atmosphere of adult encouragement and the movement and drive of Oklahoma life, the young people frequently win national honors. Again—as in the case of the farm clubs—this is not boasting but sober fact, and a necessary part of the Oklahoma story. The year 1947 is as good as any, and a very brief list will suffice.

In that year twenty-year-old George Elno Ladd of Cushing won the one-thousand-dollar first prize of the Veterans of Foreign Wars Auxiliary for the best essay on "What Can I Do for My Country?" He was managing a 750-acre farm and finishing a high-school course deferred by his father's illness when he wrote at night by a kerosene lamp: "We the people, are the country. Any fault we find with our country's actions we must find with ourselves. . . . It must therefore follow that the only way to build a better country is to build a better citizenship. I am only one individual but I must not fail to do my part. . . . The best education obtainable will be my foundation; unselfishness, honesty, and integrity my framework; and I will crown it all with a willingness to assume my responsibility in charting the course of my nation. No more can I do; no less should any man do."

Oklahoma girls have enjoyed participating in the Girls' State sponsored by the American Legion Auxiliary. In 1947 for the first time its scope was extended to a Girls' Nation, meeting at Washington. Here in the "presidential" election both "political parties" nominated Oklahomans: seventeen-year-old George Ann Hicks of Edmond, who had served as "governor" in the state meet, was her party's choice for first place; and Helen Mary Walker of Enid was the "vice-presidential" candidate on the opposing ticket. George Ann's party won, and thus she became the first "president" of Girls' Nation. When she returned, more than three thousand people met her in the Union Station in Oklahoma City; there was an armful of roses from Governor Turner, a formal welcome by the mayors of Oklahoma City and Edmond, and affectionate greetings from the throng. Then fifty cars packed with Edmond people escorted her the twenty miles to her home town, where the whole population attended a reception in her honor.

The year 1947 is also typical of young Oklahomans' honors in journalism. The *Oklahoma State Engineer,* published by the engineering students of A. and M. College, was awarded the "highest rating for excellency" by the association of engineering college magazines. *The Oklahoma Daily,* student newspaper at the University, won second place in both feature writing and straight news writing at the national convention of the honorary journalistic fraternity at Chicago. And *Tulsa School Life,* published by the students of the city's three high schools, was rated one of the seven best in the United States by the Columbia University Scholastic Press Association at the annual meeting of three thousand high-school editors in New York. At the same time, at the University of Minnesota the yearbook of Classen High School of Oklahoma City was awarded top rank among high-school annuals.

Beginning in 1945, the United Christian Youth Movement, representing forty Protestant denominations, has awarded each year two four-year college scholarships, known as the Parshad Awards, one to a boy and one to a girl in the United States, selected for their Christian character and service and their essays on a

practical religious theme. Young Oklahomans have won three out
of the eight awards made through 1948: Charlene Schick of Dun-
can, in 1946; Bill Barrick of Enid, in 1947; and Imogene Young of
Chickasha, in 1948. It might be stretching a point to add that the
other award in 1947 went to Winona Frazier of California, an
Oklahoma-born Indian girl whose parents are conducting the
Friends' Osage mission at Hominy.

Oklahoma's young men did not win the recent war by themselves, but the people of the state have taken as their own the exploits of the Forty-fifth Division. It was made up of the National
Guard units from Oklahoma, Colorado, New Mexico, and Arizona,
with Oklahoma far in the lead because of its greater population.
Its organization was completed in 1923, with headquarters at
Oklahoma City and Major General Baird H. Markham, oilman of
Ponca City serving as adjutant general of Oklahoma, as the commander. It continued with Oklahomans as commanders until shortly before it went overseas.

At this time Oklahoma's own part of the outfit was carrying
out all manner of orders: taking over the government in Ku Klux
Klan strongholds, dispersing an impeachment-minded legislature,
putting out fires from wild oil wells, and shutting down the oil
fields for the price to rise. The National Guard that carried out the
orders of Oklahoma's embattled governors during those hectic
days had a great deal of combat experience—all bloodless.

Then came the war in Europe, and the United States went into
training for defense. By that time Major General William S. Key,
Oklahoma City oilman, had become the commander of the Forty-
fifth. The division went into camp at Fort Sill. I remember visiting
the place in 1940, when its tents were sprawled out over the prairie.
I talked with the daughter of a regular army officer, a very young
girl who took her army tradition too seriously. She was "sorry" for
General Key, who was doing the best he could with "unsoldierly"
material. Some of the men had even asked her, an officer's daughter, to dance. They were "ignorant," and they would "never learn."
Truly, I think she was right. The Forty-fifth has written its history
in flame since those days, but through it all it never learned to be
"soldierly." It only learned to fight.

Early in January the division was sent to Camp Barkeley, near Abilene, in the rugged hills of West Texas. Then came maneuvers in Louisiana, and camps in the East (where the dances of the Indian soldiers created unusual interest), and overseas. By this time it had received recruitments from the Middle West, New York, and New England. Later the appalling battle losses were made up with replacements from everywhere. In addition, when the Forty-fifth became a working part of the army, officers were interchanged from division to division without regard to place of origin. But to the people back home in Oklahoma it was always their own unit.

The Thunderbirds stopped briefly in North Africa, and made their first amphibious landing in Sicily in the summer of 1943. They fought their way across that island, and landed in the fall on the blazing beach of Salerno. The next January they established the Anzio beachhead, and for four months they held that strip of bloody ground. Eventually other American troops broke through to their rescue, and they joined the army that went on to clean up the rest of Italy. By this time their battles had become household words throughout the United States. In August they made their fourth amphibious landing on the south of France and fought north across that country. (Here Lieutenant Clarence Coggins of Poteau, finding himself surrounded by Germans, bluffed them into surrendering to him and singlehanded herded one thousand prisoners back to the American lines. Later he was killed in Alsace.) The following March they cut the Siegfried line, crossed the Rhine north of Worms, and moved southeast through Germany. In April they stormed the Nazi shrine city of Nuremberg, and rescued 32,000 living skeletons from the horrors of Daschau. Then they attacked Munich, and on May 2, after two days of furious street fighting, they came to the end of their trail in the Koenigsplatz of that birthplace of naziism. They had been in combat 511 days, fought for 2,000 miles, and captured 103,367 prisoners; and they had left 3,650 white crosses along their way.

In the early training days at Fort Sill, Lieutenant Colonel Walter M. Harrison, managing editor of the *Daily Oklahoman* and *Times* in civilian life, started the *45th Division News*. It was the first army newspaper of the "national emergency," and no other gained such a hold on its readers. To the end of the fighting it was the unit's own local newspaper. In a few months twenty-five-year-old Sergeant Don Robinson, also late of the *Daily Oklahoman-Times,* became the editor. Sergeant Bill Mauldin of Phoenix, Arizona—eighteen when he joined—became his staff artist. Then there were two reporters and a photographer—and that was all. The *Daily Oklahoman* and the *Oklahoma City Times* were the first general newspapers to notice and copy Mauldin's cartoons. Later, in battle days his weary, slogging infantrymen were known throughout the land. Ernie Pyle called him the finest cartoonist of the war. The paper was published at the front under almost incredible difficulties, but somehow it got to press. Right in the midst of its fame, the University of Oklahoma Press published Don's delightfully humorous account of the venture together with a selection of Bill's cartoons in a little book, *News of the 45th,* which preserves for all time the spirit of that indomitable outfit.

Altogether about 100,000 Oklahomans have belonged to the division at one time or another, either in prewar days or combat service. In the fall of 1946, a year after they returned from Europe, they held a reunion at Oklahoma City and formed a permanent organization. Here the army formally returned their battle flags to the state. Meanwhile the new Forty-fifth is the foremost unit in the United States in carrying out the reactivation plans of the Department of the Army. Again an Oklahoman, Major General James C. Styron of Hobart, is in command.

Although Oklahoma had only this one unit it could claim as its own, individual Oklahomans fought as heroically in other outfits. It was a long, long trail that led from the old school geography to some crumpled city or battered isle. My own town of Marshall saw this graphically through a service news sheet.

When the boys first left for the camps, they found it natural to write to C. T. ("Tibbie") Shades, the young school superintendent. Soon the correspondence grew out of hand, and the paper was launched as a community enterprise. Letters from the service men and women along with some home-town happenings furnished the news, Mr. Shades served as editor, the Lions Club assumed the responsibility and supplied much of the labor, and the whole neighborhood willingly chipped in to pay the printing and postage. It started in August, 1942, with six men overseas; three years and two months later it was traveling regularly to home-town boys in Rome, Berlin, and Tokyo.

Oklahoma was one of the first states in the Union to take advantage of the so-called G. I. Bill of Rights. The intention of the law was good. There were boys who entered the Forty-fifth when barely eighteen, and spent five years learning nothing but battle training and combat. How could a young man of twenty-three with no job experience except a little vacation work in long-past high-school days be expected to fit into a peacetime economy?

The law provided that he could go to college. And veterans thronged the schools, where they studied as fiercely as they had fought. This, of course, is an experience not confined to Oklahoma. But the state does rank fourteenth in veterans' college enrollment; and Veterans Village at A. and M. with 180 packed acres of hutments, an estimated four thousand inhabitants, and an elected town government is unique in postwar educational developments. The University of Oklahoma also has several housing developments for veteran students and their families, including Niemann Apartments, apartments on the North and the South Campus, a trailer town, and Sooner City, the last containing two hundred double and three hundred single prefabricated units.

Other veterans chose job-training to develop the skills they might have acquired had their youth been free. The government would cushion their inexperience by a subsidy. It was in this field that "rackets" developed. The men who wrote the law had not included provisions for supervision or restrictions. Its application was left to community initiative, through the public school and volunteer committees. Each town set up its own standards, and the government paid—and paid. Some shied away when they saw the inherent dangers, only to have their veterans grabbed off by a less scrupulous neighbor. Some tried to make the training real, but high standards were soon swept away by the rising tide of pressure. The boys themselves showed more hesitation than a cynic would credit. But their first reaction of "Why that's not right" soon succumbed to a "Well if the government is going to pay everybody, I'm entitled to it as much as anyone."

This experience likewise was not confined to Oklahoma, but it was Oklahoma that made a notable protest. In April, 1946, when

171

the program was in full swing, the *Oklahoma City Times* carried a series of articles by the hard-hitting Mike Gorman and Bob McMillan, which General Bradley pronounced the best exposé of these abuses published in the United States. Congress then set a ceiling on subsidized wages, and appropriated money for supervision. This action cleared out some—but by no means all—of the rackets. Some men are actually learning all the ins and outs of a business they expect to follow. I know several such instances myself. And the agricultural trainees are receiving the best practical farm apprenticeship ever given to young Oklahomans.

Officials of the Veterans Administration, the Department of Agriculture, and the A. and M. College set up the standards: four hours of classwork every week and two hours of individual instruction on the farm. Most of the instructors are A. and M. graduates; all have had college work in agriculture. At the close of 1948 the number of veterans reached 16,047—working under 729 instructors—and for the first time the waiting list was virtually absorbed. These trainees are applying soil-conservation practices, planning a balanced economy, and keeping books—all under expert guidance. And they are putting their government checks back into their business. The seriousness of these young farmers and of the veterans who went back to school shows what could have been done in other fields if a well-planned job-training program had been ready.

Even at its best, the cost of the training is rather frightening, for government standards of expenditure are not Oklahoma standards. This is evident in the grant to the local community. Here is the way the program worked out in one small-town farm center in 1947. Seventy-two veterans were taking agricultural training under three full-time instructors, A. and M. graduates; and ten others were in business training under the supervision of their employers plus two hundred hours of night classes taught by a high-school teacher. These eighty-two men were receiving about $6,500 a month, and the school was paid about $1,500 a month for teaching them. This adds up to $96,000 a year. But this same community maintains an excellent school for its 120 grade-school and 90 high-school children at a cost of only $30,000 a year. The veterans themselves are a little appalled; some say they would rather forego the whole program than to pile up a load which as citizens they will have to bear.

This may be the short view. As nobody can calculate in figures the moral damage of "training" that becomes a fraudulent scheme, so nobody can appraise the benefit of training that is truly educational. To care for the land—the survival of the human race hinges on that. To acquire economic independence—whether in farming, business, or labor—the survival of society is linked with that. There has always been a dangerous slack between school years and work years in Oklahoma.

When the first generation took the land, there was none left for their sons. Why didn't they save money and buy a farm? Simply because the price of land rose faster than they could pile up savings. It was like Alice in the Looking-glass running to keep up with the world and losing ground in spite of her puffing. They went to the cities or oil fields because there was nothing else to do. Then when industry did not expand to take up this new labor crop, they went to California.

Worst of all, there has never been a demand for superior talents. Oklahoma still distrusts, or at best undervalues, the expert. It produces strangely gifted people—and fails to use them. Some trim their ambitions and settle down with a minimum of frustration, not so much wasting their sweetness on the desert air as aiding in reclamation. (How many Pierian springs does it take to reclaim a desert?) More are lured away by salaries and opportunities—it is surprising how many former Oklahomans are found in every kind of intellectual and artistic endeavor. But there is one form of superiority that is appreciated at home. That is athletic prowess.

173

XV

They Play to Win

WITHOUT DOUBT, Jim Thorpe in his prime was
Oklahoma's greatest athlete. One can go on from there and say he
was the greatest athlete of all time. Some sports writers have said
just that. Oklahoma is full of legends of this Sac and Fox Indian,
who trained no more than Humphrey Pennyworth, and of his effortless exploits in everything he tried. He lives in Chicago now, sixty
years old and portly, but trailed by autograph-seeking children,
who heard about him from their grandfathers.

When he played football for the government Indian school at
Carlisle, Pennsylvania, he had a pregame stunt that used to strike
terror into the opposing team; he would walk out on the fifty-yard
line and drop kick goals alternately at both ends of the field. And
there was the time Carlisle accepted a challenge to a track meet
with a big college, and threw the challenger into dismay after the
tickets were sold by appearing with only five quiet-looking Indians; but Thorpe was one of the five, and Carlisle gave the fans
their money's worth and won 71 to 40 against the field. And there
were the most astounding Olympic victories ever chalked up by a
single athlete, since erased from the record because of a "professional" technicality. Probably even Oklahoma will never see his
like again.

But there is always baseball. First came Pepper Martin, whose
feats filled the home papers when he ran wild on bases for the St.
Louis Cardinals in 1926. Then there was Carl Hubbell. During the
thirties while he was southpawing the New York Giants to world
series victories, I passed through the village of Meeker. It was so

174

plastered with signs proclaiming itself the home town of the great
Hubbell that to this day I remember nothing about the place except its huge baseball park. It was like an Old World city in the
shadow of a cathedral. But it was more calm in 1947 when its
famous son headed the ballots (140 out of 161) of the Baseball
Writers' Association of America for a place alongside forty-nine
immortals of all time in baseball's Hall of Fame.

Oklahomans were only a little less excited when Paul and
Lloyd Waner of Harrah were slugging for the Pittsburgh Pirates.
For the famous brothers were the sons of "Pop" (O. L.) Waner, and
that great early-day sandlot player was until his death in 1948 a
beloved figure at sports gatherings. Now the idols are Harry
Brecheen of Ada, who pitched in three world series victories for
the St. Louis Cardinals in 1946; and Allie Reynolds, Creek Indian
and former A. and M. football star, who hurled nineteen victories
for the New York Yankees in 1947 and then went on to win the
game with the greatest margin in the world series.

These big-league players develop from a baseball-conscious
population. One can walk down the street on a quiet afternoon
without losing a play of the world series as successive radios blare
forth from the open doors. Sometimes it is hard to drive through
the towns on summer evenings because most of the male population is out in the street catching flies. For Oklahomans have always loved their baseball, minor though it is. They have always
played. Town and country. In the earliest days the new cities gave
enthusiastic support to semiprofessional teams; and every rural
neighborhood had its team that played for fun—such fun that the
yelling fans crowded the diamond until the players had to run in
curves to reach the bases.

It still goes on. There is the American Legion series (age limit,
seventeen) blanketing the state in districts and culminating in a
state tournament, from which the winners go on to further contests.
There are the hilarious sandlot games, initiated in 1927, finishing
each season with a state meet in Oklahoma City. There are the
semipro games with their state finals at Enid. Enid usually wins
here and then goes on to try for the national championship (won
four times since 1937) at Wichita, Kansas. And Oklahoma's professional teams belong to the Cimarron, the Sooner State, the KOM,

or the Texas League, or the Western Association. Several of them are farms for big-league organizations.

Unlike baseball, which sprang up from the soil like a crop of weeds, football was cultivated in the colleges and planted in the high schools. But it has made a lusty growth.

The game began at the University of Oklahoma in the fall of 1895. It is said that Jack Harts, a young "elocution" teacher and student, organized it in a Main Street barbershop. (In those days there were pastures and plowed fields between the new little town and the one-building campus.) Certain it is that Harts was the first coach as well as captain of the team. In those hard-scrabbling days the legislature had no money for athletics, and Harts' efforts were purely voluntary. He remembers that it was even necessary for him to recruit two non-students to fill out his squad. However, he left Norman shortly and went to look for gold in the Arctic. At the close of the 1945 football season, the University of Oklahoma Athletic Association held a fiftieth anniversary celebration and awarded him a football blanket. Then living in California, he was unable to attend, and it was presented by the University of Oklahoma Alumni Association of Los Angeles—a sizable group, by the way—at a special recognition banquet.

The University football teams have been good since about the time of statehood. The school stands high in the Big Seven Conference, and wins its share of outside victories. Its most spectacular bid for national fame was in 1946, when for its first game it tackled mighty Army—outstanding team in the country with two all-victorious seasons behind it. Seven hundred Oklahomans went by chartered train, plane, and automobile to help along, and hundreds more living in the East converged upon the Hudson. The Sooners went wild—fifteen hundred in the cheering section at West Point, thousands more hanging on their radios at home—when their team made the first touchdown and held the lead through most of the second quarter. There it stood on the score board: Oklahoma 7, Army 0! But the game finished 21 to 7, and the 21 was not Oklahoma's.

Deflated to its normal size, the team tied with the University of Kansas that year and the next for the conference championship. Then in 1948, after losing its first game, it won nine in a row, clinched the conference championship, and went on to defeat North Carolina in the Sugar Bowl on New Year's Day. At the end of the season the Associated Press ranked its team fifth in the nation, and chose Paul ("Buddy") Burris of Muskogee, a serious-minded student in the School of Business, as an all-American guard. Incidentally Oklahoma was the only state in the Union to place two men on that mythical first eleven; for Bobby Stuart of Tulsa, playing with Army, was chosen as an all-American back.

A. and M. was slower getting started in football than the University. There was no time for such frills in that early-day vocational college. It was not until 1901 that a dean and a professor—Dean L. L. Lewis and Professor John Fields—coached a little in their off hours to get the first team on its way. The big stadium that now towers above the campus is named for "Old Doc Lew"; but at those early games the spectators stood, and a strand of wire was stretched along the side lines to keep them from tangling with the players. In 1904 the Aggies had their first clash with the Sooners at Guthrie—two little struggling schools meeting in a little territorial capital to begin a rivalry that has lasted to the present time. But it was all one-sided then: Sooners 75, Aggies 0.

Aggie football has come a long way since those days. A. and M. still loses most of its games with the University; but it wins its share of championships in the Missouri Valley Conference, and holds its own against strong outside teams. Its peak years were 1944 and 1945, when it lost only one game—not to a college, but to an undefeated service team—and topped each season with a major bowl triumph. Most of the publicity went to Bob Fenimore, a handsome, likeable, blond lad from Woodward. Both years he was an all-American back. Oklahomans were comparing him with Jim Thorpe. But hopes were raised a little too high. The three following seasons were good but undistinguished. In 1948 the Aggies won the conference pennant, gave the conquering University team its biggest scare, and lost to William and Mary on New Year's Day in the Delta Bowl.

The Tulsa University team is one of the Aggies' most consistent opponents in the Missouri Valley Conference. It defeated them in 1946 and 1947. At the end of 1946 it stood as eleventh in the nation by the Williamson rating. It has often participated in

177

major bowl games—but not in 1948. This was a bad year for Tulsa, so bad that it even surrendered a preseason bowl contract.

Most Oklahoma football stars graduate into professional playing. (Lately the "pro" scouts have taken to raiding the campuses to sign up the undergraduates.) Oklahoma is used to the headlines: "Glenn Dobbs Shines for Dodgers," "Spec Sanders Tops All-America," "Jack Jacobs Scores for Packers." When the Philadelphia Eagles and the Chicago Cardinals met for the National League championship playoff in 1948, the lineup held eight familiar names: for the Eagles, Tommy Thompson and Johnny Green from Tulsa University, Neill Armstrong and Jim Parmer from A. and M.; for the Cardinals, Bill Campbell, Jake Colhouer, and Plato Andros from the University, and Lloyd Arms from A. and M. The best known of all Oklahoma professionals is Steve Owen, who grew up in the sand hills along the Cimarron south of Alva. In the nineteen twenties he left Phillips University to play for the New York Giants. He has been coaching that team since 1931. More recently Carl Voyles, A. and M. graduate from McLoud, left the collegiate field to take over the Brooklyn Dodgers. But even with so many Oklahoma recent stars and past stars studding the teams, the general public has never become excited about professional football. It is the college games that roll out from the radios and make the roads to the school towns so many swift-flowing streams. Even greater is the interest in high-school contests.

When Oklahoma painfully built up its high-school system—each town adding a grade or two every few years as it could—young teachers with a taste of college brought in football, yells, "pep," school spirit, and all the related activities. It seemed like "foolishness" to the adults, but the pupils ate it up. Now any talented high-school senior is a marked man, and the games are so important that they rate whole pages in the sports news of the city dailies. There are duels between traditional rivals, district championships, state championships—with everything closed on Main Street and the whole town out on the field yelling. Then along in the summer comes a match between all-star teams representing the North and South of the state, and an all-star game with Texas. (Texas has always won this one.) In recent years these North-South contests have included both baseball and basketball.

They Play to Win

Oklahoma's tall young men from the hinterlands make good basketball players. In the nine or ten years since the NCAA worked out a system showing clear-cut national championships, A. and M. has won twice—the only school in the country with two top rankings—and the University came out with one second place.

The Aggies won their NCAA crowns in 1945 and 1946. Their star was seven-foot Bob ("Foothills") Kurland, named the outstanding college cager of 1946 at the Los Angeles *Times* sports award dinner that year. But A. and M. had great teams in pre-Kurland days; counting back twelve years, they had chalked up 252 victories to 69 defeats. And they have continued to play basketball since their skyscraper's lamented graduation. In the 1947–48 season, for the seventh time in twelve years they took the championship of the Missouri Valley Conference; and their captain, A. L. Bennett of Holdenville, was chosen captain of the West team in the annual all-star game in Madison Square Garden. The previous year their coach, Henry P. (Hank) Iba was selected to coach the West team. This Missourian, who has been at A. and M. since 1934, was named in 1945 to the Helms Foundation's all-time Coaches' Hall of Fame.

The 1946–47 season was the University's big NCAA year. The team won the Big Six championship and the Western regional championship, but lost the national championship at the end of the road through a defeat in the finals by Holy Cross in Madison Square Garden. On the way up they defeated St. Louis University, Missouri Valley champions; the University of Texas, Southwest Conference champions; Oregon State, Pacific Coast champions; the University of Wisconsin, Big Nine champions; and broke a thirteen-year jinx with their old rivals, the Oklahoma Aggies. And all this, said the sports writers, "without an abnormally tall player." Six-foot, four-inch Gerald Tucker from across the line in Winfield, Kansas, was their best man. He made the all-American team in 1943; then spent three years in the army, serving in the Southwest Pacific, and came back to make all-American again. Their coach is Bruce Drake, a Sooner himself, who captained the 1929 team.

The Negroes also play good basketball. Eight years out of the past ten first place in the National Negro High School Basketball Tournament has gone to an Oklahoma school: Tulsa, four times;

Sand Springs, twice; Oklahoma City, once; and Cushing, once. Langston University has won the championship of the Southwestern Negro Conference for five straight years; has not placed lower than second since 1936. Several of its players have graduated into the hilarious, barnstorming professional colored teams that delight fans as much by their antics as their ball-handling dexterity.

Phillips Petroleum Corporation picks off the best of the graduating white players—Tucker, Bennett, Kurland, and others—for its well-known "66" team. The men must have good characters and convincing scholastic records. They start at the regular beginner's salary and attend practice sessions after working hours; and they play until the increasing responsibilities of their jobs crowd them out of the game. It is a good business opportunity. In 1921 K. S. Adams, just out of the University of Kansas, took a minor job with Phillips and organized and played on its first basketball team. Now he is president of the company, and all but two of his original players are still working in the organization.

Phillips has the best amateur team in the United States. For six straight years since 1943 it has won the AAU championship. In the 1946–47 season, the team lost only two games out of fifty-four; the next year it won sixty-two out of sixty-five, and emerged victorious over all in the Olympic trials. Then five of the "66" players served on the fifteen-man Olympic squad that won the world championship at London. Here the "66" coach, Bud Browning, a former University of Oklahoma star from Enid, coached the American team; Lou Wilke, who came from Phillips University, served as manager; and Cab Renick, an Indian A. and M. graduate from Marietta, was the captain. Of course not all members of the "66" team are Oklahomans; but except for the first few years of Kansas influence, Oklahomans have been dominant. That is not the whole story; the line-up of their out-of-state opponents sometimes shows so many former Oklahoma college stars that the matches savor of an old-home week.

Why should one cleaver-shaped tract of prairie and timber grow the best basketball players in the United States? A few years ago *Life* magazine[1] found the reason in the "natural ball-handling ability" of a population "most of whom shoot at homemade baskets

[1] December 17, 1945.

before they start school." All one winter and spring as I sat at my desk writing this book, I looked across the street at my neighbor's son, twelve-year-old "Pewee." He had a ring of regulation size and height fastened in a tree in the back yard, and all the time when he was not at school or running errands, he was shooting goals. Occasionally his father came and helped, frequently neighbor boys joined in, sometimes he patiently coached his six-year-old sister, more often he worked alone; but always it was serious practice—dribbling, passing, and shooting from every angle. Multiply this instance by the thousands. Certainly *Life* is right so far. But what gives young Oklahoma the urge to shoot at goals? Perhaps we need to look deeper.

Oklahomans enjoy all physical activity—a result of their frontier heritage—but their favorite contests involve team play. This is not a denial of their basic individualism. They have always worked together in small groups—to help a neighbor or to build a city. It is in looking beyond their community to the state as a whole that they have failed. Just so, their support of "the team" is localized in the University or A. and M. or Podunk High. It is only in times of supreme effort as in the Oklahoma-Army game or the Aggies' NCAA triumphs that they unite as Oklahomans.

The state has never produced but one Jim Thorpe in track events. Its one great tennis player was Don McNeill of Oklahoma City, winner of the United States amateur title in 1940. In golf, Zell Eaton and Walter Emory came close—but not quite—to the top; and young Charles Coe, recent University star from Ardmore, reached the semifinals of the National Amateur Tourney at Memphis in 1948. For the colleges consistently hold their own—without much fanfare or public notice—in these contests. The scores help to build up the totals in all-sports championships. Thus Oklahoma has won the Big Six (or Big Seven) all-sports crown for eleven years out of the nineteen since the conference was organized; and the Aggies have won their conference championship every year during the same period. But the most unusual record of all is the Aggies' wrestling.

Their winning streak began in 1920 under the late E. C. (Ed) Gallagher, whose name now lives in the big field house. Since then they have finished all but three seasons undefeated. Between 1921

181

and 1932 they won sixty-eight dual meets in a row. Their next string of victories ran for five years. In 1937 they started another, which is still rolling; they closed the 1948 season with fifty-eight straight victories. They have won the national championship fifteen years out of the eighteen since the NCAA meets were inaugurated. Eighteen Aggies have served on Olympic teams; three have won Olympic championships. In the national Olympic tryout of 1948 they won three first places and two alternates—giving them the un-official team title—and their coach, Art Griffith, was selected to coach the Americans for the London meet. Griffith is himself an A. and M. graduate, but never a wrestler. He came to his college job from coaching at Tulsa Central High School where his wres-tling team had won two national championships.

Aggie wrestlers find some of their toughest competition in Oklahoma. In 1936 when they dropped to third place in the NCAA tournament (only two times have they fallen so low), it was the University of Oklahoma that won the championship and the col-lege at Edmond that placed second. Another strong contender in national meets is the former teachers' college at Weatherford, now known as Southwestern Tech.

Young Oklahomans also like to let off their excess energy in boxing—both AAU and Golden Gloves. The Golden Gloves, be-cause of newspaper milk-and-ice-fund publicity, attracts the more general interest. The season opens with a Labor Day jamboree between hand-picked boxers at Oklahoma City. Then follow inter-city matches between Oklahoma and Midwestern teams. At the same time six districts are holding elimination tournaments for the state meet in Oklahoma City in February. The winners then go to Chicago to compete for—and often to win—national titles; and Oklahomans frequently serve on the Chicago team in the intercity match with New York, and on the national team that meets Euro-pean champions at Chicago. About one thousand young boxers swing wild and eager fists in the district meets, and close to two hundred compete for the state title and a place on the eight-man Chicago team.

Here is an interesting fact about Oklahoma boxing: so many Indians emerge at the upper levels that the engagements become practically all-Indian melees. Even the intercity meets with Kansas City become battles between Indians, for the Kansas City team is often made up largely of former Oklahoma Glovers attending government school at Haskell Institute in near-by Lawrence. In 1947 both coaches and the entire team that represented Oklahoma in the Golden Gloves tournament at Chicago were Indians. The next year, Hubert Halfmoon, a Delaware, and Earl Grinnell, a Potawatomi, were the coaches; and on the team were three Choctaws, a Chickasaw, a Comanche, a Caddo, a Kiowa, and one lone paleface.

Thus Oklahoma athletics grow out of the life of the people. There are the muscular precision of the Indian, the strong bodies of a frontier heritage, the youthful zest for living expressing itself in play. The athletes are not hired entertainers, professionals in all but name, but young men who enjoy the game. One cannot say that every institution is free of hidden subsidies, but certainly most of the players are Oklahoma boys attending Oklahoma schools, and their home-town addresses dot the state.

There was a time not far back when Oklahomans felt left out of the national sports news. The writers, they said, never looked in their direction; if Oklahoma won a conference championship, that was small-time; if Jim Thorpe piled up records, the credit went to Carlisle, Pennsylvania. In sports as in other fields there was that unsatisfied craving for "recognition." When the A. and M. basketball team got its first bid to Madison Square Garden in 1938, the Stillwater newspaper came out with an extra edition and the whole quiet little town dropped everything to celebrate.

All this is changed now. Probably it was the Aggies' wrestling that first opened the eyes of Eastern writers. Then came those bizarre Aggie seasons of 1944–45 and 1945–46, when two national basketball championships, an undefeated football team with bowl triumphs, plus five victories and no losses in dual track meets from West Point to California, and a rifle team that won first place in the army's national intercollegiate matches all built up a legend of Oklahoma invincibility. Thus glory accumulates like a snowball; the mere fact that a man is from Oklahoma now adds to his renown. And this is not a true evaluation either.

The Oklahomans themselves seem to be settling down to a steadier view. They know they have good athletes—they have always been sure of that—but they are beginning to realize that other states have their heroes, too. Now they can watch the game without keeping one eye on the national cheering section. A little outside notice no longer wrecks a community. But they still enjoy their sports. A high-school boy unable to learn any other history can recite the chronicles of sports events back as far as statehood; and any sober citizen knows the ins and outs of the sports news better than he knows his business. These are the ones who cheer the stars. But they play on their own, too, and Oklahoma has many playgrounds.

XVI

They Play for Fun

PUBLIC PLAYGROUNDS have been established in Oklahoma by cities, the state, and the federal government. They vary as widely in scenic features as the state itself varies in topography and climate. Seven are state parks. Three of these are in the west where they are needed most.

Out near Woodward at the ragged edge of the High Plains is Boiling Springs State Park. It is on a bend of the North Canadian River and its nine hundred acres are surrounded by sand hills and sagebrush. Here in a treeless land is a sheltering tract of heavy timber. An immense spring bubbling up through the sand once made a historic camping place for early-day travelers; now the water fills a four-acre lake with built-up rock walls and a commodious bathhouse. The lake is always in use, for dwellers in that semiarid country know how to appreciate water. Like all the other state parks, it is a game sanctuary, and wild quail mothers have found it is a good place to raise their striped, downy broods. One might even glimpse a road runner or chaparral *(Geococcyx californianus)*, that strange bird of the West that makes its nest of snake skins, joints of cactus, cow manure, and sticks; feeds its young on grasshoppers, tarantulas, centipedes, scorpions, and small snakes (with possibly a baby quail or two); and instead of flying, streaks through the brush with long tail dragging, like a huge, darting lizard.

A few miles away is another recreation area surrounding the Fort Supply dam and reservoir constructed by the federal government on Wolf Creek as a link in its flood control plans for the North

185

Canadian River. People drive long distances for the fishing and boating on this 1,700-acre lake. Woodward even has a troop of Sea Scouts who come here for training; and these boys from the high, dry plains recently won first place in a national Sea Scout meet.

Farther down on the North Canadian the federal government has just completed the great Canton dam and reservoir. Designed for flood control and extensive irrigation of the land downstream, it also has fine recreational possibilities. Probably by the time this book goes to press, some of its facilities will be in use. Not so far along are the Hulah reservoir on the Caney River near Bartlesville, the Fort Gibson dam on the Grand, the dam at Tenkiller Ferry on the Illinois, and the Wister job on the Poteau, but the dirt is flying in all of these places.

Southeast of Canton, in the gyp hills of Blaine County, is Roman Nose State Park—named for a Cheyenne war chief. Here one drives through level wheat land until the plain is suddenly gashed by rugged canyons with candy-colored walls. Cedars grow along the sides, and at the bottom are cool valleys shaded by graceful chinaberries and tall cottonwoods and watered by everlasting springs. (Do not try to drink the water!) This also was a favorite early-day camping site; and later when the farmlands were homesteaded, the gyp hills became a favorite rendezvous for the outlaws who stole settlers' horses and robbed frontier stores. Now the springs feed a four-acre lake and a concrete swimming pool.

Fifty miles north, on the Salt Fork of the Arkansas near Jet and Cherokee, is the Great Salt Plains Wildlife Refuge. Here early travelers found a strange setting—a crust of salt ten miles long and twelve wide lying on the flat floor of the valley, in winter like a covering of snow, in summer a sheet of blinding white light shimmering to blue under the blazing sun. Biologists came to study the meager life supported on its barren acres—plants and insects exactly like those of the salt marshes along the ocean. The Cuban snowy plover and the least tern nested there, the only place where they were found in Oklahoma. In 1930 the federal government established a refuge there for migratory wild fowl, and eleven years later it completed a flood control dam on the river that backed the water up over 10,700 acres of the area. This lake attracts myriads of ducks and geese during the fall and winter. Other water birds—the handsome avocat and the large, black-crested cormorant—once listed as rare transients in Oklahoma have begun nesting here. There are few recreational facilities, but the place is worth seeing. It made a fine bombing range during the war. Some of the best goose shooting in the state is in the vicinity.

In the southwestern part of the state is Quartz Mountain State Park, near Altus, at the tail end of the Wichita uplift. It is a wild, picturesque 3,300-acre tract of massed granite hills and boulders, with mesquite and cedar growing on every toehold. Strangely enough, in a sheltered spot of this rugged place is a grove of live oaks, green all winter, the only ones in the state. All through the park is a great profusion of wild flowers. Redbuds line the creeks, and the showy gallardia—cultivated plant in Eastern gardens—flames through the grass. On the edge of the park is the 6,000-acre lake of the Austin Irrigation Project, with a bed of solid granite and a natural sandy beach, where swimming, fishing, and boating are provided; and outside are lush green fields of that watered Eden.

Thirty miles east, the most notable peaks of the low-lying Wichita Mountains are enclosed in the Wichita Mountains Wildlife Refuge of the federal government. This 61,000-acre tract is close to the city of Lawton and joins the military reservation of Fort Sill. Here among the granite crags are picturesque lakes well stocked with fish. Scenic drives circle the area and wind to a magnificant view from the summit of Mount Scott.

The refuge was established primarily as a home for buffalo. The herd was started with 17 head brought—humiliating fact!—from New York in 1905. The number is now more than 500—second only to the herd in Yellowstone Park—with a yearly calf crop of about 120. Longhorned cattle also graze over the area as in the old days—293 head, the largest herd in the United States in 1948. Other wild life includes white-tailed deer (735), elk (241), antelope (40 head waging a losing struggle against coyotes, although 121 coyotes were trapped there last winter), two wild mustangs, and turkeys; and there is even a thriving prairie-dog town, one of the few places in the state where the chubby little rodents can still stand in the entrance of their burrows and "bark" at the passer-by. Enough surplus buffalo, elk, and longhorns are sold every year to pay the operating expenses of the refuge.

Every foot of this ground is storied with Indian history. Alice Marriott's *Ten Grandmothers* closes with an unforgettable passage in which the aged Spear Woman is taken to see the buffalo herd. For years she had found the prairies dead, all one color. But here in this virgin place the short buffalo grass was "like changeable silk, the kind the Delawares used to trim their blankets. Yellow as the wind struck it, rose-color as it died away; then a sort of in-between color, with patterns that moved like the patterns in silk when you folded it. . . . It was the old kind of grass, the old rippling, running prairies." Then she saw the buffalo, and she began to sing of the days when "we were all free on the prairies together." But the herd milled about, not knowing. Then she said: "Of course you don't understand my singing. . . . You don't remember. You were born inside the fence, like my own grandchildren." But it is this herd that furnishes meat to the Indians for their tribal gatherings.

In the tilted rocks of the Arbuckles just north of Ardmore, several civic and religious organizations own camp grounds. Within sight of U. S. Highway 77 is Turner Falls, the best-known waterfall in Oklahoma. This spot is owned by the little town of Davis, northern gateway to the region, and the State Park Service helps in its maintenance. Nine miles east of Davis and adjoining Sulphur —a town of hotels and bathhouses—is Platt National Park. Here are medicinal springs (sulphur, iron, and bromide to choose from) and shining brooks cascading over rocks. Thousands of redbuds have been planted along the trails, and in the administration building is a herbarium containing specimens of six hundred species of wild flowers found in the park. On the books are the names of 731,861 visitors, representing every state in the Union, who registered there in the 1947–48 season.

On the southern edge of Ardmore is Lake Murray State Park. It is a large area of untouched scrubby timber running out on pronged fingers into an artificial lake of six thousand acres. Here are motorboat racing and swimming and organized group camps for both white and colored; and fish too large even for Paul Bunyan's frying pan jump out of the water to attack the angler.

Almost touching Lake Murray is one of the great branching arms of 93,000-acre Lake Texoma, created by Denison Dam on

188

Red River. Another arm backs up to the city of Tishomingo. Others enter from the Texas side. The fishing here rivals that in Lake Murray. The whole region is under the National Park Service, and the cities along the 1,400-mile shore line—Kingston, Madill, Tishomingo, and Durant—are rapidly burgeoning into resorts. Official records show that it draws well over two million visitors a year, leading by more than one million the Yellowstone, the Grand Canyon, the Great Smokies, or any other recreation area under the National Park Service.

Far to the north in the hilly eastern margin of the Red Beds is Lake Carl Blackwell, ten miles west of its sponsoring A. and M. College. It also has excellent fishing. And a member of the college faculty carried on such important research on the growth of fish there that the government recently sent him to Japan to build up the Japanese fisheries.

Osage Hills State Park is in the heart of the spacious ranch country midway between Pawhuska and Bartlesville. Here the sides of the great rounded hills are covered with blackjack and post oak, and at the bottom of a deep gorge flows clear, winding Sand Creek with its fringe of alluvial timber. Not too far away is the FP Ranch, private playground and game preserve of Frank Phillips; and here the Woolaroc Museum, open on certain days to the public, attracts visitors from all over the state.

In the spring when all northeastern Oklahoma is white with dogwood, people come a long way from the prairie cities to make pilgrimage along its winding roads. In the heart of this region, but easily accessible from Muskogee and Fort Gibson, is the Cookson Hills Playground surrounding a 900-acre flood-control lake of the federal Soil Conservation Service. During the war Camp Gruber was located there. Now it is in the process of being turned over to the state. Wild flowers grow so profusely that they make solid patches of color on the grass. In the surrounding timber are the hidden cabins of Creek Indians who took refuge with the Cherokees in Georgia and Alabama at the time of the Creek Removal, only to be uprooted and dragged to the West with their hosts.

Another playground in the Ozarks belongs to the city of Tulsa. It is the by-product of a brilliant engineering feat of the early nineteen twenties. The Tulsans wanted pure mountain water. They

189

voted seven and one-half million dollars in bonds and hired Major
General George W. Goethals of Panama Canal fame. Then they
dammed Spavinaw Creek to form a lake, blasted a tunnel through
the hills, and brought their water sixty-five miles by gravity to the
city. They bought the woods around their lake in order to guard
its purity, stocked it with fish from their own municipal hatchery,
built some cabins—and here was camping, fishing, and boating
all before flood control, PWA, CCC, and other playground-build-
ing measures of the thirties and forties had ever been thought of.

The largest recreation area in northeastern Oklahoma stretches
sixty miles from Miami to Pensacola along the 55,000-acre lake
formed by the Grand River Dam. The 1,300 miles of wooded shore
around its branching arms at certain seasons are lined with happy
fisherman, and every little town sells bait and rents cabins. At its
dedication by Governor Turner in 1947, there were motorboat
races, water skiing, and a massed flotilla of fifty cabin cruisers on
the big lake, and a parade of roundup clubs across the mile-and-
one-eighth-long dam.

Beautiful as are the Ozarks, there is a wilder beauty in the
mountains of the southeast. This scenic paradise takes in the whole
corner of the state—fully seventy-five miles north and south, east
and west. All of it is worth visiting; as for public playgrounds, besides the Ouachita National Forest and the State Game Preserve,
there are two state parks.

Robbers' Cave State Park is six miles north of Wilburton in
the timbered—in spite of the name—Sans Bois Mountains. It takes
in 8,400 acres of pine forest and leafy grove and tumbled rock. The
clear-flowing Fourche Maline ripples through over a rock bottom.
In one place it has been dammed to form Lake Carlton, a jewel
of a lake set in wooded bluffs. Legend says that Belle Starr, the
Youngers, and Frank and Jesse James holed up at various times in
the natural cave from which the park gets its name. If they did not,
they overlooked a good hide-out, for the place is snug and dry with
a south-facing entrance commanding the valley, and even the roof
is shaped just right to carry the smoke out through this door.

Beavers Bend State Park is in the mountains twenty miles
north of Idabel. If one may make comparisons, this is the state's
most scenic playground. The Mountain Fork loops around and

then cuts through its 1,300 acres. A more beautiful river does not exist—could not exist—anywhere. Pellucid water beating itself to foam on huge boulders, cliffs with pine tops piercing the blue sky, brooks cascading down the rocky walls. Here in still pools grow the cypress trees, knees coming up above the clear water. The magnolia also grows here, and Spanish moss festoons the forest. Wild deer tread daintily over the leaf-flecked shadows, and the wild turkey struts around his shy mate.

I cannot name all the beauty spots outside the public playgrounds in the Ouachitas and the Ozarks in this volume. Neither can I name all the picturesque places that break the prairies of the west—the purple cliffs of the Black Mesa with the Cimarron lying like a green snake on the floor of the empty valley, the glistening barrens of the salt plains east of Buffalo, the petrified trees lying about on the bare ranches of the High Plains—and so on. Oklahomans visit all these places. They are also beginning to learn that beneath their land is a gleaming world of caverns.

The only cave that has been explored and lighted commercially for tourists is the Alabaster Cavern near Freedom in the northwestern corner of the state. The crystal rooms and passages are like a Carlsbad in miniature—and not so very miniature either, for the bottom levels are 180 feet down—underground streams, and a great funnel of bats pouring out every night. All the way along the Cimarron from Freedom to Fairview there are caves discovered in early days by cowboys, but never fully explored. Others underlie an unknown area from Corn to Vinson in the southwest. All of them erupt clouds of bats, and contain gleaming columns and pinnacles of unearthly beauty. These are gypsum caves. Fully as dazzling are the caverns of the limestone regions. One has been found in the Arbuckles south of Sulphur. An unknown number are in the Ozarks—three around Lake Spavinaw. Exploring caves is a favorite adventure of hardy souls, who work their way from room to room flashing their electric lanterns on a scene literally "out of this world."

If one does not care to travel afar for outings, nearly every city has a near-by artificial lake for its water supply. All of these have fishing and swimming, and the largest have motorboat races attracting entries from distant states. Once the National Outboard

Motor Regatta was held on the lake at the edge of Tulsa; and Frank Vincent of Tulsa has won nine national outboard championships, and has held, at one time or another, world's records in classes A, B, and C motorboat races.

Perhaps the first territorial legislature was not so far off after all in enacting a maritime code for Oklahoma. Come to think of it, Indian Territory's first sportsman was the owner of a steamboat. The story of his great race has passed into "east side" legend, with as many versions as there are narrators. But this much is true. Joe Vann, mixed-blood Cherokee, owner of many slaves, lived on a rich plantation along the Arkansas and his boats plied the river to outside cities. In 1844 his pride, the *Lucy Walker,* was steaming down the Ohio below Louisville when a lesser craft attempted to pass. Joe ordered his slaves to shove in the fuel. When this was too slow, he threw in sides of bacon. Then the boiler blew up with a bang that killed Vann and about fifty of his passengers. Thus aquatic sports came very early into Oklahoma history. Vann was only anticipating the time when the scarcity of water would drive the cities to construct municipal lakes.

Surrounding these lakes and at other places around and within the cities are fine parks. For few Oklahoma towns grew up of themselves; they were consciously and quickly built, and the need for beauty entered into the initial planning of many of them. Tulsa especially is dotted with parks, where a combination of great wealth, civic spirit, and rich soil produce an exuberant growth of tree and flower. Muskogee, strangely modest for an Oklahoma city, says very little about a park worth driving across the state to see. On the edge of town is one of the rugged hills that rise in that region like gigantic haystacks above the Arkansas flats. Every possible advantage has been taken of the terrain: a long approach by lily ponds and through avenues of trees; a wooded ridge with shaded paths and tumbling falls; at the foot, still pools with floating lilies and fringing willows.

Many of the county-seat towns are built around courthouse squares. Here are flower and verdure at the heart of the business district; or—if civic spirit has not progressed so far—at least a place for the country people to meet and mingle. Other towns take pride in growing some particular shrub. Thus Hugo in the Red River country has six thousand crepe myrtles—enough to veil the face of the whole little city with plumes of color. In the same way Shawnee plants redbuds, and Edmond has exactly the right soil and climate for roses. These are the up-and-coming cities. Many a little town is stretched far out over weed-grown vacant lots, eloquent of its failure to grow into the plans of its builders.

Oklahomans love outdoor scenery, whether in city park or mountain wilderness. It revives for them the virgin beauty that fell before the plow. It is a short step from covered wagon to trailer camp. And outdoor exercise is their substitute for the horseback riding and farm work of their youth. No wonder they are inveterate hunters and fishers.

Not so long ago the whole country was an anglers' paradise. Then except in remote mountain sections the fish were all gone from streams muddied by erosion or polluted by city sewage and oil-field waste. Now the sport has come back in the big lakes. The state now ranks thirteenth in resident, eleventh in nonresident fishing licenses.

Once the Indian Territory was alive with game. Hunters came from surrounding states for glorified outings; or they killed for profit hauling wagonloads of turkeys or prairie chickens to the railroads to ship to outside markets. Of course this practice violated the Indian Intercourse Acts, but nothing was done to halt it. Some of David L. Payne's "homeseekers colonies" were little more than game-slaughtering excursions. Irving's *Tour on the Prairies* shows a supposed military expedition interested mainly in cutting an ugly trail of destruction across a new, fresh land. The buffalo went first; the last herd was reported around present Oklahoma City in 1876, but a few were left in the Panhandle until the late eighteen eighties. The rest of the wild life survived until the coming of the settlers; then it vanished suddenly and almost as completely. Now the state is in the slow process of restocking.

The duck population has increased greatly with the filling of the new lakes. The hunters have fair success with quail and doves. They also go in considerable numbers to Northern states to shoot pheasants, and the State Game and Fish Department is now experimenting with those birds in the High Plains area. About seven or eight hundred deer are killed legally each year in a five- or six-

193

day season in the seven southeastern mountain counties—one to every dozen or so hunters. An estimated two million squirrels are taken annually, and hunting with 'coon dogs is so much fun that one hunters' association bought every live raccoon brought in and turned it loose until they found they were only stimulating trappers. Rabbits have never been protected and are still plentiful in most places. Even yet in the prairie sections the jack rabbits graze on the wheat and alfalfa until they become pests. Sometimes they are thinned out by "rabbit drives," in which the hunters surround a six-mile-square township and work in toward the center shooting them down by thousands.

Coyotes are hunted partly for sport and partly to destroy a predatory pest. Some are surrounded by "drives," others are shot from planes, still more are killed with dogs at organized hunts, and a few are even run down and lassoed from horseback. Organized fox hunts are also held, but foxes are regarded as game animals and protected in closed seasons. One sees fine dogs everywhere in the hill country; and the Wolf and Fox Hunters Associations hold bench shows and field trials that attract entries from many states.

Oklahomans also take their bird-dog field trials seriously. The dogs run in regional tests, the annual state meet, and in National and All-America contests. At the National amateur trials in 1948 the championship went to an Oklahoma dog: Carolina Doughgirl, owned by Powel Briscoe of Oklahoma City. Several Oklahomans within the past year or two have served as officers of field-trials associations: Cecil Proctor of Oklahoma City as a director of the Amateur Field Trial Clubs of America; Charles E. Griffith of Big Cabin as president and C. E. Duffield of Tulsa as a director of the All-America Club; Dr. A. C. Hirschfield of Oklahoma City as president of the Midwest Championship Field Trials Association. Proctor is known as one of the leading judges in the United States, and Fred Lasiter of Wewoka served as one of the two judges through the National amateur trials in 1948.

A bizarre sports event in Oklahoma is the Annual Rattlesnake Roundup sponsored by the Okeene Junior Chamber of Commerce. The setting seems unpromising. Rattlesnakes long ago disappeared from the settled places; and Okeene is a typical prairie town with grain elevators towering above it, and the surrounding level farms usually win the outstanding wheat honors in the state. But not far away are the gyp hills, and diamond backs six or seven feet long—every inch packed with concentrated malevolence—still infest the rugged canyons. The hunt is held in the spring when the reptiles are up and stirring. People come from quite a distance to join in the excitement, and hundreds of snakes are taken. They are captured alive and turned over to zoos or else to laboratories, where the venom is extracted and used for medicinal purposes.

The administration of Oklahoma's fishing and hunting laws is entrusted to a Game and Fish Department. This consists of a commission of eight members appointed by the governor and serving for staggered terms; a director appointed by the commission; and rangers and other employees appointed by the director. With the exception of a small appropriation for the dynamiting of crows and the payment of a bounty for the killing of wolves and coyotes, all the expense of the program is borne by license fees. A resident hunting license costs $1.25 (it takes an extra $7.50 to hunt deer); a fishing license is $1.25; and there are larger fees for nonresidents and commercial fishermen and trappers. This revenue pays for fish and quail hatcheries, the rangers' law-enforcement service, and public education through bulletins and a monthly magazine. All conservation measures require an uphill fight, for the frontier conviction that wild life is meant to be wiped out still gives trouble.

The state parks are administered by a division of the Planning and Resources Board. This agency has become very active in advertising the state's beauty spots through folders, photographic slides, and moving pictures. Several Oklahoma cities, especially Tulsa, are engaged in the same promotion. But the most active salesman of the Oklahoma scene is Arkansas-bred R. G. Miller, who writes "The Smoking Room" column of the *Daily Oklahoman* and *Times*. For fifteen years he has been describing places of scenic or historic interest, and working out tours to reach them. People have developed such confidence in his judgment that now he and his publishers practically run a free travel bureau, answering hundreds of queries and sending out folders to assist the vacationer.

This service is needed. Oklahoma's public playgrounds are so new and general knowledge of the state is still so meager that its own people are not fully informed about its recreational facilities. What shall be said then for people outside who believe that the whole area is one unending plain? Overenthusiastic citizens would like to launch an intensive campaign to make it a resort center. The 1947 legislature, in fact, appropriated $150,000 for advertising it throughout the nation. But it would be a calamity if the tourists should all come at once. Supply points are few and far between, resort hotels are nonexistent except at a few of the older parks, and cabins are booked months in advance. The Planning and Resources Board is now spending $200,000 authorized by this same legislature for more boat docks, cabins, and group camps in the seven state parks, but this will not enable them to catch up with the demand. However, while there is scenery to spare and fish to catch and game to shoot, Oklahomans will continue to tour their state. They do not mind roughing it, and they do enjoy outings. They also enjoy the many celebrations in their cities.

XVII

They Drive to Town

EVERY OKLAHOMA COMMUNITY has its distinctive celebration. Usually this is historical: in the east it is oil superimposed on the vanished institutions of the five Indian republics; in the west it commemorates the great runs, old settlers' reunions, or the native Indian ceremonials. Then there is the natural urge of every Oklahoman to load the family into the car and drive to town.

In the "east side" everybody goes to Tulsa. It has a beauty unique among American cities. Its towers soar into a smokeless sky. Its churches are right in design and mature in architectural concept. The dwellings of the rich are palaces set in woodland splendor. The more humble houses are spic and span and shining as new glass washed in soap suds. The shops are of Fifth Avenue elegance. The manner of the place is suave and worldly, but underneath it is the happy sense of a job well done.

For this generation of Tulsans saw their city rise. They remember it as a former cow town shorn of its open range and determined to find a substitute. They saw its early throes of growth. I remember the impression it made in 1916 when some of us from the University went there for a student conference. A stream of wealth was pouring in from the Cushing field and running over in bricks and mortar, and the soul of the city was fairly bursting at the seams. On the way back we stopped at Oklahoma City and looked over the busy, orderly streets. Said my roommate, "After Tulsa, this seems just like being in church." Those were the inchoate days. It took its present form in the nineteen twenties. No wonder the sky

197

line is as symmetrical as an architect's drawing; it was built to scale, and its measure was the posted price of crude oil.

Tulsa still claims to be the "oil capital of the world," for no matter where the fields may be, the management of the industry centers there. It is surrounded by rich Arkansas Valley farmland, and the fine cattle of the upland ranches probably produce more beef than the longhorns that once grazed on the open range. It is tied in with the new industrial growth of all eastern Oklahoma. In 1947 the headquarters of the Junior Chamber of Commerce of the United States were transferred there from Chicago. Just now it is breaking out in another surge of building, the expression of its newest industrial cycle.

Tulsa made itself a city by brass and brawn. It had its early rivals. Red Fork had the better location when both were cow towns, and it got the first taste of oil. Indeed, Tulsa has never had even one oil well. Now Red Fork is a part of the greater city. Then Sapulpa was dangerously close to cashing in on the Glenn Pool strike. Tulsa was farther away and on the wrong side of the river, but its leaders bridged the stream and captured the business. Now Sapulpa is a prosperous small city making brick and glass and Frankhoma pottery, but by no means a rival to Tulsa. In the first years of the century Muskogee was far in the lead. The Five Tribes agency and the varied activities of the Dawes Commission all centered there. But the Indian business eventually slowed down, and by that time Tulsa had gained ascendancy. Now Muskogee is a quiet city, with its beautiful park and its surrounding truck farms, and recently it has captured some solid new industry. It is still the third city in Oklahoma; but the census of 1940 gave it 32,000 people to Tulsa's 142,000.

Muskogee is the gateway to much of historic Indian Oklahoma. Just across the Arkansas is old Fort Gibson, with the stone barracks of Civil War days still standing on the hill overlooking the Grand River, and on the flat the earlier log stockade recently restored by WPA and the Oklahoma Historical Society. Thirty miles northeast is Tahlequah, former seat of government of the Cherokees, where the tribal capitol erected in 1869 now serves as the county courthouse, and the girls' boarding school, once the pride of the Indians, is the main building on the beautiful, wooded campus of the Northeastern State College. Every spring the graduates of the old school assemble for a nostalgic home-coming—graying gentlewomen, who have never forgotten the well-bred graces of the Cherokee Female Seminary. In the opposite direction, forty miles southwest of Muskogee, is the thriving glass-making farm center of Okmulgee. This completely modern city is built around the square where stands the old Creek capitol, erected in 1878 and now used as a museum. The whole region west and south of Okmulgee is dotted with Creek churches and squares, and people drive out from town to attend their "stomp dances."

Far to the south at Tishomingo the Chickasaw capitol, like the Cherokee, is used as a county courthouse. It was built rather late in Chickasaw history to replace a brick building that burned down. This one ought to stand forever, for it is made of immense blocks of native granite, which contrast strangely with gingerbread turrets growing out of the roof. People used to take trips to Tishomingo for the fishing and picnicking at Devil's Den, where great heaps of granite boulders line the canyon of clear-flowing Pennington Creek. Now they add the fishing of Lake Texoma, which reaches almost to the door of Murray College.

The Seminoles had their capital at Wewoka. Nobody knows much about the government or history of this conservative tribe after its forced removal to the Indian Territory. Their council house for at least part of the time was a small double log cabin with a clapboard roof and a stick chimney at each end; and the chiefs of the different bands came and camped in the woods near by while they carried on the tribal business. All trace of this is gone now and the Seminole County courthouse dominates the square, but a large pecan tree still standing there is said to have been used as the tribal whipping tree where lawbreakers were punished.

Wewoka shows unmistakable signs of oil money, as do all the towns of Seminole County. The city of Seminole is in the heart of the great field, and in its roaring heyday it set a record of a bigger and better hell-on-earth never surpassed in Oklahoma oil history. Now it is a lively, prosperous town with fine buildings and one of the best school systems in the state; it has an impressive oil-field payroll and is a center of natural gasoline and butane manufacturing, oil-field supplies, and machine-shop repair. Every summer it holds a big celebration on the anniversary of its famous strike. It has somethirg to talk about: the discovery well made 2,348,914 barrels during its nine years of flowing, and the production of the Greater Seminole area has reached 900,000,000 barrels.

Here the old tribal days have been forgotten, but traces still survive in the back country. There is for example the huge, ornate house of John F. Brown now standing deserted in the blackjacks, with the dust lying thick over the pianos and rich furniture. Brown was a mixed blood who joined the Seminoles after the Civil War and lived among them like a feudal overlord. He preached to their congregations, served as their principal chief or as the power behind the throne, and—with other members of his family—ran trading posts that gathered in most of their cash. Near his house is a Seminole church surrounded by brush arbors, where the Indians still camp for their all-day, all-week meetings. But the Indian village of Sasakwa that grew up around his trading post has been displaced by a white man's town of the same name two miles away on the railroad.

None of the Civilized Tribes was interested in cities. They built their capitols in the woods somewhere, and the cities slowly grew up around them—after all, the white man did the same at Washington. But the Choctaw capitol now stands by itself in the beautiful mountain valley of the Kiamichi. The tribe erected it in 1884 close to the site of the earlier log council house, and named it Tuskahoma (Red Warriors). A lively village grew up around it in the old days when chiefs and lawmakers met there. But again a railroad came through and established the Tuskahoma station two miles away. Then when the Choctaws lost their tribal government, their settlement faded out. They still own the sturdy brick building, and meet there occasionally to discuss matters of interest to their people.

Also important in Choctaw history is the old church near Millerton. Many Oklahomans stop on their travels to see it. The stanch, thick-walled building is as gracefully proportioned as a New England meetinghouse. It looks as though it might stand for several more centuries. Close by are the tree-shaded buildings and velvet grounds of the old Wheelock Academy, a boarding school founded in early days by the American Board of Commissioners for Foreign Missions, later taken over by the Choctaw tribe, and now operated by the government.

These nostalgic Indian memories are a far cry from the exultant pioneer celebrations of the "west side." Those who entered the great runs knew at once that they were making history. In 1889, twenty-one-year-old James K. Hastings had taken a claim and made some improvements, and returned to his Ohio home to report. He was full of his subject. He is full of it now. He treasures every sight and sound of that April morning: the glory of the sunrise, the booming of the prairie chickens, and the clear song of the meadow larks; the new green of the timber and the misty splendor of the blooming redbud; the bunch of white-tailed deer flashing their signals as they fleeted by. He rode in almost alone, selected a good claim in a valley, and slept that night on his own land with his saddle horse grazing on the lush grass. All this he told, and of his plans and hopes for the future. His little sister listened, her eyes like saucers. She had just attended an Old Settlers' picnic. Suddenly she clapped her hands, "Oh, Goody! Goody!" "Well! What started you off?" she was asked. And she said, "Now James is going to be an Old Settler."

Even a child could sense it back in 1889. And it has all come true. Mr. Hastings has retired from his farm and lives in Stillwater, but he is active in all eighty-niners' doings. When I met him he was taking part in a program of the Payne County Historical Society.

Norman, Edmond, El Reno, Oklahoma City, Kingfisher, and Guthrie are all entitled to "Eighty-niners' Day," for each came into existence the same tumultuous afternoon. All of them do have reunions and parades. But by common consent the main celebration has been left to Guthrie.

On every April 22 this quiet little city recalls the boundless ambitions, the social gaiety, and the political turmoil of its young, brave days. It fought a twenty-year duel to the death with Oklahoma City. For the first decade the two slugged it out on equal terms; then the enemy began to gain in population and business; next it "stole" the capital; and Guthrie's spirit died. For years afterward, the two towns hated each other—the victor with boastful insolence, the loser with festering bitterness. Now an hourly bus

201

service can hardly handle the crowds of Guthrians that go to "the City" to work or shop; and Oklahoma City defers to Guthrie's historic primacy and the importance of its eighty-niners' celebration. And this last is worth seeing.

Here the pioneers register—old couples from the country, city builders mellowed by time. A long parade moves through the unchanged streets that seemed so grand in the eighteen nineties when the town sprang up full-grown on the hillside. Roundup clubs from over the state ride in matched costumes; Indians from the neighboring Iowa settlements march in their gay finery, just as they have helped in every celebration since the city's first birthday; historical floats, covered wagons, uniformed bands from many schools—all are there. Thousands of visitors jam the sidewalks, old-timers recalling other crowds—the throng that swarmed over the prairie the day of the Opening, the holiday-makers that packed the city at the inauguration of a territorial governor or welcomed the birth of the state. Then all repair to the Jelsma Stadium, where first the roundup clubs fill the great arena with a weaving pattern of beautiful horseflesh, and then skilled riders compete in rodeo contests.

Oklahoma City has grown beyond any one-event attraction. Visitors swarm to it at all seasons. For shopping, for business, to attend shows and lectures, to visit the state historical museum and the capitol, to see the zoo, for conventions, to attend the state fair, or just to be in "the City." Always its streets are blocked with cars and its sidewalks are thronged with shoppers. And everyone looks happy. For it is still a country town, an immense country town. All the towns of western Oklahoma are its suburbs; all the people in that half of the state are its inhabitants. Their houses may be far away, but their cars shuttle back and forth to "the City" oftener than the average Chicago dweller takes the streetcar for the Loop.

Its sky line is as irregular as the teeth of a six-year-old, and as eloquent of future growth. Those evenly-spaced ten- or twelve-story buildings are the first set, built by agriculture, meat packing, small manufactures, and wholesale and retail trade; the two or three skyscrapers, thirty or more stories high, throwing the others out of proportion, are the products of the oil era, the beginnings of the permanent set. And, as at Tulsa, in that clear, smokeless atmosphere all are clean and shining. From this center the city spreads in every direction, its growth pattern as easily read as the rings on a tree. First a circle of frame dwellings of the nineties running to seed with towers and spindled balustrades; then gracious, beautiful houses shaded by big trees; next the younger trees and newer houses of the "California" era, all windows and eaves; then street on street of new, bare lawns and sun-scorched dwellings shouting FHA; present rows of languid construction, where desperate housing needs contend with shortages of materials and labor; and on the outskirts, country estates with large houses and unfinished grounds. And through and around the city are the great oil fields—lines of derricks, burnished silver tanks, and the complicated structure of refineries. The shop windows are beautiful with everything that money can buy—and money is there to buy it. The population was 204,000 in 1940; then an unreckoned number came in to work in war plants, and stayed to develop the new industry.

Oklahoma City had no reason for growth except that its leaders willed it so. Any one of twenty towns that sprang into being that momentous April day had an equal chance to become "the City." Some of its rivals have long been ghost towns; the others are its willing tributaries. In the nineteen twenties it waged its last duel with Tulsa. This time it did not win. Now within the past years both have come to realize that they are actually partners instead of enemies.

East of "Old Oklahoma" and its eighty-niners' traditions is another group of pioneers, who celebrate September 22 as their natal day. They are the ones who waited at Guthrie and Perkins and Oklahoma City and looked across the border until they could enter the Sac and Fox, Iowa, and Shawnee-Potawatomi reservations in 1891. Perkins, although on eighty-niner ground, is one of the most active on this anniversary; every fall it holds an Old Settlers' Reunion honoring the pioneers from its trade territory across the Cimarron. The tiny village of Goodnight, on the Iowa side of the river, also takes its September 22 seriously; this is a real homecoming with former residents coming from long distances to greet old friends and talk over old times. Chandler and Tecumseh also remember that they belong to the Run of 1891. But Shawnee, the largest city in the area, has developed older loyalties.

203

Long before the Indian Territory was opened to homestead-ers, there was a Shawnee Town on the North Canadian. First came the Quakers, who established a mission and a day school for the Indians about 1872. Then the government opened a boarding school there. Next came trading houses, a blacksmith shop, and a post office. The present Indian tubercular hospital and the govern-ment agency for all the tribes in that section have grown out of this early center.

When the land was opened for settlement, a girl homesteader from Oklahoma City staked the timbered claim that became the site of the present city. The town grew slowly at first, but at state-hood it was a leading convention city and a serious contender for the capital. It had another period of rapid growth during the flush production of the Greater Seminole oil field.

Strangely enough, except for a few years about the time of statehood, it has generally stayed out of the news. It has always been an attractive city with its big trees and comfortable houses. In the early nineteen twenties it was adjudged by an educational foundation as the best city in Oklahoma in which to bring up chil-dren. (How chagrined its noisier neighbors were!) It has long been an educational center: besides its public schools there is the Oklahoma Baptist University, and just outside the town is St. Gregory's College for Young Men, a small junior college of very high rank, maintained by the Benedictine Fathers. Its Lake Shaw-nee, the source of its water supply, has the most cabins and other conveniences of any recreational area in the state. Just now the city is fighting to prevent oil drilling around the shores and under the waters of this lake.

In general the people of the Cheyenne and Arapaho country in western Oklahoma also find other developments more important than their Run of April 19, 1892. That land was never designed by nature for the 160-acre homestead. Except along the eastern mar-gin it remained for a long time a ranch country, and although the nesters eventually had their try, it has reverted again to the larger unit. But every five years the town of Cheyenne holds holiday with all the trimmings to celebrate the Run. In 1947 an estimated four thousand visitors were present—a good many people to collect in one place from that land of sun-scorched distances. Four hundred pioneers and their children signed the register, two or three of whom had actually dashed across the line at noon on the opening day to claim their quarter-sections. They came from all over the dry Southwest. At the head of the parade was Governor Tom Mabry of New Mexico, who lived in the Cheyenne-Arapaho country when it was still fairly new in 1901, and later attended the University of Oklahoma.

Other towns concentrate on Indian celebrations. Clinton and Canton sponsor important Cheyenne-Arapaho festivals where white visitors gather to watch costumed dancers from many tribes. Others hold horse-racing meets, with entries from all the southwestern country.

In the Cherokee Strip all lesser holidays lead up to the Sixteenth of September. Even the eighty-niners' celebrations pale beside the exuberant rejoicing of the 1893 pioneers at Enid, Perry, and Ponca City. Each of these Strip cities always had a county or more of prairie as its community. Take Enid, a typical center of the region, with its massed grain elevators rising in haze above the wheat waves—like a seaport. The very first anniversary of its riotous birth found the sod houses through a wide radius all deserted as the whole country came to town to celebrate. It was the same on circus day. The people might have to leave their homes at three o'clock in the morning; but when the parade started, they were standing on the square, packed as close as the eggs they brought to market. They drive faster now, but the spirit is still the same. On September 16, or band festival day, or any day, a walk around the square is an Old Settlers' Reunion.

The small towns are likely to be emptied on these special days, but sometimes they also hold celebrations. A community I know, but dare not name, was planning to do the thing right. It seemed a good idea to reconstruct—for exhibition purposes, only—one of the thriving saloons of territorial days. But the chairman in charge of the celebration found out that the "saloonkeeper" planned a little bootlegging on the side. He went to a woman active in religious circles. "We want some o' your church women to help us," he said. "We're goin' to have a saloon, and we want you all to dress like Carry Nation and smash it up."

All Oklahoma remembers Carry Nation. With a preacher

husband, who soon disappeared from public view, she lived on a claim near Seiling before she moved to Kansas and began her saloon-smashing activities. Then shortly before statehood she returned to Oklahoma and settled at Guthrie, where she edited a militant newspaper and sallied forth to lecture against Rum, Tobacco, Sin, and the Republican party. I heard her speak once in my own childhood; and I have a vivid recollection of the dumpy little woman with the brisk manner and the keen wit.

The church women thought it would be fun to take the part of Carry Nation. They dressed up in long skirts and old-fashioned bonnets, armed themselves with hatchets, and marched to the "saloon." The leader began a long harangue in Carry's style as they started to smash bottles. The crowd watched delightedly. A few knew what was happening, but to the women the whole setting was stage property. When the "saloonkeeper" tried to save his stock, they thought he was a good actor and they redoubled their efforts. He was more helpless than the real Carry's victims had been in prohibition Kansas. The law was against him, and so was public sentiment, for "Carry" was the doctor's wife and one of the most loved women in the community. When they got through, his place looked like a preview of the atomic bomb. It was several days before they discovered that their "raid" had been real. Then they were embarrassed but not too sorry, and the community had something to laugh about for years.

Woodward is the one Strip city that does not take September 16 seriously. It came into being on that historic day as riotously as Enid or Perry, with five thousand people fanning out over the townsite; but in a country too dry for quarter-section farming, it became more appropriately the capital of the ranching counties of the northwest. The annual meeting of the Cattlemen's Association was held on May 26 in 1947, less than seven weeks after the laughing, lusty city had been leveled to earth by the tornado. The usual two days' session was squeezed into one because of housing and restaurant shortages, but the schedule was not broken. And a three-day racing meet was held on July 3–5. The only concession to the tornado was the use of half the proceeds to replace instruments and music lost when the school-band building was torn to shreds. In August the rodeo went on as usual. More than one hundred new graves are in the cemetery, and the whole city has been fighting back to life, but its heart beats to the old rhythm.

A hardy breed of people inhabits northwestern Oklahoma. The weaklings moved out. But the ones who stayed stick like the burrs in a bronc's tail. Probably there is a higher percentage of old-timers in this section than anywhere else in the state. It includes the northwestern corner and the Panhandle—the region of former "dust bowl" notoriety and present "gold bowl" wealth in wheat and cattle. It is so much a unit economically that Oklahomans have formed the habit of calling the whole area the Panhandle. Well, that suits the real Panhandle dwellers all right. They feel fully competent to annex the rest of the state.

The Panhandle proper is 170 miles long and 35 miles wide, and it has a population of 22,000. The towns are few and far between; the county seats, Beaver, Guymon, and Boise City, each has from one to two thousand people. The United States agricultural statistics of the mid-decade showed its per capita farm income as the largest in the nation, and it has gone up since then.

Its wheat harvest is a nerve-wracking strain, with every home-owned combine at work and custom machines pulling in from farther south. One traveler there in the summer of 1948 counted more than one hundred combines moving along on less than fifty miles of highway. Weeks before, the one east-west railroad begins filling every spur and siding with empty cars; then when the trucks start dumping into the elevators, the elevator men begin to demand more cars, and there is a two-way shuttle of empties going in and long, loaded trains pulling out. But in spite of all preparations, the system clogs and the elevators fill up and the trucks wait and then the wheat begins pouring on the ground. In 1947, with the greatest harvest of all, seven and one-half million bushels at one time were piled in the fields according to the estimate of the three county agents. It is almost as hard to find a place to stack the farmers' income. In Boise City of the western county (population of the county, 3,654) the bank's June 30 statement showed: capital, $25,000; surplus, $25,000; undivided profits, $47,943; loans, $518,-800; and deposits, $2,555,709. Remember this was before harvest.

Socially the Panhandle is more closely bound to the neighboring Texas Panhandle and the Plains counties of southwestern Kansas than to the rest of Oklahoma. It has always resented the map makers' device of detaching the area and placing it in a vacant space below the Red River; and it has about won its fight to change the system so far as official state publications are concerned. This wastes a great deal of paper or reduces the scale of the whole map, but the people feel the cause is a righteous one. For the Panhandle is intensely self-conscious. And no pioneers are more active in preserving their history. They can remember when they lived in a No Man's Land of open range and cattle trails, sod-house villages, and starveling nesters.

Their greatest celebration is held at Guymon on May 2 to commemorate the passage of the Organic Act of 1890, which gave them their first organized government. The long parade reviews their past: chuck wagons, stagecoaches, covered wagons, and historical floats. Hundreds of individual riders participate, and school bands from the neighboring High Plains towns of the three states. Sometimes there is barbecued buffalo, and always there is a rodeo. In 1947 the celebration was dedicated to the memory of Boss Neff, old-time trail driver, cowhand, and ranchman of near-by Hooker, who had died the preceding March.

Other celebrations with a Texas flavor are held in old Greer County, which now forms three and one-half counties in the southwest. Mangum is the center of these activities. The former cowhands hold a chuck wagon reunion, where they eat in the old way squatted on the ground with their plates and coffee. Early-day nesters and cowmen swap yarns in the town square, forgetting the old battle over open range and herd law. And there is the inevitable parade and rodeo. Best of all is the Old Time Fiddlers' Contest. This gay art has never died out in Oklahoma. When one of these fiddlers saws out the familiar folk tunes, head nodding, body swinging, foot tapping, it is indeed a lame toe that can hold still. No wonder square dancing and old-fashioned couple dancing have become a craze with city groups. Talk about their "revival"! They never declined in places like old Greer County.

Mangum has forgotten an older history as dim as the marks of a Spanish trail that once passed up the east bank of the North Fork. As late as 1830 caravans of pack burros and creaking ox-drawn wooden-wheeled *carretas* inched along this prairie thoroughfare that connected Nacogdoches in East Texas with Santa Fé; and hardy traders came out to traffic with the wild Indians of the Southwest. Just below the Austin Dam and about twelve miles east of Mangum the route crossed the place where Devil's Canyon opens into the river; and here was a Spanish village so remote in time that even the Indians have forgotten it. Apparently it represents that perennial search for gold in the Wichita Mountains. The abandoned site was afterwards occupied for many years by a Wichita Indian village, but even that was moved away in the eighteen thirties. The canyon extends back into the granite hills to the northeast—a wide, beautiful valley with spring-fed streams and lofty trees and grassy meadows enclosed by craggy walls three hundred to five hundred feet high. It is almost inaccessible now, for the Spanish Road has gone to join the Spanish village in the mists of history, and only rarely does some adventurous traveler explore its solitudes.

But very much alive on this side of the North Fork are the traditions of the Kiowa-Comanche and Wichita reservations. The Indian center of the region is Anadarko, a busy little county seat laid out when the country was opened to white settlement in the land lottery of 1901. Here is the Agency, first established in the vicinity in 1859. Across the Washita is the Riverside boarding school opened by the government in 1872; and farther up the river is St. Patrick's Mission school founded in early days by the Roman Catholics. This is the setting for the Indian Fair; and white visitors have learned to make provision beforehand for this celebration, for every room in Anadarko is reserved weeks in advance.

On the north edge of Lawton is another Indian school, where little Plains redskins have been instructed ever since 1871 in the ways of agriculture and peace. Just beyond is Fort Sill with its old stone buildings erected in Indian fighting days, and its newer stucco structures familiar to soldiers of both world wars. The post library has an important collection of Southwestern books and manuscript material built up by Master Sergeant Morris Swett, who has become a specialist in the history of the region. These records and the memories of living Indians furnished the principal sources when Captain (now Colonel) W. S. Nye wrote *Carbine and Lance,* published by the University of Oklahoma Press in 1937.

209

In a style as exciting as any "Western" fiction, it tells the story of the Indian wars and of Fort Sill. And the visitor still feels that "The stone walls of the Old Post stand as an everlasting monument to the cunning of the red dwellers of the prairie, to their perversity and valor, and to the memory of those blue-clad troopers who wrote the final chapter of their primitive life."

These are the memories on the edge of Lawton; but Lawton itself cherishes August 6, 1901, as the day of its founding. There was no Run to stake homesteads, but thousands of people came and camped about their covered wagons to test their luck in the "drawing." Then on August 6 the government began the auction sale of lots in the townsite, and a tented city sprang up immediately on the sun-scorched prairie. This is the day that Lawton celebrates each year with its pioneers' reunion.

But strangely enough Lawton sponsors Oklahoma's most notable observance in a field far removed from Indian or frontier history. It could have been set in any state, but it belongs to Oklahoma; and the Wichita Mountains provide a perfect backdrop. It is the annual Easter pageant.

Can it be possible that this great miracle play is only twenty-three years old? An estimated two hundred thousand people from all parts of the United States now come to watch and worship on the hillside while the radio sends out its message to the world. The idea for the pageant originated with the Reverend Anthony Mark Wallock, Austrian-born, Chicago-educated, who came to Lawton to serve as pastor of the little Congregational church; and it grew out of his feeling that this bare, rugged land was like the sacred hills of Palestine. He began in 1926 by holding his Easter morning service in the mountains. Something of his own spirit must have moved the worshipers, for in a few years these services had grown into a community pageant and its fame had spread through Oklahoma. Then came WPA and Lawton's chance to build a fitting setting. Strange documents have gone into the WPA files, but nothing stranger than the forms and specifications for a project marked "Holy City." The planning was superb: the walls and gateway of the ancient city, the sinister Judgment Hall of Pilate, the Garden, the Tomb—all of natural rock merging into the background, as ageless as the granite hills.

210

They Drive to Town

On the night before Easter many thousand cars are parked on surrounding slopes. The people range themselves about a huge natural amphitheater, some in quiet talk, some sleeping a little in their blankets. At midnight two trumpeters on a tower sound a call to worship, and a service of organ and song is carried by an amplifier through the open night. Then a floodlight picks out the old city with throngs of people moving about its cobbled streets. For the rest of the night the story unfolds—the shepherds with their flocks on the hillside, the worried couple seeking quarters in the crowded town, the Wise Men coming over the horizon following the star—all the vital scenes to the tragic last week with the three crosses on a barren height. Just as the dawn begins to light the east, the women walk through the empty streets to the tomb, and the pageant ends in the brightness of an Oklahoma morning.

Until his death at Christmas time in 1948, Mr. Wallock wrote a new pageant every year, adapting his message to the troubled world situation. It has had as many at 65 scenes, 75 speaking parts, and a cast of more than 2,500 persons from many towns of southwestern Oklahoma. All Lawton residents, regardless of creed, work on its production, whether directing, making properties, or acting in the cast. About two thousand costumes and five thousand properties have been accumulated—all made by volunteer labor. Here at last under an Old World leader, restless Oklahoma has created a tradition that seems to be permanent. Can it do the same with other forms of art?

XVIII

The Fine Arts in Oklahoma

WHEN IT COMES TO MUSIC, Oklahomans are like their mockingbirds—more interested in getting it out of their system than in a finished performance. (Remember how a mockingbird sings for fun, one tune after another, raucous squawk or limpid trill, not caring?) In early days they sang everywhere they met, and they played every instrument that came to hand. The quality varied from the lively melody of the rural genius who rigged up a wire to hold a harmonica to his lips leaving his hands free for the accompanying chords on the reed organ, to the great oratorios sung by a cultured group that gathered from the tents and shacks of new Oklahoma "City." And in spite of the passing years the spirit is still the same.

In the rural areas the people hold singing conventions, meeting turn about in the churches of a county, listening to quartets and duets from the different delegations and joining in group singing that practically loosens the rafters. Their songs are unknown to musicians, but they carry plenty of rhythm, they drip with religious sentiment, and they virtually sing themselves. Allied to this, but consciously humorous, is the SPEBSQSA (Society for the Preservation and Encouragement of Barber Shop Quartet Singing in America) founded in Tulsa a few years ago by O. C. Cash. The organization has spread to other states and foreign countries with 315 chapters and 23,000 members, and its national headquarters are now at Detroit; but it held its 1948 convention in Oklahoma City. Meanwhile the women met in Tulsa recently with quartets from as far away as Chicago and Florida and formed a

212

national organization of Sweet Adelines. This is not very classical, but what could be better fun?

The interest taken in the school bands is almost as spontaneous. True, as a rule they do have paid instructors, but often big football huskies enjoy band practice better than athletics. In my home town the children spend all their spare time in the band room working hard at their instruments. Making a boy practice is about as hard as compelling him to eat cake. These young people like to sing, too. In 1947 the girls' quartet from Oklahoma won first place in the American Legion Auxiliary contest at the New York national convention. They came from Clinton; a school board member was their coach, one of their mothers was their accompanist, and their home town (population, 6,736) raised $1,250 to send them to the meet.

The cities have more formal musical education in the schools. The colleges also have good music departments. All the larger cities have choral societies capable of fine musical performances. From this more serious musical background a number of Oklahomans have gone out to win a place in the larger world. One thinks first of Roy Harris, born near Chandler of parents who came in one of the land rushes. His career has taken him far afield, but—to quote a Chicago critic—there is still "something of the crudeness and strength of pioneer America" in his compositions, "as completely outside European experience as the prairie morning itself." He drew consciously on this heritage when he composed "Cimarron" for Enid's Tri-State Band Festival. But there is little chance for a musician to make a living in Oklahoma except by teaching. Again like the mockingbird, he may make all the melody he wants, but he is seldom paid for his tune.

The Oklahoma Symphony Orchestra is the most notable musical organization in Oklahoma. For four years it has been classed as one of the twenty major symphony orchestras in the United States. Young Houston-born Victor Alessandro has been its conductor since the beginning. He knows how to make good music popular, for although he has become a significant national figure, he has never got away from his understanding of the Southwest.

The orchestra has its headquarters in Oklahoma City, but is supported by a statewide Symphony Society. It was started in 1938 as a WPA project sponsored by the University and helped along by the Oklahoma City Chamber of Commerce; and it was designed to take care of unemployed musicians, and to grow into a permanent institution. When the WPA financial support was withdrawn, it staggered dangerously for a time. Now it seems to be firmly established. It is completely out of debt, but its budget is relatively small; it collected about $125,000 in membership fees and contributions to finance the 1947-48 season. Its musicians make their living at outside jobs—in a bank, a lumber yard, a real-estate office, a cleaning establishment—if not in teaching at one of the near-by colleges. Their serious work in the orchestra thus takes the status of a hobby.

Oklahomans also like to act. From earliest times they presented plays in churches and country schoolhouses; later in some of the cities they joined the Little Theatre movement. Tulsa's Little Theatre has had the longest continuous history. Established in 1922, it worked up from old storeroom, beer parlor, even a tent, to its own building with elaborate sets, a professional director, and standing-room-only crowds. It was the first Little Theatre in the nation to recognize the genius of Lynn Riggs, by presenting his *Big Lake*—a play about Indian Territory days—in 1928. The youthful author would come over from Claremore and drop in at rehearsals; it was then that news came to him of the Guggenheim Fellowship that sent him to France to write *Green Grow the Lilacs*. From that time on he was claimed by New York, the world, and Hollywood. For Oklahoma is not theater conscious; few of its people ever see a good play.

Moving-picture and radio stars also grow up in Oklahoma and find their living elsewhere. Will Rogers and Tom Mix started out by way of the Wild West show; Gene Autry sang his way to cowboy fame a little later. Lon Chaney lived in early-day Guthrie and then worked as a photographer in still newer Lawton before he found his career in Hollywood. Texas-born Joan Crawford spent her childhood in Lawton, where her stepfather ran a vaudeville theater. Once when she tried to dance on the rain-drenched grass, she cut her foot so badly on a broken bottle that she fainted, and young Don Blanding picked her up and carried her home. The ardent, gifted child must have made an impression on the budding

214

poet, for it was about her that he wrote "The Little Girl Who Lived across the Street."

Van Heflin entered the movies in the more modern way by serious study at the University of Oklahoma. Jennifer Jones went to school in Oklahoma City and Tulsa, then East to a dramatic school. For a time she worked at Tulsa's radio station KOME. Cathy O'Donnell, sweetheart of handless Harold Russell in greatly-Oscared *The Best Years of Our Lives,* grew up in Oklahoma City. Recent magazine articles have described her as an awkward little waif from the wild spaces coached into a civilized personality by Hollywood; but she herself gives the credit to excellent public-school teachers and Professor Wayne Campbell of Oklahoma City University.

At the present time Governor Turner is carrying on a one-man campaign to bring the moving-picture industry to Oklahoma. His talking points are the sunny climate, the clear atmosphere, and the diversity of physical setting. Certainly it would be a change from the system that has driven the state's talent to other centers.

There is dancing, for example. Lovely Yvonne Chouteau of the famous French-Osage family grew up in Oklahoma City, studied dancing as soon as she could walk, and appeared on local programs from babyhood on. When she signed with the Ballet Russe de Monte Carlo in 1943, she became the youngest dancer in professional ballet. She still calls Oklahoma City "home." Maria Tallchief, half-Indian, half-Irish, all-Oklahoman, reached the Ballet Russe by way of a Los Angeles dancing school; she is now a premier danseuse of that famous group. Ballet is completely foreign to Oklahoma culture, entirely unrelated—or is it?—to the hilarious square dance of the early settlers or the serious ceremonial dances of the Indians.

One also wonders about the prospects of an indigenous painting in Oklahoma. A discriminating interpretation by an outsider is found in a survey made in 1943 by Lura Beam of the American Association of University Women.[1] She found a landscape suggesting "the illimitable"—"wild, harsh, and strident. . . . Speaking very plainly of a long past," but still untamed, "as if Nature had

[1] Lura Beam, *Oklahoma: An Impression of Her Arts,* circulated in mimeographed form by the American Association of University Women.

not really given in to man." The feelings evoked by this background made "freedom, storm, and fighting seem inevitable." The sociological factors—Indian heritage, rural life, oil, and migration —brought about "unsettled and exciting conditions," and she found in the people "an inherent inability to stay still" and a "compulsion for making new forms in religion and politics." All this, she concluded, should some time "produce an art on the magnificent scale." It has not done so yet.

The elements were there from the beginning. The Indians had a strong art consciousness; their pottery, tepees, clothing, baskets, and even their bodies were ornamented with symbolic and highly stylized designs, and their pictographs throbbed with basic rhythms. Several painters came to the territory during the nineteenth century—George Catlin, John Mix Stanley, Frederic Remington, and Elbridge Ayer Burbank—to record the life of the Indian villages and army posts, just as one would now do with a high-grade camera. Then the settlers came, more concerned with making a society than interpreting it. It was not until about the time of statehood that art in the accepted sense of the word began to develop.

The first resident white painter doing original work was Nellie Shepherd. She grew up in early-day Oklahoma City, studied abroad, and returned in 1910 to paint the rolling prairies and settlers' cabins of her own Oklahoma landscape. Her girlhood friend, Martha Avey, also studied abroad; then came back to become in 1906 the first art supervisor in the city's public schools; and later organized the Art Department of Oklahoma City University. Tulsa had its first art supervisor in 1907. Other cities followed slowly.

Meanwhile Father Gregory Gerrer was building up the first art collection in the state. When this young Alsatian came to Guthrie in 1891, he became interested in the Sacred Heart Mission and Abbey established fifteen years before by the Benedictine Fathers on the Shawnee-Potawatomi reservation. He was ordained to the priesthood in England, studied art in France and Italy, and painted the official portrait of Pope Pius X to hang in the Vatican; then back at Sacred Heart shortly after statehood, he began to bring strangely beautiful pictures to the remote establishment in the blackjacks along the South Canadian. In 1915 the Benedictine

Fathers moved to Shawnee and opened St. Gregory's College, and
Father Gerrer became the curator of its museum and art gallery.
He died in 1946, but his collection lives on. Here are examples
of ancient and Oriental art; canvases by Raphael, Murillo, and
Guido Reni; Spinello Aretino's "Madonna and Child" and Guilio
Romano's "Adoration of the Magi"; and seventy-five paintings—
Indian portraits and Oklahoma landscapes—by the artist-priest
himself.

An even more surprising collection was accumulated in a
little town on the Arkansas. Laura Rutherford, daughter of a homesteader near Marshall, became a rural school teacher and married
Ike Clubb, but continued her studies. The couple established a
ranch near Kaw City. Then they struck oil. They built a three-story,
brick hotel in town and moved there to live. Mrs. Clubb had always
loved pictures. Now she could enjoy them to her heart's content.
She bought carefully; and she bought only what she liked—portraits, landscapes, farm scenes, children, and Biblical subjects—
old masters, some more recent canvases, but no modern vagaries.
There were Titian's "Self Portrait," a Botticelli, a Murillo, Sir
Joshua Reynolds' "Infant Samuel" and "Mary Horneck," Corot's
"Avenue of Trees," two Gainsboroughs, Sir Peter Lely's "Mrs. Hudson," probably the largest collection extant of Thomas Moran, one
of Gilbert Stuart's portraits of Washington, a Benjamin West,
several landscapes by Inness, a Daubigny, a number of paintings
by Henry Balink, and many others—almost two hundred in all.

She hung them around the lobby so close they almost touched,
one above another up to the high ceiling; then she ranged them
along both sides of a dark, narrow hall to the dining room; next
she paneled the walls of this busy room; then upstairs along every
hallway and overflowing into the rooms, to the top floor. Here and
there on the walls between them were mounted cattle horns,
souvenirs of Ike Clubb's cowboy past.

Everyone was welcome to come and look. And they did come
to the remote little town from many states. Some were a little
supercilious about the setting; others saw here a love of beauty
so elemental that it formed the fabric of everyday life. Mrs. Clubb
received all comers with unaffected friendliness, and her lively
comments ranged from art to pioneering. But when she realized

that old age would soon overtake her, she cast about for the best way to continue her gift to the public. In 1947 she turned over the collection to the Philbrook Art Center in Tulsa.

While these collections were developing art appreciation, an indigenous art was being fostered by the colleges. It began at the University of Oklahoma, but the inspiration had to come from abroad. The first art courses were offered in 1910. First came Samuel Holmberg of Sweden, who stayed one year; then Peruvian-born Patricio Gimeno, who soon shifted to teaching Spanish. Oscar Brousse Jacobson took over in 1915. Born in Sweden, educated in Lindsborg, Kansas, then Yale, Paris, and the world, he immediately made the young university conscious of a vigorous personality and an art of broad strokes, clear, bright colors, and Homeric simplicity suited to the elemental strength of the setting. He imported artists of like mind, each a sturdy individualist expressing himself in his own way with seriousness and integrity.

The year after Jacobson came, he took the lead in forming the Association of Oklahoma Artists. The society now has over one hundred members, all active artists, and for the past thirty years it has held an annual exhibit of Oklahoma work. In 1948 there were 214 entries, from which a one-man jury selected 48 oils, 38 watercolors, 27 graphics, and 14 pieces of sculpture to form the show. Good exhibits, but almost never a sale. Oklahoma artists must find their market outside the state.

Four years ago Jacobson resigned as director of the School of Art. But he still teaches art history, directs the museum, and arranges exhibits. His artistic creed in its optimism, its nearness to the earth, its forthright character is typically Oklahoman. Returning from a recent summer of painting in the West, he said: "I found the pine needles and the sagebrush sweet and fragrant, the mesas and the sky secure in their places. I have come back convinced that life can be endured without escape into abstractions." He spends much time working on some notes for publication. He should tell an interesting story. He saw the artistic landscape change from a desert to a cultivated field. It just might blossom as the rose. But that is still in the future.

Doel Reed is doing a somewhat different thing for the Agricultural and Mechanical College. Born in Indiana, he studied in

Cincinnati, France, and Old Mexico; he came to the college to teach in 1924, and became head of its Art Department in 1939. He, too, is at home in Oklahoma, steeped in its history and folklore, responsive to its wild sweep of earth and sky. His landscapes show a primeval scene, remote but all alive with its own color and movement; his people are strong, simple, and unafraid.

Although he paints in oils, his specialty is etching. After careful research he has revived the difficult, tricky technique of the aquatint, neglected since the time of Goya. He has received many honors. Every year since 1929 he has exhibited with the Society of American Etchers; always since 1932 his aquatints have been chosen in the one hundred etchings of the year. When the Associated American Artists held its first national competition in 1946, his aquatint was selected for publication as one of ten out of 1,200 entries, and again in 1947 he repeated the performance. He has won the Charles M. Lea Prize of the Print Club at Philadelphia, the most coveted award for etchings in the United States. He has been invited to exhibit in the art centers of Europe and Latin America. But he is scarcely known in Oklahoma outside his Stillwater circle.

Several of his students, trained in his aquatint courses, have won important honors. Young J. Jay McVicker, now an assistant professor in the Art Department, received all his training at A. and M., made his first print in 1940, and then spent three years in naval service during the war; but he has won a number of awards in national and regional competitions, has exhibited in shows throughout the country, and is classed in the Britannica Book of the Year as "outstanding among American etchers." Through such influences, little Stillwater is becoming an art center, with no less than eleven studios and a genuine community interest. When a recent number of *La Revue Moderne,* a magazine of art criticism published in Paris, discussed the work of six Americans with reproductions of their paintings, two were Stillwater artists with water colors of Oklahoma landscapes: J. Jay McVicker and Dwight E. Stevens, who teaches architecture at the college and paints in his spare time.

A third Oklahoma art movement is the development of the Indian painters. In the strict sense, this did not originate in Oklahoma; for Indians around Santa Fé had begun as early as World War I to paint pictures and to sell to tourists. But to most of the world outside, their work was merely an ethnological curiosity. It was Oklahoma that accepted its importance as an art movement —just as it had appropriated the history of the Choctaws or the genius of Sequoyah. The movement was launched through the insight of Mrs. Susie C. Peters of the government school in Anadarko. In spite of Washington blueprints for making young Indians into white children, she encouraged her pupils to paint after the tribal manner, and some of them did so well that she wrote to Professor Jacobson about them. The result was that five young Kiowas came to study art at the University under a financial grant from Lew Wentz. Jacobson arranged special classes for them, and placed Edith Mahier of his department in charge.

The Indians ranged in age from sixteen to twenty-four years. Spencer Asah was a full blood, the son of a medicine man, steeped in tribal legends. Jack Ho-ke-ah, also a full blood, was an orphan reared by his grandmother and sent to school at St. Patrick's Mission. Steve Mopope was three-fourths Kiowa, the grandson of a Mexican captive; all of his family could draw, and his mother was a fine bead worker. James Auchiah, a full blood, was the grandson of Satanta, Kiowa orator and war chief, famed in Oklahoma story. (It was Satanta who said, "When I roam the prairies I feel free and happy, but when I settle down I grow pale and die," and who killed himself when shut up in a Texas penitentiary for a raid on a wagon train.) Monroe Tsa-to-ke, son of Hunting Horse, had one grandmother who was a white captive; he had drawn pictures all his life, but had his first formal instruction from Mrs. Peters. He was the most gifted of the five young artists, and it was a great grief to his friends, both Indian and white, when he succumbed to tuberculosis in 1937.

Here was something new in art. These young men painted spontaneously, joyfully, with deep religious instinct and a feeling for the beauty in nature and the soul of man. They used flat water color, applied thickly with a beautiful jewel-like texture. Their pictures had no depth, but they were so alive they almost seemed to sing. Miss Mahier helped them to perfect their art without changing it. In 1930 Jacobson edited some exquisite reproductions of their paintings and had them printed in France in portfolio form; and their original work was exhibited in a number of European countries. They were employed to paint murals in the University auditorium and in the Historical Building in Oklahoma City. Father Gerrer purchased some of their paintings for St. Gregory's collection, and their work adorns the chapel at St. Patrick's mission. The Indian Office, with its new emphasis on native expression, became their active sponsor; and they were commissioned to paint murals in the Federal Building at Anadarko and the Department of the Interior Building at Washington.

Their successors found the going easier. And some of them have gone farther. Acee Blue Eagle, part Pawnee, part Creek-and-white (of the tribally prominent McIntosh family), attended Haskell and Chilocco Indian schools, Bacone College, and the University of Oklahoma. His work shows the same singing rhythms of the earlier painters, but a greater development. He has won many honors in both Indian and general exhibitions; once he lectured at Oxford University; and his chaste mural, "The Buffalo Hunt," adorned the library of the ill-fated battleship *Oklahoma*. For a time he headed the Art Department at Bacone, but he has recently opened a studio in New York.

Woodrow Crumbo, half-white, half-Potawatomi, grew up in Shawnee and graduated as valedictorian of his class in the Shawnee High School. Then he received a government scholarship to Haskell Institute, and later studied at the University of Oklahoma. He made a serious study of tribal dances, and took his dance troupe on a government-sponsored tour to Indian reservations throughout the country, teaching classes in Indian art to each tribe he visited. Then he was employed to paint murals in the Interior Building. He also taught at Bacone, where he created an unusual stained-glass rose window of Indian inspiration above the chapel altar. He paints wild animals with loving interpretation and Indian dancers that are poems of movement and yet meticulously correct in costume and action.

Archie Blackowl is a full-blood Cheyenne, born in 1911, who as a boy attended the government schools at Concho and Seger. He began painting much later at home, first as a pastime, then with serious purpose. He received advice and encouragement from

Woodrow Crumbo and Professor Jacobson, and from 1938 to 1941 he studied and painted at the Fort Sill school under a government scholarship. Then he went to teach at Riverside. In 1944 he won third prize in an all-state exhibition—competing with Indian and white artists—at Philbrook; then he took first prize among Plains Indian artists of the United States in Philbrook's first all-Indian show, and the next year he served on the three-man jury. He is a real Indian in his reactions. Recently Jacobson was preparing an article about him for the *Daily Oklahoman* and wrote him for some biographical details. Instead of writing, he came, saying, "I'd rather drive two hundred miles than write a letter."

Walter Richard West, also a Cheyenne, was born at Darlington in 1913. He graduated from Bacone, and then from the University of Oklahoma, receiving the degree of Bachelor of Fine Arts in 1941. He served four years in the navy, then came back to paint. Now he is head of the Art Department at Bacone. His lively "Cheyenne Children's Games"—little redskins swarming all over a setting of tepees and gyp hills—won first place in the Plains division at the Philbrook show in 1947.

Allan C. Houser is a descendant of the fighting Apaches who kept most of the United States Army busy in Arizona and New Mexico until the last holdout band with the chief and the famous Geronimo with sixteen warriors, fourteen women, and six children surrendered in 1886, and the whole group of 514 was held as prisoners of war in Florida, in Alabama, and finally at Fort Sill. In 1913 they were freed and settled in New Mexico, but 78 chose to remain in Oklahoma, and here near Apache Allan Houser was born in 1916. A spell of sickness during his high school days started him to drawing. Recently he completed a statue for the campus of Haskell as a memorial to its students killed in World War II. In 1948 he received a Guggenheim Fellowship to continue his work in sculpture and painting.

Younger Indian artists are springing up everywhere in Oklahoma. How do they manage to live in a state where there are, strictly speaking, no professional artists, but only school teachers, museum directors, Catholic priests, and others who paint? Well, for one thing, an Indian is less concerned about making a living than a white man. Then the government commissions of the friendly nineteen thirties gave a financial boost, substituting for the support white artists find in college teaching. When the war came, like their white brethren the Indians used their skills in defense plants or the armed services. Now they are finding opportunity at Tulsa through Philbrook and the Gilcrease Foundation.

The Gilcrease Foundation owns exquisite fabrics from the ancient Ancon site in Peru; pre-Columbian figurines, ornaments, and pottery from Mexico and the Southwest; tribal records of the Sioux painted on buffalo skins. Its art galleries contain pictures that the Smithsonian would be proud to own: by William De la Montagne Carey, who painted the Plains Indians and the fur trade; by Alfred Jacob Miller, who traveled through the Rocky Mountains sketching aboriginal Indian life in the eighteen thirties; by Charles Bird King, who painted portraits of the tribesmen visiting the Great Father in Washington; and by George Catlin, John Mix Stanley, E. A. Burbank, and Frederic Remington. There are Western scenes by Wimar, Blakelock, Russell, and Moran; the work of the present Taos group; and paintings by the greatest of contemporary Mexican artists. And growing out of this setting are the galleries devoted to modern Indian art. Here is not only a market, but soul-satisfying recognition.

The Philbrook Art Center was first opened to the public in 1939. It grew out of one of the first art-appreciation clubs in Oklahoma. In 1908 a few women, culture-bent, organized the Ruskin Club. From it branched the Tulsa Art Association, and then the Southwestern Art Association, with sustaining memberships; and Waite Phillips' dramatic gift did the rest. It is a beautiful place—an Italian palace set in twenty-one acres of landscaped grounds—with completely adequate facilities in galleries, library, lecture room, studios, and period rooms. The director is Bernard Frazier, a sculptor in his own right, who grew up on a Kansas farm and thrilled to the tales of a buffalo-hunting grandfather. In 1948 he was awarded the first prize of the Thirteenth Ceramic National at the Syracuse Museum for two animal figures—a bison and an untamed horse—in native clay. He has worked out a schedule for nine exhibits a year in each of the five galleries—a total of forty-five exhibits. In 1947, 43,520 persons came to view them.

The Indian wing with its sensitive murals by Woodrow Crumbo and Archie Blackowl, houses one of the important permanent collections of the center. It contains pottery, basketry, costumes, jewelry, beadwork, metal work—not curios, but true art objects showing Indian craft at its best. And a collection of fine Indian paintings is being accumulated through the purchase awards of the annual Indian exhibition.

The first of these Indian shows was held in the summer of 1946. The exhibition is open to all Indians on the North American continent, and also to the Eskimos; but entries must carry out the native art traditions. It is a task to spread the word around to remote Oklahoma farm, Navajo hogan, or Alaska igloo, but a good many Indians hear about the show and enter their pictures. Ten purchase prizes totaling $1,250 are awarded. The first year the "Best Painting in the Show" award went to Fred Kabotie, a Hopi of Arizona; the next time the winner was Oscar Howe, a Sioux of South Dakota; and in 1948 the prize was won by Allan Houser. The exhibit attracts much attention in Tulsa; then it goes on a tour of art museums over the country, where it seems to be creating strong interest. The Philbrook management believes this show will benefit not only Indian art but general American art. In 1943 Lura Beam predicted that the white man would absorb from the Indian "nearness to nature, a sense of the eternal, respect for ancestors, a style of life beyond fashions." Certainly these timeless qualities are strongly felt by the visitor to the exhibit.

Philbrook co-operates closely with the Art Department of the University of Tulsa. The latter is headed by Alexandre Hogue, who grew up in Texas and virtually taught himself. With lines as clear-cut as a rattlesnake's coils, he began painting what he knew—the metallic sky, the drifting soil, the dead farmsteads of the "dust bowl," or the gullied wastes of sheet erosion. His pictures became powerful, moving documents, not only for what they showed, but for the meaning behind it—the horror of a fair earth raped by violence and flung aside in scorn. He came into public notice when *Life* magazine reproduced some of his paintings in 1937. The next year his "Drought Survivors" was the only picture purchased from the International Exhibition in Paris to be hung in the Louvre thirty years after his death, as is the custom. He has shown in New York, London, Venice, and the twenty-one capitals of the New

World, and in Scotland, Sweden, and Germany. Texas recognized his abilities and gave him college positions. Now he has come to Tulsa. If he can resist the gracious living of that suave city, he should have a bracing message for Oklahoma.

Oklahoma City also has an art center. It really belongs to the state, and was started in 1936 as a WPA project sponsored by civic organizations. Now it is precariously supported by memberships; no doubt it could use some of the solid financial backing Philbrook received through the generosity of Waite Phillips. It is located in the new, modern classic Municipal Auditorium, also built with WPA help. The director is Nan Sheets, wife of an Oklahoma City physician, who has studied at art colonies at home and abroad, and paints with a real feeling for the Oklahoma landscape.

This Oklahoma Art Center was the first in the state to keep continuous exhibitions before the public. The Association of Oklahoma Artists holds its annual exhibit here. For the past six years there has been a competitive exhibit from the public schools sponsored by the American Association of University Women. Characterized by Miss Beam as "very near the beginning," the quality of these paintings has improved steadily. Miss Ida Hoover, art director of the East Central State College at Ada, has been the leader in this unheralded task of helping art grow up from the grass roots.

The Oklahoma International Salon of Photography also has an annual show at the Art Center, which attracts entries from the best photographers of the Western Hemisphere. Oklahomans enjoy good photography. In 1947 the Photographic Society of America held its annual convention in Oklahoma City—the first time it had ever been held west of the Mississippi—bringing an exhibit that filled all the space in five galleries.

Here and there in Oklahoma—in hotels, restaurants, and theaters—one sees sprightly, half-humorous murals depicting the history of the state. Each of these marks a spot where an artist got a commission. Oklahomans, in fact, have their best commercial opportunity in any art connected with building. For building has been very rapid, and much of it is good by any man's standards. Thus young graduates in architecture often find a place for their services with architects in their own state.

Recently a strong new influence has come to Oklahoma architecture through the return of Bruce Goff. Growing up in a Tulsa firm, young Goff had shared the exhilarating experiences of that city's building decade. When the depression struck, he worked in Chicago, then later on the West Coast, where he shocked or fascinated people by his strange designs. Returning to the University in 1948, first as professor, now as director of the School of Architecture, he encourages his students to throw tradition overboard and start free. Nothing could please Oklahomans better than such an opportunity to create new forms. The appraisal of his work is still in the future, but the impact of his personality is already being felt in the developing taste of his state.

Before he left Tulsa, Goff drew the plans for the Boston Avenue Methodist Church. This building was a collective creation. The pastor and congregation rejected copies of European architecture; they wanted to build what young Tulsa felt. They enlisted Adah M. Robinson, public-school art supervisor. She drew a design using the Oklahoma tritoma and coreopsis as its decorative motif, the pioneering history of Methodism as its sculptured symbolism, and the spirit of the modern age as its plan. But she was not an architect. She called on twenty-two-year-old Goff, one of her former pupils. Another pupil, Robert Garrison, was employed to execute the sculpture. (Later he served as sculptor of the Riverside Church in New York.) Thus the church expresses the worship of a people—I have said this elsewhere—"not mystical or contemplative, but strong and confident, coming, through joy of achievement into harmony with the Creator."[2]

As new, as completely satisfying in their way, are the buildings of Christ the King church and school, also in Tulsa. Here it was the Roman Catholics who discarded Gothic forms to express the religious faith of the Oklahoma builders. And appropriately enough a young priest has come there—the Reverend John L. Walch, born in Oklahoma City, trained in the Chicago Art Institute—who uses painting, sculpture, stained-glass designing, and ceramics as dramatic mediums to express a powerful modern Christian message.

The Central State College at Edmond, using gifts of students and alumni for the financing, is now building a chapel as a creative

[2] In *Tulsa*, 106.

campus project. It will be a "Chapel of Song," for a hymn has been chosen as the theme for each of its windows, and the subjects stress the idea of youth and modern America. All of the art work on the windows, the designing and firing of the stained glass, is being done on the campus by students. Other students have carved the ends for the pews and panels for the pulpit, and still others are making the tiles for the floor.

Nothing could be more hopeful than such community expression. Miss Beam pointed out the danger of a cleavage between an art intelligentsia and the great untrained masses, which would develop an esoteric art and leave the rich experiences of the people unexpressed. Such a separation, she said, had occurred in other societies; but Oklahoma, just beginning its art development, could avoid it "by preceeding along universal lines."[3]

Public-school art, exhibits, and collective building—all these should help. Published art criticism should broaden the base further. The University Press published a penetrating appraisal of Berber art by Jeanne d'Ucel, wife of Professor Jacobson, and a fine study of the Navajo and Pueblo silversmiths by John Adair; but no book has ever been written about Oklahoma art. The Oklahoma City *Daily Oklahoman* and the Tulsa *World* and *Tribune* carry art news and art criticism, but one doubts that these columns are read as assiduously as the sports page. These are voices crying in an artistic wilderness. Oklahoma art cannot be said to be a general movement until a resident artist can make a living at his profession. Does an analogous condition exist in literature?

---

[3] I am quoting this visitor frequently because few outsiders have seen so deeply into the soul of the state.

XIX

Oklahomans Write, Too

IT HAS BEEN CLAIMED that Oklahoma ranks second only to New York in its literary output. Oklahomans savor this statement. Probably it is not true, but it still sounds good. The rest of the assertion gets lost somehow. It is that Oklahoma ranks forty-seventh in its reading. This is the law of supply and demand that must be bucked by Oklahoma authors. But in spite of it, they write.

The area figured largely in the reports of travelers from Coronado on. The University of Oklahoma Press has rescued a number—dust-covered government documents or forgotten manuscripts—and published them, usually in its American Exploration and Travel Series. They paint a scene as exotic as any modern explorer's adventure against the familiar shape of an Oklahoma background. Take, for example, the journal of Captain Randolph B. Marcy, edited by Grant Foreman.

Here is his entry for July 22, 1852, when he visited the Wichita and Waco villages in the present neighborhood of Rush Springs. There "in the rich fertile valley"—now a truck-gardening area nationally known for its watermelons—the Indians were cultivating "corn, pumpkins, beans, peas, and melons. . . . These people have no ploughs, or other agricultural implements, but a small hoe, with which they prepare the ground for the reception of the seed, and do all other necessary work in its cultivation; yet the prolific soil gives them bountiful returns." Their grass-thatched lodges looked from a distance like "a group of hay-stacks," but the interior arrangements were comfortable, with a raised couch covered with buffalo hides for each person. "When seated around their fires in the centre of the lodges, they have an air of domestic happiness about them which I did not expect to find."[1]

Then the settlers came, deeply stirred by their experience and eager to record it. They still are; a surprising number of the old-timers, whether literate or not, intend to write a book some day. Naturally perhaps, it was newspaper writers who took the lead. The eighty-niners wrote and published two histories of the new frontier within a year: *The First Eight Months of Oklahoma City* by "Bunky" (Irving Geffs, or possibly Irvin Jeffs), a reporter; and an *Illustrated History of Oklahoma*—"Oklahoma" meaning the little tract then open to settlers—by Marion Tuttle Rock, a society writer who later became Oklahoma City's first Carnegie librarian. In 1893 the Oklahoma Press Association, meeting at Kingfisher for its annual convention, voted unanimously to organize an Oklahoma Historical Society to preserve the current newspapers of the two territories. The collection grew, and other material was placed with the newspapers. It was precariously housed here and there until the present Historical Building flanking the capitol was erected by the state in 1930.

For a long time few people knew how to use these records. As soon as the Society was organized, the curator began sending out a thin folio called *Mistletoe Leaves,* which he followed later by *Historia*—mainly for listing his accessions. It was supplanted in 1921 by the *Chronicles of Oklahoma,* a historical magazine. Joseph B. Thoburn, who served for a number of years as secretary of the Society, was actually the state's first historian. He came first in 1889, undertook various kinds of work, and finally settled down to studying Oklahoma history and archaeology. At statehood, with the help of a collaborator he wrote as a school text the first connected history of Oklahoma. Later he carried on more extensive writing with Muriel H. Wright. He died about 1940. Miss Wright now edits the *Chronicles,* except for a recent leave of absence to prepare a handbook of Oklahoma Indians under a Rockefeller grant.

Meanwhile, out-of-state scholars like Annie Heloise Abel and

[1] Grant Foreman (ed.), *Adventure on Red River* (Norman, 1938), 123–28.

Solon J. Buck were finding the unwritten history of Oklahoma a good subject for monographs. In the middle nineteen twenties Edward Everett Dale and Grant Foreman joined them as serious writers of Oklahoma history. The trickle of monographs grew into a deluge of specialized studies by many Oklahoma authors during the next decade. These later writers have been fortunate in having a publisher at hand.

The University of Oklahoma Press ventured into the real business of publishing books in 1929. The president of the University at that time was scholarly, Texas-born-and-reared William Bennett Bizzell. He invited young Joseph A. Brandt of Tulsa, University alumnus, Rhodes scholar, and newspaper editor, to direct the plan of creating a scholarly publishing arm of the University. It was about what the government had offered the homesteaders—mostly unturned sod and blue sky—but Brandt accepted. The Press had very little money, but somehow it published outstanding books. Brandt directed the work for ten years. Then he left the state for wider publishing fields, returning once to serve briefly as president of the University. His successor is Savoie Lottinville, his former assistant, also a Tulsan, University alumnus, and Rhodes scholar. And the titles multiply.

The Press started out in the field of regional publication— hence the emphasis on Indians, oil, ranching, agriculture, and local history. But all these subjects extend beyond the boundaries of the state. The Southwest may include New Mexico, Texas, Old Mexico, and even extend to older Spain; the frontier may take in the Rocky Mountains; the American Indians may live in Labrador or the Black Hills. Then, since Oklahomans served on all battle fronts, there are books of the recent war—fighting and diplomatic aspects. Mr. Lottinville now frankly accepts all the intellectual interests of the University as the province of the Press: literature, economic theory, philosophy, political science, sea power, American and world history. If Oklahomans won't read their own books, why not publish for more general reading? And how the Texans do buy the Oklahoma books about their state! Two of them have been adjudged "Best Texas Book of the Year" by the Texas Institute of Letters.

The Press, in fact, never did confine itself strictly to regional

230

subjects. In 1927 Roy Temple House, head of the Modern Language Department, founded *Books Abroad,* an international quarterly devoted to reviews of foreign books; and the Press soon took over its publication. It is now published for a world-wide clientele and goes to all continents. It was one of the first of the Press publications to bring international notice to the University.

Five University Press books were selected in 1947 by the American occupation authorities for use in former enemy lands. Contracts have been signed for German-language editions by German and Austrian publishing houses, and translations of part of the list will probably be made into Japanese and Korean. The titles chosen are: Ferdie Deering's *USDA: Manager of American Agriculture,* a study of good aims and bureaucratic ineptitude; Faulkner's *Plowman's Folly,* advocating a simple tillage suited to machinery shortages; A. J. Hanna's *A Prince in their Midst,* showing how Napoleon's nephew, Achille Murat, became an enthusiastic American frontier citizen; Edward Dumbauld's *Thomas Jefferson, American Tourist,* of the Exploration and Travel Series, giving the reactions of the great democratic philosopher as he viewed the European and American scene; and Nelms Black's *How to Organize and Manage a Small Business,* a practical antidote to communism. Thus Oklahoma may have an influence in shaping another kind of frontier.

The Press prints its books in its own plant on the campus. Until a modern building was finally completed in 1948, every publication strained its meager facilities until it was a wonder the whole set-up of men and machines did not fly off in pieces. But the books are beautiful. The present art editor is Will Ransom, who came from New York in 1941, bringing a love of fine books and the ability to design them. Every year since 1944 a Press book has placed among the "Fifty Best Books" chosen annually for "excellence of design and manufacture" by the American Institute of Graphic Arts. Incidentally Joseph A. Brandt, who published Oklahoma's first beautiful books, was elected president of the Institute in 1947.

The University of Oklahoma Press is virtually self-supporting. This is not an ideal condition, for a university press should be able to give to the world books that deserve publication but will not become profitable sellers. Both Brandt and Lottinville have maintained that "scholarly" writers should write well enough to reach the public; otherwise, why write? But this is not the whole story; some well-written books are in fields too highly specialized for general reading. To further such studies, in 1944 the Rockefeller Foundation made a gift of $25,000, to be administered by the University of Oklahoma, to provide fellowships so that Oklahoma and Southwestern scholars and writers might prepare books on the life and culture of the region. Several grants have been made, and about a dozen books (including this one) are in progress. Two have been released: Alice's Marriott's *María: The Potter of San Ildefonso* and *America's Heartland: The Southwest* by Green Peyton of San Antonio.

These are nonfiction. The University Press has not published imaginative literature, except when it was feeling its way. And Oklahoma writers in general have been slower to develop along imaginative lines. A few have written plays. It is interesting to note in passing that Russel Crouse of the Pulitzer Prize-winning *Life with Father* team got his first newspaper experience during high-school days in Enid. But only Lynn Riggs' plays grew out of an Oklahoma setting. Poems came easier; then short stories and novels.

Indians should be poets, for they compose the rhythmic chant of the tribal dances. Even yet, as we have seen, Christian full bloods compose songs—words and melody—for their religious services. And two educated Oklahoma Indians became the state's first poets. John Rollin Ridge was born in 1827, the son of a full-blood Cherokee who went away to school and married a New England girl. In 1849, with other mixed-blood Cherokees, he joined the California gold rush—the first "Okie" invasion—and became one of the leading newspaper editors of the new settlement. All the time he wrote verses, which were collected and published posthumously by his wife. The background is classic and conventional with no Indian or frontier influence; only the feeling is real. And this feeling is revealed more in letters to his Cherokee relatives than in his conscious literary work. Alex Posey was born in the Indian Territory in 1873, the son of a white ranchman and his full-blood Creek wife. He spoke only Creek until he was twelve years old; but a few years later as a student at Bacone he was editing the school paper and writing poetry. Then he went into the newspaper business in Eufaula and Muskogee, where he became a leader in the "booster" element, demanding "progress" and the end of the Indian regime. But his poetry was entirely Indian in feeling, marked most of all by a mystical union with nature. He was drowned in the North Canadian in 1908. Not so long before, he had written:

> *Why do trees along the river*
> > *Lean so far out o'er the tide?*
> *Very wise men tell me why, but*
> > *I am never satisfied;*
> *And so I keep my fancy still*
> > *That trees lean out to save*
> *The drowning from the clutches of*
> > *The cold, remorseless wave.*

There is certainly a connection between the way the untutored Indian feels and the way the educated Indian turns instinctively to poetry. But the machinery is too complicated; the circuit has always been broken. Some time the spark may leap across, and then we shall have great literature. I have a friend, Mary Hartshorne Shank, who is a daughter of the prominent Choctaw McCurtain family. She now lives in Chicago with her husband and son, and concentrates on her home and all its ramifying interests. But when she was a very young girl she wrote like this:

> *Look how the clay reflects the colors of the sky:*
> *Red-gold and dusky purple for a perfect moment. Why?*
> *What is this molded moment? What is clay?*
> *Out of it God made the body of man one day,*
> *Body of man red-gold and dusky purple, and alight,*
> *Then clay again under the sudden night.*

Even her colors are Oklahoma and Indian, but her thought is universal.

The early white settlers also turned to poetry. Sometimes it was an outlet for personal grief when a new grave was made in the tall grass. More consciously it expressed the sense of drama and joy in the making of a new society. It was published in the local

233

newspaper and forgotten. Only one of these writers made a lasting literary impression. In 1902 George Riley Hall settled in the new town of Henryetta and started the *Free Lance.* In a land where newspapers sprang up and bloomed and faded like desert weeds, he established a journalistic influence that was felt for more than a generation. And one day in 1906 to express his pride in the developing commonwealth he wrote the flamboyant "Land of my Dreaming," which is still quoted and loved by Oklahomans.

While adult poets were finding the home-town newspapers a means of publication, the school magazines were encouraging the youthful versifiers. Again one must go back a long way in Indian history. *Cherokee Rose Buds* was published by the Cherokee Female Seminary at Park Hill at least as early as 1854. Its school-girl contributors wrote in this vein:

> *The Seminary, our garden fair,*
> *And we, the flowers planted there.*

We have seen how Posey found opportunity at Bacone. But it was only at the University of Oklahoma that this student undertaking grew into a literary movement.

In 1897 when most of its students were of high-school rank, the University started a magazine called *The Umpire.* One of its most enthusiastic contributors was Zoe A. Stratton, a homesteader's daughter, who served as literary editor for the year 1902–1903. After she left school and married the famous territorial peace officer, Bill Tilghman, she was active in writers' clubs and poetry classes, and she still exerts a strong influence over youthful poets. And the fire smoldered along at the University until it burst into flame about the time of World War I.

It was in 1915 that *Poetry: A Magazine of Verse* first published the work of Oklahoma contributors. The young authors were Muna Lee, who grew up at Hugo, attended the University, and then taught school; and Ardmore-born John McClure, who graduated from the University that year and then became assistant librarian. Three years later McClure's *Airs and Ballads* was published. It had a profound influence on Lynn Riggs, who entered the University in 1920. McClure also became a regular contributor to H. L. Mencken's *Smart Set.*

Oklahomans Write, Too

In 1921, Joseph Francis Paxton, Greek professor, edited a *University Anthology,* published as a bulletin by the Print Shop—mentioned previously as the forerunner of the University Press. Among the contributors were McClure, Riggs, Mrs. Tilghman, Professor House, and Oklahoma-reared, Oxford-trained Walter S. Campbell, then a young instructor in the English Department. Other anthology bulletins were published in 1924 and 1929. Meanwhile young Boston-born, Harvard-bred B. A. Botkin, recently come to the University English Department, had become excited about Oklahoma's literary possibilities; and he used the first of these latter volumes as the basis of an article on the poetry of the state. H. L. Mencken—already interested in Oklahoma through "Jack" McClure—read this analysis, and invited Botkin to select a group of poems for the May, 1926, issue of the *American Mercury.* This was the beginning of a Mencken-Oklahoma literary entente that is apparent even at the present time.

I am not sure that this relationship has been altogether wholesome. Mencken's generous recognition certainly stimulated the growing literary movement in Oklahoma; but too many of the young authors began writing to please Mencken rather than to please themselves. In my opinion a few have missed greatness by that narrow margin. The "Oklahoma manner" (Mencken's phrase) at that time seemed to be a sort of Villon-like quality evoked by wanderlust and an independence of tradition. It grew naturally out of the restlessness and freedom of Oklahoma experience. A synthetic sophistication, however, is something else again, as unnatural as the New England mold that confined the genius of John Rollin Ridge.

In 1929, Botkin edited *Folk-Say: A Regional Miscellany* of old-timers' stories, old songs, and local-color sketches and poems. It was the first publication of the newly created University of Oklahoma Press, so new that the book came out without the Press imprint and colophon. It was issued annually for four years, and more young Oklahoma writers appeared there, were spotted by Mencken, and started on their way to a professional career. Few remained with poetry, however. Still fewer remained in Oklahoma.

John McClure went to New Orleans about 1921, and became city editor of the *Times-Picayune.* Muna Lee went to New York during World War I. There she met and married Luis Muñoz Marín, of Puerto Rico, destined to be chosen in 1948 as the island's first elected governor. From her West Indian home she became very active in Pan American relations, and contributed poems and articles to the leading magazines of the hemisphere. Botkin's accomplishments in the field of folklore took him to Washington and the Congressional Library. Lynn Riggs was in and out of the state for a few years; he left for good before 1930. Campbell stayed at the University and concentrated on other forms of writing.

After the nineteen twenties the Pierian spring at the University had almost dried up. But poetry broke out spontaneously here and there over the state. Many of the writers were housewives. A number of them achieved publication in the better magazines; a few published slender volumes of verse; several won national literary prizes. If there was any "Oklahoma manner" in this new movement, it showed itself in a passionate love of the soil, especially a love of the prairie.

There were at least two unifying influences in all this writing. One was the authors' clubs. Ever since 1914 there has usually been an organization of state writers with chapters in various towns. Zoe A. Tilghman started the Poetry Society of Oklahoma with 140 members in 1934. Two years later it sponsored the publication of a *State Anthology* with poems by 169 Oklahomans. Now it has about 200 members, who come together for mutual encouragement and stimulation. The other unifying influence came through the work of Kenneth C. Kaufman.

Kaufman was the son of an Oklahoma homesteader. He taught school, worked his way through college, joined the modern language faculty of the University, and became co-editor of *Books Abroad.* He began writing a column for the *Daily Oklahoman;* then from 1932 until his death he served as literary editor of that newspaper. Everybody interested in writing read his book page, and budding authors crowded his office and jammed his mail for his never failing help. He himself began writing poetry in the middle twenties; and his *Level Land* was chosen (with one other) from 197 entries in the Kaleidograph Fifth Book Publication Contest. Even his prose is touched with poetic magic. Thus in his newspaper column he wrote of his western Oklahoma boyhood:

Days were mostly golden that spring, with the sun drenching the flat green floor of the world and the sky making up three-fourths of it. . . . The wind too was bright, dancing along, singing a barely perceptible song in the tall bluestem of the low places, tossing this way and that the thousand heads of the Mexican wine cups. . . . Even the birds, the meadow larks and the little grass sparrows, sang bright liquid notes, as if they came from golden flutes.

The three mules sloped along, their heads straining out in front, drooping their ears back, patiently. . . . The boy had the lines tied together over his right shoulder and under his left arm; around his right wrist was the rawhide thong of the whipstock, and the long lash trailed in the furrow behind him. The flat, wide share of the sod plow cut the grass roots just under the surface, and the slender steel fingers that served as mould board laid the long black line of sod in an endless smooth ribbon.

The boy was not thinking. . . . His ears were filled with the endless slow roaring of the iron beneath the grass, falling and rising in a kind of soothing hum, and his mind was filled with a slow kind of joy. Then all at once, out of nowhere, out of the sea of cloud overhead, the air was full of silver wings. The boy had never been to the coast, and he had never seen a sea gull in his life, but he knew them instantly for what they were. He could never see one come into sight; every time there would be simply a flash of pearly white like the inside of a shell, and there were the long sweeping wings, with the short curved beak and the red eyes hunched down between them, peering at this strange heaving ocean of grass that was so like the sea. . . .

Silently they came and as silently disappeared into the nothingness of distance. . . . In their place was an emptiness vaster than ever the prairie and the sky had been before. And the prairie boy's heart was filled with an infinite sadness and a wild sweet yearning such as he had never known.[2]

[2] *The Daily Oklahoman,* April 7, 1944. Used with the courteous permission of the Oklahoma Publishing Company.

Oklahoma poets like Oklahoma artists must make their living at something else. Only two can honestly cite "Poet" as their only profession, and neither now lives in the state. Welborn Hope kept himself alive by asking handouts—literally—at back doors. Only Don Blanding makes his poetry pay.

Hope was born at Ada in 1903. His father was a banker and civic "booster"; his mother served as president of the State Federation of Woman's Clubs. He himself went to college, studied pharmacy, and owned and operated a drugstore. But he wrote verse that appeared in *Poetry* and other magazines; and when he was thirty-seven years old, he struck out for the East without a dime in his pocket, begging for his food and sleeping in fields and ditches. When he reached Boston, he was lionized, and lectured in his rags before a cultured audience. Thus he has gone on—working for brief snatches, and then taking to the open road, sending his poetry back to friends and publishers. For a recent April 22 he wrote "To Oklahoma—1889–1947" idealizing the pioneer years, condemning oil and its profits, and pleading for financial support of the gifted young. It sounds peevish and a little bilious, but for the life of me I cannot see any poetry in it.

Don Blanding was born in Kingfisher, but grew up in Lawton, where his parents moved at the opening of the Kiowa-Comanche country. He worked in a bank, studied at the Chicago Art Institute, and traveled over the world. His first volume of poems, *Leaves from a Grass House,* was written in Honolulu and published in 1923. Since then he has written more than a dozen volumes, charming books illustrated by his own facile pen. His poems are mostly sensuous descriptions of far and romantic places colored by his own zest for life.

More Oklahoma poets have turned to fiction for a writers' market. Louis L'Amour of Choctaw traveled as widely and lived as zestfully as Blanding, and saw his poems published here and there. Then he began writing for the pulp magazines. Now he lives in Hollywood. When he came back to Oklahoma to lecture recently, he had six stories and one article in magazines on the newsstands and a record of forty stories sold during the preceding twelve months. Edward J. O'Brien listed his work in the *Best Short Stories* series for four consecutive years before the war.

Oklahomans Write, Too

The first important fiction writer in Oklahoma was John M. Oskison, a mixed-blood Cherokee born on a ranch near Tahlequah in 1874. He spent most of his adult life in the East, but most of his novels and short stories have an Indian Territory setting. Written with almost studied realism, they yet show the same nostalgic quality—the "visible golden emanation"—that appears in Lynn Riggs' plays.

The new settlers of the land rushes also experimented with fiction. The first Oklahoma writer to grow up against this background was Vingie E. Roe of Fallis. She was the first of a remarkable literary succession.

Fallis is a little town in the blackjacks southeast of Guthrie. It hangs precariously on the side of a red hill, and one reaches it by the worst dirt road in Oklahoma. Once it was a live little town; now it is somewhat less than a village—population, 137—half of them colored—in 1940. But it has been the home of a number of writers of national note.

Young, ardent Vingie Roe was an eighty-niner child. Her doctor father settled first at Guthrie, then—after the Iowa country was opened—at Carney and Fallis. She grew up on horseback when there were "no fences to stop a rider," and began very early to scribble verses. President Angelo C. Scott of A. and M. saw one of her poems in the newspaper of near-by Perkins; he wrote the girl an encouraging letter, and sent the poem on to Victor Murdock of the Wichita (Kansas) *Eagle;* and Murdock also became her friend. That was all the help she ever had. But soon she was selling stories to New York magazines. She left Oklahoma about the time of statehood and eventually settled on a ranch in California. She has written more than a dozen novels, not about Oklahoma, but always about the outdoors and full of horses and action. Her latest volume—published in 1948—is dedicated to Dr. Scott.

Jennie Harris came to Oklahoma in 1898, taught school a while, then married Lloyd Oliver and settled in Fallis with her husband. She was much older than Vingie Roe, but the girl's success fired her imagination; and with Vingie's encouragement she borrowed a typewriter and began to write. She, too, was almost without formal education, and she wrote, as she typed, by instinct. Her writing was all joy, an entrance into an enchanted world; and as long as she lived, this thrill of creation never failed her. Her success was extraordinary; and eventually her income was running into five figures. Her setting was the "Red Earth" of Oklahoma, but her subjects were whimsical, imaginative, almost disembodied. Her "Mokey Delano" stories of a gifted, neglected child were collected in book form, and then used on the screen by Metro-Goldwyn-Mayer. Others were collected and published as *It is Morning.* Her volume of poems, *Red Earth,* ran into several editions. She died in 1942 at the age of seventy-eight, beloved of Fallis and Oklahoma.

Nobody knows how many writers Jennie Harris Oliver sent on their way by her encouragement. In Fallis people turned as naturally to writing as in other places they turned to oil or wheat. In the nineteen thirties Beulah Rhodes Overman was a semi-invalid with big medical bills, and her husband was caught in the depression. She could not hold a regular job, and writing seemed a good way to make money. So she wrote love stories and sold them to the pulp magazines. Then she recovered her health and her husband recovered his finances; and they went to New Mexico and invested in a tourist court and a bank.

Meanwhile, energetic little Blanche Seale was growing up in this atmosphere of writing. When she was still playing with dolls she wrote a story, "Love versus Duty," copied it many times in ink, and sent it to a confession magazine. Her father and grandfather laughed so hard when it came back that she definitely abandoned the writing business. Then she grew up and started teaching. One day she made up "Little Brown Koko" for a little girl to use in a storytelling contest. The child won the contest; the young teacher wrote more stories, and her pupils always won. Then Beulah Rhodes Overman sent one of the stories to a magazine, and a check came back. This was about twelve years ago. Every month since that time the magazine has carried one of the adventures of the lovable little Negro; and two volumes of the collected stories have reached a circulation of one-half million. Meanwhile the author married Gene Hunt, and the young couple bought an acreage of red sand and set out an orchard. They find Fallis "an ideal place for meditation, writing, gardening, flower-growing, and a happy life in general."

For the little town itself is greater than anything that has yet been written there. One senses this in the conversation of Blanche Seale Hunt. There is almost a family pride in "Vingie." "Her mother is buried in the Carney cemetery a few miles from here, and on her headstone is a lovely poem Vingie wrote." There is all of a family love for "Jennie" and "Lloyd." "I'll never forget the many grand times I've had at their home. And when she was entertaining the governor and a little colored boy happened along, she had time to talk with him and see that he had all his little stomach could possibly hold." There is a fine friendship for Beulah Rhodes Overman. "I used to visit her almost every day. She and her husband used to help me with my sixth-grade arithmetic problems." And there is a community confidence in Cecil Brown, who runs the grocery store and writes homely verses for newspapers. "He is one of our best friends," and his mother "is one of the best persons I have ever known."

Very little of this has been told by Fallis writers. None but Jennie Harris Oliver has even tried to tell it. It remained for the University to attempt a literature distinctively Oklahoman. And here again it has been hard to write in what John Joseph Mathews calls "the rhythm of the earth; in the sap-filled, living language of the earth."[3] This is what Botkin attempted in *Folk-Say*.

In Botkin's first volume there appeared some short, sketch-like stories by George Milburn of Coweta, then a student at the University. John McClure reviewed them, H. L. Mencken read the review, and young Milburn began to sell to the *American Mercury*. Since then his stories have appeared in many periodicals. He collected some of them in *Oklahoma Town* (1931)—published also in Berlin under the title *Die Stadt Oklahoma*—and *No More Trumpets* (1933), and wrote a novel, *Catalogue* (1936). For ten years he lived in Chicago and Hollywood writing radio and moving-picture scripts. Recently he brought out another novel, *Flannigan's Folly*. He has a photographic accuracy of observation, a swift, terse style, and brilliant characterization. Nearly all his settings are of rural and small-town Oklahoma—to him very unpleasant places filled with disagreeable people. Naturally he is not loved in his home state.

[3] *The Saturday Review of Literature*, May 16, 1942.

Walter S. Campbell (Stanley Vestal) writes in a happier vein. He can sell an adventure story to a pulp magazine or a critical appraisal of Western psychology to *The Saturday Review of Literature*. He has written novels, ballads, poems, short stories, biography, history, and even a detective story. But his enthusiasms are easy to discover beneath the quick movement of his prose and verse: his enjoyment of the color and drama of the Western scene.

In the nineteen thirties Campbell began offering courses in professional writing at the University. Soon Foster Harris, born at Sulphur, geologist-turned-writer, became his assistant. Students come to them from Oklahoma and neighboring states. They have been most successful in closing the gap between the good English theme marked with "A" and discarded, and the salable manuscript. A bizarre example is Earnest Hoberecht's Japanese best-seller, *Tokyo Romance*. The author is a twenty-nine-year-old newspaper correspondent from Watonga, now representing United Press in Tokyo. He wrote a torrid love story in English, got a Japanese friend to translate it, and sold it to a Japanese publisher. It has sold more than 300,000 copies, a song of the same name has already gone out over the Japanese radio, and there is talk of a film version and a dance.

This, of course, is not Oklahoma writing. There are young people all over the state writing to a larger public than they can find with regional literature. For outsiders do not care about the state, and the home people—who do care—do not read. The wide general reading of *Cimarron* and *Grapes of Wrath* is not an exception; neither had any real connection with life in Oklahoma.

A few radio beams are going out to pierce this darkness: Lewis Meyer of Tulsa's KVOO works as much Oklahoma book news as possible into his "Values We Live By," and even sends out lists of recommended titles; Henderson Leake, director of A. and M. College's radio service, reads selections from state authors in his "Oklahoma Almanac"; and the University's radio station WNAD regularly broadcasts information about Oklahoma writers. Henry G. Bennett, president of A. and M., also included Oklahoma literary selections in the readings he compiled as high-school English texts. Several of the city libraries are building up Oklahoma collections, and the Library Commission, which maintains a traveling service from the capitol, has always tried to spread information about Oklahoma books. The bug under the chip is that most Oklahomans do not use their libraries.

Oklahoma has not yet filled the gap in literary criticism left vacant by the death of Kenneth Kaufman. Burton Rascoe is the best known literary critic to come from Oklahoma, but he left soon after he graduated from Shawnee High School in 1911. He has not forgotten his early years. "Oklahoma and Shawnee in particular, will always remain to me a sort of enchanted spot, because . . . I spent an extremely happy childhood and youth there and there I first experienced a vast, aroused curiosity about life and literature. . . . I had to work hard but I have always worked hard. Tenderness, sweetness, hospitality, encouragement and appreciation I have always found in my Oklahoma friends." This feeling shows when he takes up an Oklahoma book; his interest is so great that he is more likely to write a general essay on the subject than a specific criticism.

Marquis James, Pulitzer Prize-winning biographer of Sam Houston and Andrew Jackson, has the same feeling for Enid that Rascoe has for Shawnee. His recent *The Cherokee Strip* is a delightful account of his boyhood in that lively young city: his father's story of the Run, early life on the claim, high school, and newspaper writing. George B. (Deak) Parker was another young newspaper reporter who went far in journalism—to the editorship of the Scripps-Howard chain and the Pulitzer Prize for distinguished editorial writing. Parker LaMoore, brother of Louis L'Amour, began as a reporter on the *Daily Oklahoman;* now he is foreign editor for Scripps-Howard, recently assigned to the Far East.

A matter of ninety thousand words back we began to explore the Oklahoma scene. Since then we have seen the power, the drive, the joy of the creative forces that center here. No wonder Oklahomans have an urge to write. And no wonder they have not settled down to read. But some day the twain shall meet. Then it will not be necessary for the Rockefeller Foundation to encourage anyone to "interpret Oklahoma."

Thirty-two Years After

The passage of years since this book was published has caused me to ask myself whether events since that time have changed the Oklahoma character. It was not possible for me to present these reflections in the printing now in progress, but I want to include them in any future printings. And at my age (ninety-one) it would be unrealistic to delay the writing until that time.

I have always had a special affection for this evaluation of Oklahoma as I saw it in 1949, for it marks the golden anniversary of the day when I became one of its citizens. I was nine years old when, sitting beside my mother and my younger brother on November 8, 1899, I watched wide-eyed as our covered wagon lumbered down the road past the new little town of Marshall to the farm my father had purchased in the area opened to lusty growth ten years before. While our parents were unloading, we children ran to the creek and selected the site for our playhouse, but it never occurred to me in that childish act of settlement that one day I should be asked to write an interpretation of the society I entered. And by a strange coincidence the publication date was November 8, exactly fifty years from that beginning.

Now, as I glance through the pages, I see that many outward changes have come to Oklahoma since it was written. But the more I examine the spirit of the state, the more I am convinced that the 1949 setting forms the base. Here are the roots, not only of the present but of the future. Take, for example, the athletic chapter with its shift of interest from the home-grown baseball of that writing to the grafted football of today. The total commitment to the team, whether of the small town to its high school or of the statewide citizenship to one of the two great rival universities, remains constant—and fundamental. And the almost universal corruption of county government being revealed at this time and the tendency of the general public to condone it, whether of the probate courts of the "East Side" in early statehood or of the county commissioners now, is a continuing pattern. It is also typical that attempts to streamline the structure of government that seemed promising in 1949 were lost without a trace. At the same time the creative drive, the ready friendliness, the practical common sense, the community loyalty—all the traits that distinguish the Oklahoma character—are also changeless. Its faults and virtues as events have shaped it still stand. But on this last American frontier—opened typically by a horse race—these events occurred in such rapid succession that they tempted outside writers to fabrication. And misrepresentations trouble me, for they tend to their own fulfillment.

In the early years the home people did not mind the wild West trimmings. They even contributed to them by showing these outsiders what they wanted to see. One is reminded of the time when the National Editorial Association was lured to Oklahoma in 1905 by an excursion to the 101 Ranch to see Geronimo stage a buffalo hunt, watch hair-raising stunts of riding and roping, and see three hundred obliging Indians sweep yelling over a hill and engulf a wagon train. Oklahomans could smile at the lurid stories these newspapermen wrote when they returned home, but clumsy ignorance in presenting the facts of their history and the quality of their heritage was something else. This was their own experience, and they insisted that, good or bad, it be recorded accurately. The dispute might have settled down into more honest writing and less local sensitivity had it not been for Edna Ferber.

She later described her writing methods with amazing—and unashamed—truthfulness in *A Peculiar Treasure* (this "peculiar treasure" as she defined it was the knack of writing about something of which she was ignorant). It was in 1928 that she came out to Kansas to visit the William Allen Whites. Incredible as it may seem, she had never before heard of Oklahoma except that she knew there was a state of the Union by that name. What she was told intrigued her, and so she came here and spent all of thirteen days in research (this is her own story). Then she retired to New York and France, and with her undoubted facility as a writer, she produced *Cimarron.*

The book begins with an exciting narrative of the Run of 1889. This occurred, as all Oklahoma knows, on April 22. It had just rained, and the spring was far advanced. The grass was green. The wildflowers made solid drifts of color. The trees were soft green plumes. The sun shone in a freshly washed sky, but the people waiting along the border for the day and hour of opening found the warmth of their fires good at night.

Edna Ferber's homeseekers were not spaced along some 250 miles of border. They were packed in dense crowds and [for no discernible reason] formed themselves into a queue. They were scorched by the [April] sun, and [with the creeks all full of clean water] suffered agonies from thirst. When the race started, they were choked by a dust cloud [rising from land that had never felt the plow], and fires set in the six-feet-tall [wet] bluestem burst into walls of flame. And this wierd perversion of nature continued throughout the book. For example, there was Sabra's farm that because of the surface features never felt the drought. But because of the same trick of topography it produced no oil. [Such freaks of nature would have been an easy guide to the wildcatter, saving all the expense of the geologist and the geo-physicist.]

With its publication the whole two million Oklahomans writhed collectively and then raised one concerted denial. Only forty years had passed since the events so flagrantly falsified in its opening pages had occurred. Active couples were cultivating the farms they had staked on that great day, and business firms still bore the proud date on their letterheads. In Oklahoma City even a mule was living that had carried its rider to the place where a leading family had established itself in the community; probably it was the only eighty-niner that did not join the protest.

But perhaps Oklahomans were too literal in their objections.

247

The author herself explained that she was not trying to create an exact setting but was seeking to capture the spirit of the state. In this we are dealing with imponderables, where errors are harder to pin down. But one example will show how far the book misses the truth even here.

The tarnished hero of *Cimarron* was a *champion of the red men*. He constantly bewailed their lot, rotting on reservations, herded up like sheep in a pen; and when he might have been appointed governor of the territory, he antagonized official Washington and thereby renounced his chances with an editorial advocating full United States citizenship for them. Years later his wife, Sabra, advocated the same breathtaking idea in Congress, where it was received with wonder and no little approval by the most advanced thinkers.

Actually the whole history of white Oklahoma was based on that policy. For it was the fixed policy of the federal government, and it was fervently supported by the Oklahoma settlers. "Break up the reservations, give the Indians United States citizenship and turn them loose, and open the land to homesteaders" had been the cry of the Boomers and all the surging forces of the shrinking American frontier. The Indians fought it desperately, but they lost. Otherwise there would have been no state of Oklahoma; it would have remained Indian Territory. Yancy Cravat's crusade to break up the reservations was about as daring and revolutionary as an editorial in Hitler's Germany advocating the annihilation of the Jews.

This complete reversal of the facts regarding Indian policy is more serious than a false physical or historical setting, for it miseducates even conscientious citizens in their attitude toward helpless human beings. Nobody can estimate its influence in inspiring the disastrous "termination" policy of the 1950s. Considering its small Indian population, one may conclude that the white settlement of Oklahoma was inevitable, but it should be told truthfully. A reservation is not a prison; it is simply a tract of land owned by Indians.

Perhaps it was the immense circulation of this book depicting a physical and historical setting that none of them had ever seen that caused Oklahomans to develop an abnormal sensitiveness to outside opinion. At least I was not aware of this before, and it was still very noticeable at the time of my own interpretation. It might have developed into a healthy self-criticism except for *The Grapes of Wrath*, published in 1939. The spiritual insight that makes this book great literature—the heartbreaking compassion for the dispossessed of the earth, the triumphant faith in ultimate human goodness—all this was lost on a people who saw only errors of fact.

When John Steinbeck wrote his compassionate novel about California berry pickers, he apparently decided that he would have to bring them from somewhere, and so he simply invented their Oklahoma background. It would not have required thirteen days—even half a day of honest work reading an encyclopedia or a ninth-grade Oklahoma history text would have given him some idea of the original setting of his Joads.

These buffeted people were the victims of a mass eviction from around Sallisaw, in Sequoyah County. Their ancestors had killed off the Indians [in what had been an Indian Territory and remained the home of many fullblood Cherokees, with the log cabin of the great Sequoyah still preserved as a sacred shrine]. Then they had wrested from the wilderness their sterile forty-acre farms. [Forty acres! Telling that to an Oklahoma homesteader.] The next generation had borrowed money from Soulless Banks, which had foreclosed the mortgages, and they themselves had lived in poverty and degradation as sharecroppers on the land their grandfathers had so hardly won. Then came the drought of the 1930s that turned their country into a dust bowl, and Impersonal Capital used caterpillar tractors to plow long furrows across boundary fences and farmyards, pushing the families out of their houses and leaving the country one great field of cotton managed by a hired superintendent.

The dispossessed people then went to California in search of new opportunities. Here Steinbeck dealt with facts. Oklahoma like its neighboring states lost population during the desperate drought and depression thirties, and for the "Okies" the road to California was an old trail. It began as early as 1849, when a number of leading mixed-blood Cherokees joined the gold rush;

and after 1889 it became an important extension of the Oklahoma frontier as restless white pioneers moved on to invest the profits from their homesteading venture in that westward trek. Now it offered hope to the victims of the Depression. Steinbeck related their experiences on the road with the accuracy of one who understood the problems of travel in an old jalopy, and he depicted truthfully the hostility they encountered when they arrived. But not one item of his Oklahoma setting has any basis in fact.

His book, translated into many languages, was to stir people throughout the world with a sense of human values, and it was certainly a factor in winning for its author the Nobel Prize in Literature. But all of these readers accepted without question the Oklahoma setting. I remember an article by one of the greatest English literary critics, stressing the importance of the relationship between land and people in fiction writing and the necessity of an accurate portrayal of background. I was reading it with enthusiastic approval. "Just what I have been saying." Then I came to his major example of a great novel projected against a true setting. And the novel was *The Grapes of Wrath*! I have even read that Hitler said there was nothing to fear from the United States and cited *The Grapes of Wrath* for conditions there.

At the time of publication Oklahomans raised one voice to point out the falsity of this setting just as they had done with *Cimarron*. But I have become troubled these past years to see that they have come to accept both invented portrayals. It is still true, as I said in 1949, that Oklahomans do not read; but even so, the influence of these books has reached them. Thus I hear statements by public officials lauding the state's present prosperity to show that the conditions depicted in *The Grapes of Wrath* are no longer true [as though they ever were]. I find articles describing the years when Oklahoma was in the dust bowl. These are illustrated by dramatic photographs, but a little tracing of the sources will show that they all come from the Panhandle. (I know from personal experience the fearful phenomena of this High Plains calamity, but, although all of Oklahoma was affected by the terrible drought of the 1930s, only the Panhandle and a small adjoining area were in the dust bowl.) I also find serious books by local writers attempting to interpret the Oklahoma spirit by citing *Cimarron*, the product of thirteen days' observation. This reliance on false data is in fact my reason for writing this addendum. As Franklin D. Roosevelt is reported to have said, "Repetition does not transform a lie into truth."

I must admit, however, that even the writer who works hard to discover the facts may fail to present them adequately. I should like to clarify here a few lapses in my oil story. On page 60 I should have stated that proration was successfully practiced by the oil companies in the Cushing and Healdton fields after World War I, though statewide overproduction continued. On page 62 my statement regarding the beginning of the Interstate Oil Compact Commission is not technically correct. Representatives of the four states I named were the original signatories of the compact, but when it became official by congressional approval, it had been ratified by the legislatures of Oklahoma, Kansas, Texas, New Mexico, Colorado, and Illinois, which thereby became the original members. I find another technical error on page 71. Although the name, *The Oil and Gas Journal*, dates from 1910 at Tulsa, it had been brought there under a different name and publisher from Beaumont, Texas in 1906. This date is eloquent of the early leadership of Tulsa in the industry.

Marshall, Oklahoma
September 14, 1981

Angie Debo

Index

Index

Index

Frank, John N.: 105
Frazier, Bernard: 223
Freedom: 108, 191
French in Oklahoma: 15–16
Fruit growing: 78, 91–92
Future Farmers of America: see junior farm clubs

Gallagher, E. C.: 181
Game: see wild life
Game and Fish Department: see Oklahoma Game and Fish Department
Garber: 58, 95 f., 163
Garrison, Robert: 226
Gas: see natural gas
Geological Survey: see Oklahoma Geological Survey and United States Geological Survey
Geology: structure, 4–6; oil, 6, 65–66; study of, 70
Geophysics: 66–67
Gerrer, Father Gregory: 216–17, 221
G. I. Bill of Rights: 171–73
Gilcrease, Thomas: 148; see also Thomas Gilcrease Foundation
Glass: 106–107
Glass Mountains: 6
Glenn Pool: 57–58, 61, 148, 198
Goethals, George W.: 190
Goff, Bruce: 226
Gold, in Wichita Mountains: 14, 209
Golden Trend: 64, 67
Goodnight: 203
Goodwell: 165
Gorman, Mike: 123, 172
Government, studies in: 52–53
Grain elevators: 89–90, 205, 207
Grain sorghums: 86, 91
Grand River Dam: 50, 81, 101, 190
Granite: 5, 108, 187, 199
Grapes of Wrath: 84–85, 100, 242
Grass: 10 ff., 78–79, 85 f., 132, 188
Greater Seminole oil field: 58, 61, 199–200, 204

Great Salt Plains Wildlife Refuge: 186–87
Greer County: see Old Greer County
Griffith, Art: 182
Guardianships, of Indians: 43, 46, 55, 104–105, 109; see also Indians
Guthrie: 48, 150, 206, 239; early history, 27 ff., 203; as capital, 30 f., 37; leadership in agriculture, 76, 78–79; historical celebrations, 153, 201–202
Guymon: 207 f.
Gyp Hills: 6, 11, 186
Gypsum: 107–108

Haley, J. Evetts: 92
Hall, George Riley: 234
Hamner, Laura V.: 92
Harding, T. Swann: 93
Hargrett, Lester: 148
Harrah: 175
Harris, Roy: 213
Harrison, Lieutenant Colonel Walter M.: 169
Harts, Jack: 176
Haskell, Charles N.: 36 f., 44, 69
Haskell Institute: 183, 221 f.
Healdton oil field: 56, 58 f.
Heflin, Van: 215
Hennessey: 25
Henryetta: 103 ff., 152, 234
"Hereford Heaven": 86–87
High Plains: 6–7, 128, 185, 191, 207–208
Highways: 5, 25, 83, 111, 157, 178, 188
Historians: 21, 145–46, 229–30: see also Dale, Edward Everett; Foreman, Carolyn Thomas; Foreman, Grant; Oklahoma Historical Society; Rister, Carl Coke; *and* University of Oklahoma Press
Historical Building: 221, 229
Historical celebrations: 153, 197 ff.
Hitchcock: 108

Index

Johnston, Henry S.: 36, 48 f.
Junior farm clubs: 87 f., 94–97, 162, 165

Kaufman, Kenneth C.: 236–37, 243
Kee-too-wah Society: 151
Kerr, Robert S.: 51, 82, 88, 101
Key, Major General William S.: 168
Kickapoos: 32
Kicking Bird: 149
Kingfisher: 25, 28 ff., 201, 238
Kingston: 189
Kiowas: 22, 25, 33, 139–40, 149–50, 154 f., 183, 188, 220–21
Ku Klux Klan: 47, 168
Kupper, Winifred: 93

L'Amour, Louis: 238
Labor unions: 103, 128
Lakes: 81–82, 185–92, 204
Lambert: 96
Lamont: 92
La Moore, Parker: 243
Land: use, 83–84; prices, 98, 121; see also farm mortgages, farm ownership, farms, and Indians
Land lottery: 33, 137–38, 209 f.
Land rushes: see Indian Territory, land lottery, and runs
Langston: 118
Langston University: 76, 117 f., 165, 180
La Salle, Robert Cavelier, Sieur de: 15
Lawton: 76, 149, 165, 209–11, 214, 238
Leader, Otis W.: 159
Leake, Henderson: 242
Lead mining: 37, 104–105
Lee, Muna: 234 ff.
Lee, Robert E.: 18
Le Flore County: 103, 108
Limestone: 108
Lindsay: 91
Linguistics: see Navajos, Sequoyah, *and* Summer Institute of Linguistics
Literacy: of Indians, 17, 142–44, 154, 156; of Oklahomans, 32, 163–64
Livestock: *see* cattle, hogs, horses, *and* sheep
Llewellyn, Karl N.: 147
Lookout, Fred: 153
Lottinville, Savoie: 230, 232
Lumbering: 109–10

Madill: 189
Mahier, Edith: 220
Mangum: 33, 208–209
Marcy, Captain Randolph B.: 228
Marietta: 180
Maritime code: 31, 192
Markham, Major General Baird H.: 168
Marland, Ernest W.: 50, 58, 62, 72, 98, 163
Marriages: 124–25
Marriott, Alice: 146, 188, 232
Marshall: 97, 129, 166, 170–71
Martin, Pepper: 174
Mathews, John Joseph: 146, 241
Mauldin, Sergeant Bill: 170
Mazie: 107
McAlester: 18, 23, 87, 101, 103, 166
McCarty, John L.: 92
McClure, John: 234 f., 241
McDonald, Angus: 94
McFarlin, Robert M.: 72
McGraw, James J.: 72
McLoud: 92
McVicker, J. Jay: 219
Medicine: 115, 122–24, 132 ff.
Meeker, 174–75
Mencken, H. L.: 234–35, 241
Mental hospitals: 22, 118, 122–23
Meyer, Lewis: 242
Miami: 82, 87, 101, 104 f., 190
Milburn, George: 39, 241
Miller, R. G.: 195
Millerton: 19, 200

259

Index

94, 96; honors won by students, 96, 167; in forestry, 110; organization of Flying Farmers, 112; veterans in, 171; supervision of veterans' agricultural training, 172; in athletics, 175 ff.; in art, 218–19

"Oklahoma Bills": 26

Oklahoma City: 8, 47, 68, 104, 106, 123 f., 153, 157, 160, 168, 170; history, 27, 29–30, 40, 197, 201-203, 212; population, 29, 37, 203; as capital, 30, 37, 201; agricultural leadership, 76, 82, 93; industry, 101 f., 111, 202; aviation, 112–13; Indians in, 153, 157; schools, 167, 215 f., sports, 175, 180 ff., 194; description of, 202–203; as music center, 212–14, art in, 216, 225; *see also* Oklahoma City oil field

Oklahoma City oil field: 37–38, 58 ff., 67, 203

Oklahoma City University: 165, 215 f.

Oklahoma Game and Fish Department: 109, 193 ff.

Oklahoma Geological Survey: 70–71, 100 ff.

Oklahoma Historical Society: 198, 229

"Oklahoma Lands": 26–30, 130–31; *see also* "Old Oklahoma"

Oklahoma Planning and Resources Board: 101 f., 109, 196

Oklahomans: faith in the future, *ix-x*, 29, 121, 140, 165; humor, 9, 120; sensitiveness to public opinion, 13–14, 51, 183–84; rural mindedness, 36, 39, 82, 86–87, 94, 102, 202; physical characteristics, 51, 124; restlessness, 54–55, 111, 119 ff., 216; mechanical aptitude, 101, 111; friendliness, 116–17, 137, 139; social classes, 117, 125–26; dialect, 119–20; energy, 120–21, 123; family life, 124–25; morals, 125; religion, 126–27; individualism and

particularism, 127–28, 164, 181; interest in sports, 174–84; love of outdoors, 193, 196; as readers, 228, 230, 243

Oklahoma Symphony Orchestra: 213–14

Oklahombi, Joseph: 159

Okmulgee: 22, 106, 199

Old-age assistance: 122

Old Greer County: 32–33, 137, 208–209

"Old Oklahoma": 32–33, 203; *see also* "Oklahoma Lands"

Oliver, Jennie Harris: 239–41

Oologah: 145

Order of the Rainbow: 166

Organic Act: 30 f., 163

Osage County: 43, 85

Osages: 22, 33, 43, 55 ff., 85, 146, 151–53, 159–60, 168

Oskison, John M.: 239

Otoes: 33

Ottawas: 21–22

Ouachita Mountains: 4 ff., 10, 16, 87, 109–10, 190–91

Ouachita National Forest: 109

Outlaws: *see* criminals

Owen, Steve: 178

Ozark Mountains: 4 ff., 91–92, 103, 108, 111, 190–91

Packing plants: 100

Page, Charles: 72

Painting: *see* art

Panhandle: definition, 3; description, 4, 7 f., 12, 76, 207–208; early history, 16 ff., 25, 30–31, 193; population, 31, 123, 207; ranching, 31, 86, 207 f.; gas field, 69; farming, 84, 89, 91, 207; education, 162, 165; historical celebrations, 208

Pardons to criminals: 45, 125

Parker, George B.: 243

Parker, Isaac C.: 24, 26

Parks and playgrounds: 185–93, 199

Index

cepted by University students, 120, 176 ff.; accepted by state, 120–21
Sorghums: *see* grain sorghums
Southard: 108
Spanish in Oklahoma: 15, 30, 33, 208–209
Spoils system: 31, 37, 41 ff., 47, 49
Sports: *see* athletics, fishing, horse racing, hunting, motorboat racing, *and* rodeos
Stanley, John Mix: 216, 223
Starr, Belle: 190
Statehood: 35–37, 69, 202
Steamboats: 18, 192
Steinbeck, John: 242, 248–50
Stevens, Dwight E.: 219
Stillwater: 32, 79, 94, 183, 219
Stilwell: 92
Stuart, J. E. B.: 18
Sulphur: 188, 191
Summer Institute of Linguistics: 156
Swett, Master Sergeant Morris: 209

Taft: 118
Tahlequah: 20, 56, 156 ff., 164, 198–99, 239
Talala: 104
Taxation: 50, 52, 98
Taylor, Joseph R.: 106
Taylor, Zachary: 18
Teachers colleges: 164–65; at Edmond, 32, 138, 182, 226–27; at Alva, 164; at Weatherford, 164, 182; at Ada, 164, 225; at Durant, 164; at Tahlequah, 164, 198–99
Tecumseh (city): 203
Tecumseh (Indian): 145, 147
Tenantry: *see* farm ownership
Texans: 32–33, 127, 230
Theaters: 214; *see also* playwrights
Thoburn, Joseph B.: 229
Thomas, George H.: 18
Thomas Gilcrease Foundation: 147–48, 223
Thorpe, Jim: 174, 177, 181, 183

Tilghman, Zoe A.: 234 ff.
Timber: 6, 10 f., 23, 34, 76–77, 84, 108–11
Tinker, Major General Clarence L.: 159–60
Tinker Field: 101, 123, 160
Tishomingo: 165, 189, 199
Tonkawa oil field: 58
Tonkawas: 32
Topography: 5–7
Tornadoes: 8, 128, 206–207
Tourists: 188 f., 195–96
Towne, Charles Wayland: 93
Townsites: 29 f., 34, 40, 102, 192, 206, 210
Trails: 18, 24–25, 28
Transportation: *see* aviation, motor transportation, railroads, steamboats, *and* trails
Trapp, Martin Edward: 48
Tri-State mining area: 104–105
Truck gardening: 92, 101
Tsa-to-ke, Monroe: 146, 150, 220
Tulsa: 104, 118, 179, 212, 215; history, 20 f., 24, 69, 134–37, 197–98; leadership in oil industry, 36, 56–57, 60, 71–72, 135, 198; population, 37, 198; civic spirit, 72, 192; interest in cattle, 87, 89, 198; interest in agriculture, 92, 94; new industry, 101, 111, 198; "booster" activities, 102, 195, 198; coal, 103 ff.; aviation, 112; as Indian center, 147–48, 151, 223–24; art, 148, 223–25; schools, 163, 167, 182, 216; water systems, 189–90; sports, 191–92, 194; architecture, 197–98, 226; Little Theatre, 214; *see also* University of Tulsa
Turner, Roy J.: 51 ff., 86 ff., 102, 167, 190, 215
Tuskahoma: 20, 200

United States Bureau of Mines: 71, 104

Index

United States Geological Survey: 71

United States Indian service: *see* Indian administration

University of Oklahoma: 88, 117, 124, 197, 205, 215; founding and growth, 32, 38, 164; influence on city government, 52; leadership in oil technology, 70; historians, 71, 92, 138–40; art, 105–106, 218; training of Indian artists, 150, 220–22; linguistic studies, 156; honors in journalism, 167; veterans in, 171; athletics, 176 ff.; architecture, 226; literary movement, 234–36; radio, 242; professional writing, 242; *see also* University of Oklahoma Press

University of Oklahoma Press: books on government, 52; oil, 71; agriculture, ranching, and soil conservation, 77–78, 92–94; history, 107 n., 209–10; Indians, 146–47, 227, 232; World War II, 170, 230; art, 227; travel, 228, 231; history of, 230–32; books to enemy lands, 231; *Books Abroad*, 231; Rockefeller grant to, 232, 243

University of Tulsa: 70, 165, 177–78, 224

Vann, Joe: 192

Vegetation: 10–12, 185–91

Vestal, Stanley: *see* Campbell, Walter S.

Vincent, Frank: 192

Vinita: 18, 145

Vinson: 191

Volcanic ash: 108

Wacos: 228–29

Wakita: 102

Wallock, Anthony Mark: 210–11

Walton, John Calloway: 47–48

Waner family: 175

Washita Valley: 90

Watermelons: 92, 228

Watonga: 242

Waynoka: 7

W. C. Austin Irrigation Project: 81–82, 187

Weather: *see* climate, drought, *and* dust storms

Weatherford: 164, 182

Weaver, James B.: 40

Weaving: 157–58

Weleetka: 92

Wentworth, Edward Morris: 93

Wentz, Lew: 72, 220

West, Walter Richard: 222

West Cement Pool: 63

West Edmond oil field: 63

Western movement: 21, 74

Westville: 20

Wewoka: 194, 199

Wheat: 11, 82, 89–90, 205, 207

Wheatland Conservation Experiment Station: 79

Wheelock Academy: 200–201

White settlement: 16, 23–24, 26, 28–34, 74

Wichita Mountains: 4, 6, 15, 108, 187, 209 ff.

Wichita Mountains Wildlife Refuge: 150, 187

Wichitas: 22, 33, 209, 228–29

Wilburton: 190

Wildcats: 64, 67

Wild flowers: 10–12, 187 ff.

Wild life: 12, 109, 133, 150, 185 ff.

"Wild Mary Sudik": 60

Williams, Robert Lee: 36, 45

Wind: 8 f., 49, 76 f., 128

Wister: 186

Woodward: 76, 86 f., 89, 128, 185 f., 206–207

World War I: participation in, 45–46; depression following, 46–47, 98; demand for oil, 59; demand for coal, 103; Indians in, 158–59

World War II: 50 f., 73, 106; demand for oil, 63, 73; effect on agriculture,

265